Bad Guys
and
Good Guys

Recent Titles in
Contributions in Criminology and Penology

Bad Guys
and
Good Guys

Moral Polarization and Crime

Daniel S. Claster

Contributions in Criminology and Penology, Number 36

Greenwood Press
Westport, Connecticut • London

Library of Congress Cataloging-in-Publication Data

Claster, Daniel S.
   Bad guys and good guys : moral polarization and crime / Daniel S.
Claster.
      p.   cm.—(Contributions in criminology and penology, ISSN
0732-4464 ; no. 36)
   Includes bibliographical references and index.
   ISBN 0-313-28489-X (alk. paper)
   ,1. Criminal justice, Administration of—United States.
2. Criminal justice, Administration of—Moral and ethical aspects.
3. Crime—Moral and ethical aspects. 4. Punishment—Moral and
ethical aspects. 5. Polarization (Social sciences) 6. United
States—Moral conditions.   I. Title.   II. Series.
HV9950.C53   1992
364.973—dc20   92-4053

British Library Cataloguing in Publication Data is available.

Library of Congress Catalog Card Number: 92-4053
ISBN: 0-313-28489-X
ISSN: 0732-4464

First published in 1992

Greenwood Press, 88 Post Road West, Westport, CT 06881
An imprint of Greenwood Publishing Group, Inc.

Printed in the United States of America

The paper used in this book complies with the
Permanent Paper Standard issued by the National
Information Standards Organization (Z39.48-1984).

10 9 8 7 6 5 4 3 2 1

For Rebecca and Andrew and the memory of Elizabeth

Contents

Preface

This is not a book about criminal behavior, nor is it about social and psychological conditions that contribute directly to the occurrence of crime. It is rather an examination of the perception of crime. Much of it is descriptive: an account of the ways in which criminals and their victims are perceived by ordinary citizens, makers of criminal justice policy, people responsible for carrying out those policies, scholars, and the press. It also considers the interplay among perceptions, for example, effects of press coverage on public attitudes and efforts by the press to give the public what it wants.

In calling these perceptions "good-guys" and "bad-guys" views, I suggest that moral judgments are closely connected to awareness of criminal encounters. The tendency to make moral evaluations is of course not limited to thinking about crime. It is widespread in matters as mundane as neighborhood gossip as well as in broad concerns like international relations and economic policy. Crime, however, seems to be a focal point for the human need to hold positive and negative attitudes toward social objects.

This phenomenon of "moral polarization" is accounted for on two levels. One is the level of historical development. Starting with moral judgments about crime as they appear in the United States at the present time, we trace some of the religious, political, and humanitarian doctrines that have led to the current perceptions.

The other level of analysis leads us to the scholarly literature. Psychologists have discerned a phenomenon that they call "psychological polarization"; sociologists, "social polarization"; and political scientists, "political polarization." The concepts seem to have developed independently; I bring them together here and emphasize their bearing on perceptions of crime.

Since societies' images of their social problems affect what they do about them, our society's perceptions of crime ought to explain some of the actions—and inactions—that are carried out in the name of criminal justice policy. In an indirect way, then, we shall pay attention to causes of crime, insofar as polarized judgments give rise to policies that encourage or discourage criminal behavior. Extremes of moral judgment will be shown as barriers to effective social action, but a rational evaluation of "harm" as "bad" will be emphasized as a proper element of criminal justice policy.

I first began to take seriously the "bad-guys" notion more than twenty years ago when, in a lecture on theories of crime, the late Arthur Niederhoffer emphasized views about criminals' evil nature as a "theory" worthy of attention. A number of my early ideas leading to this book were developed in discussions with colleagues in the summer institutes on juvenile delinquency at Brooklyn College: Professor Niederhoffer, Abraham Blumberg, and Alexander Smith.

Some time thereafter I attended a forum sponsored by the Nassau County, New York, chapter of the American Civil Liberties Union, at which the main speakers were a public prosecutor and a prisoners'-rights advocate. The prosecutor depicted criminals as dangerous people who did great harm to innocent victims. The advocate for prisoners portrayed them as having taken a wrong turn at some point but ultimately as good people deserving of compassion and support from society. This forum was far from a unique occurrence. I saw it as one example of encounters in many arenas, which crystallized my impression that encounters like this one represent a basic stumbling block in efforts to ameliorate the crime problem.

A few years after that, my interest in victims was stimulated through collaboration with Deborah David in a study of elderly victims of robbery.

As I began writing, I received encouragement and good advice from the study group on law and society at Brooklyn College: especially from its organizer, James Levine, and John Beattie, Philippa Strum, and Elvira Tarr.

I am grateful also for many helpful suggestions from other colleagues who have read parts of the manuscript: Sidney Aronson, Mark Fishman, Vincent Fuccillo, Laura Kitch, Marvin Koenigsberg, Jerome Krase, Roberta Satow, and Alexander Smith.

My wife, Flavia, and my children, Becky and Andy, were often re-sponsible for encouraging my writing, relieving me of household respon-sibilities, and making helpful suggestions. They were also sometimes re-sponsible for encouraging me to knock off writing and have more fun. I thank them for it all.

Bad Guys
and
Good Guys

1

Moral Judgments and Crime: An Overview

One institution that had an important early influence on my character—on my ideas of good and bad, of achievement and failure, of love and hate—was the cowboy film. My friends and I, in the small manufacturing town in Pennsylvania where we lived during my elementary school years, far from the deserts, canyons, and mountains of the West, would line up on Saturday mornings, hours before the box office opened for the afternoon show, eager to pay our twelve cents for the pleasure of cheering the good guys and booing the bad guys. Many of the heroes were well-known (Hopalong Cassidy was my personal favorite). But even when the faces of the men on screen were unfamiliar, we were able to begin cheering or booing because of a convention so familiar that it has since become a cliché. Often the heroes did indeed wear white hats and the villains black ones.

Why the color white identified the good guys and black the bad guys, rather than the other way around, need not concern us here. We might wonder, however, why the early filmmakers adopted a convention that denied their audiences the delicious suspense of not knowing whether the protagonists would turn out to be courageous and kind, or cowardly and mean.

Very likely, if we had the opportunity to pose the question to them, those filmmakers would respond that the people to whose tastes they catered would prefer not to be burdened with such uncertainty. The appeal of this genre, they would tell us, lies in situations appearing to make it impossible, just this once, for the hero to emerge victorious, as he has in all previous encounters with evil men, but then allowing him finally to win out once again. To present a hero of ambiguous morality would only muddy the simple plot. Assuming a short attention span on the part of youthful audiences, writers of these films would seek to let them know, before boredom began to set in, which characters were on the side of virtue and which on the other side. Keeping the audience in mind, they probably wished to avoid burdening it with subtle gradations. Since the color-of-the-hat convention, even more certainly than a sheriff's badge, provided useful information for the seasoned Western movie fan, the audience had no need to await the unfolding of events before showing its support for one group of principals in the drama, and its dislike for the other. As the story proceeded, the fans would find it comforting to be able to predict certain kinds of behavior on the basis of their early judgments. A man in a black hat could be counted on, when reaching a water hole after a hot ride through the desert, to jump off his horse, run fully clothed into the water, and drink greedily. A man in a white hat would immediately lead his horse to the water, remove its saddle and any other weight, and only then bend down and drink himself.

The cowboy film is not the only dramatic genre that telegraphs moral character at the outset instead of allowing it to unfold in the course of the play. Show us two men on stage in a nineteenth-century melodrama—one dark and middle-aged with a long handlebar moustache and a black suit and hat, the other young and blond, clean-shaven, and dressed in faded overalls and a flannel shirt—and we have little trouble figuring out who is about to foreclose the mortgage on whose hard-earned land and house.

Professional wrestling matches are another example. Even if the good guy on entering the ring does not look like a matinee idol, he smiles and waves at the crowd, and reserves his hostility for the opponent in the other corner. But the villain, even if he is not especially ugly, is likely to affect a grotesque appearance, through tattooing, a shaven streak through his hair, and so forth. He seems to anticipate boos by scowling and making threatening remarks and gestures at the crowd.

In the modern novel there seems to be a trend toward greater moral ambiguity than in writings of 100 or 200 years ago (Sperber, 1974: 9). But at the same time there persists a market for escapist literature, designed to appeal not to the minority of the population who are presumed capable of appreciating the more subtle art forms but rather to the supposedly less discriminating tastes of the masses. Such literature relies on what might be called polarized characterization—depiction of some major characters as consistently and extremely good with no bad qualities, depiction of others as consistently and extremely bad with no redeeming virtues, and an absence of characters who combine virtues and vices.

CRIME AS ENTERTAINMENT AND MORALITY PLAY

In modern urban American society with the frontier more than a century behind us, it seems only natural that cops-and-robbers fiction has largely taken the place of the cowboy melodrama for making a clear distinction between good guys and bad guys. To be sure, there is sufficient nostalgia for the traditional frontier so that Western novels have not been altogether supplanted by modern crime stories, films, and television series: Louis L'Amour's Westerns continue to compete with Joseph Wambaugh's police novels for top positions on the best seller lists. But the urban milieu is more in tune with the experiences and moral expressions of the modern public, among whom struggles between innocent crime victims or "untouchable" lawmen on the one hand and muggers or political terrorists or vice lords on the other are more popular than fights between good cowboys in shining white hats and bad cowboys in greasy black ones.

As make-believe crimes provide modern audiences with an outlet for their needs to participate vicariously in the struggle between good and evil forces, those needs are satisfied even more by accounts of real struggles between the established moral order and threats to subvert it. Sales of tabloid newspapers, it is well known, are boosted by sensational crime reporting, and it may be that the market for crime fiction represents a gap between the volume of people's needs to hear about bad criminals who hurt good victims and the paucity of real reported incidents that satisfy those needs. Indeed, one of the best things one can say about a fictional crime story is that it is realistic, in other words, so much in tune with the audience's experience that it might well have actually occurred. Thus it is not surprising that, when actual crime incidents are reported, those newspapers and other media that are directed toward the less-educated masses tend to focus on details that would reinforce perceptions of the good qualities of the victims and the bad qualities of the offenders.

In reality, however, criminal incidents are factually and morally complex. The fact of a theft naturally leads to the inference that it was done by a bad guy, whereas in some cases if the truth of the offender's altruistic motivation were known, an opposite conclusion might be drawn.

Likewise, although victims may appear at first glance to be morally blameless, further investigation may reveal "bad" motivations—initial provocation and deadly threat by murder victims, or greediness and the desire for illicit profit by con game victims.

The widely publicized case of Bernhard Goetz is instructive. A slightly built, thirty-seven-year-old white man and self-employed engineer, Goetz shot four black youths who were in their late teens on a New York City subway train in December 1984 because, according to statements he made, he believed they were about to rob him. Three of the teenagers recovered without apparent lasting disability, but the spinal cord of the fourth was severed by a bullet, resulting in his intellectual impairment and paralysis. Goetz was indicted and tried for attempted murder, but a jury found his claim of self-defense persuasive enough so that he was, in the end, acquitted of all charges except that of possessing an unlicensed handgun.

It is not unusual for an attempted robbery to end up with a turning of the tables, in which the intended victim draws a weapon and injures or kills the alleged assailant or assailants. Typically the table-turner is a shopkeeper in a high-crime neighborhood who has been previously robbed on a number of occasions. In states like New York, where the use of "deadly physical force"—that is, shooting to kill another person—is permissible if one "reasonably believes that such other person is committing or attempting to commit a kidnapping, forcible rape, forcible sodomy or robbery" ("N. Y. Penal Law," 1987: sec. 35.15; see also Klansky, 1988), there is likely to be a bias on the part of law enforcement officials in favor of the shopkeeper's "reasonable belief," so that such individuals are seldom charged.

At first glance the Goetz case seemed to be similar—one in which a law-abiding citizen who works for a living is attacked by robbers who are intent on ripping off the good people, trying to take money that they have done nothing to deserve and at the same time threatening the personal safety of their victims. Society judges the would-be robbers to be bad on the basis of their intentions to violate accepted rights to life and property. And the intended victim who uses a weapon, even if he is not legally authorized to own it, is given a morally favorable evaluation. He is judged to be a "good guy" for protecting his property, and also for performing a service to the community by conveying a message to other potential robbers that any apparently helpless target may perhaps be armed and therefore not so easy a prey as they might think.

What basis was there, in the Goetz case, for the public perception of Goetz as a righteous person and of the teenagers who shot him as wrongdoers? For one thing, Goetz was a solitary, middle-class white man in a subway, a location perceived as dangerous—a place where one might be called upon to protect one's self. For another, Goetz had actually been mugged three years earlier, after which he had tried to get a gun permit. When that effort proved unsuccessful, he bought a gun illegally, and on one occasion had used it to ward off a second robbery attempt.

And the basis for viewing the gunshot victims as bad? To begin with, they were black, in their late teens, and residents of a low-income housing project, at a time when such individuals made up a high proportion of street crime arrests. As it turned out, each of the four youths had police records. They had all been arrested at one time or another; all but one had criminal convictions. One was under indictment at the time of the incident for a prior armed robbery. Another, James Ramseur, provided the public with an opportunity to see him as a stereotype of the arrogant, defiant young ghetto criminal when television news programs showed him yelling angrily into their cameras as he was accosted by reporters on the street. And his subsequent conviction in 1986 for an unrelated occurrence of rape, robbery, sexual abuse, and assault was widely publicized, along with the twenty-five-year maximum prison sentence he was given. There were also many references made to sharpened screw drivers, presumably used to threaten or actually stab their victims, which were reported to have been found in the possession of all the injured youth.

These observations, taken together, seemed to support an image of Goetz as a good guy, of the boys who were shot as bad guys, and of the incident as a morality play in which an innocent and virtuous man appears to be at the mercy of evil forces but ultimately triumphs. In fact the term "subway vigilante" was often used as an analogy between Goetz and the vigilantes of the old West, who were justified in taking the law into their own hands because of the lack of an authoritative legal system on the frontier; the image was conveyed by Esquire magazine in an article titled "The City as the OK Corral" (Smith, 1985: 62). Therefore, when someone like Goetz, with whom citizens of the mainstream can identify, is prepared to and does prevent his victimization by the bad guys, those citizens feel a sense of satisfaction that justice has been done and all is right with the world.

And yet, as further information became available, there emerged a contrary view: In contrast with the initial impression that trouble had come to an unsuspecting Bernie Goetz, the supposition arose that Bernie Goetz went out looking for trouble. While the four young men had been behaving in a rowdy fashion at one end of the subway car, witnesses reported that other passengers had moved to the other end of the car. Yet Goetz had chosen to sit down near the youths. One of them had apparently asked Goetz for five dollars. But perhaps it was a simple request, without the threat of force that would make it robbery. The screwdrivers, originally described as sharpened, turned out to be ordinary screwdrivers known to be used by gangs such as this one to steal coins from videogame machines rather than employed in crimes of violence. To counter Goetz's claim that he acted to forestall a robbery, ballistics evidence was introduced at his trial to suggest that one of the youths was seated and two of them were retreating when they were shot. Much speculation centered on whether, had the circumstances been exactly the same but the young men white, Goetz would have used his weapon. A videotaped statement he made shortly after his surrender to New Hampshire police, in which he described his own actions as "cold-blooded," was cited to support the contention that Goetz perceived his actions as retaliation rather than prevention. And the young men, at first described as "animals" and "savages" whose appearances in themselves constituted a threat to a weak helpless victim, turned out to be appreciably smaller than he; they were all slight of build, and in comparison with Goetz's height of five feet ten inches, theirs varied between five four and five six (Rubin, 1986: 56).

And so there seemed to be a shift in some people's perceptions of Goetz, "from hero to villain" ("Subway vigilante," 1985: 14), and a corresponding shift toward viewing the gunshot victims as more sinned against than sinning. Of course not everyone went along with the shift; many continued to see Goetz as the hero and the black teenagers as villains.

But let us consider an equally likely scenario—more morally complex than either of the images reconstructed above, and in contrast with the presupposition that there is one guilty and one innocent party. It is a view in which Goetz's motives and those of the youngsters—like most people's motives, especially in tense situations—are in each case considered to be not fully formed, and to the extent that they are formed, are part social, part antisocial, and part innocuous, changing from one moment to the next, and lacking a consistent pattern.

Assuming that the teens' behavior was typical of the mode that has been described as most often reflecting the motivations of male, teenage, lower-class delinquents (Matza, 1964: 27–30), we may suppose that they did not start out with any explicit intention to commit a crime. Rather, it is likely that they were "cruising": travelling around with a mind set that was neither bent on committing criminal acts, nor committed to avoiding illegal conduct. They find themselves in a subway car, where they talk in a boisterous fashion and, perhaps noticing that passengers near them move to the other end of the car, unconsciously congratulate themselves on being "bad." Then a thin white man wearing glasses sits down near them. Why not ask him for five dollars, and see how he reacts? Maybe he'll think we're going to hurt him and give us the money for that reason. If he doesn't, what then? If he stays at this end of the car we might try to frighten him a little, but he'll probably move toward the other end of the car, among the twenty or so other passengers, and there might be a plainclothes cop down there. We wouldn't take a chance and go after him. We're just fooling around, after all.

Now consider the possibility that Bernhard Goetz also approached the situation with intentions that are morally ambiguous. He enters the subway car, notices that a group of rowdy teenagers are congregated at one end of the car and a score of additional passengers at the other, and surmises that the older people are trying to avoid the youths. He sees this as part of a familiar scene which he has come to resent in the past, in which respectable people find it necessary to accommodate to young punks who intrude on other people's sense of well being. With the knowledge that he has a gun to defend himself if need be, he demonstrates bravado by sitting near the noisy kids, half hoping that he will have a chance to show them he cannot be pushed around, but not really believing it is going to happen. When asked for the money, however, he says to himself, "It really is happening!" Automatically he pulls out the gun and starts shooting. On later reflection he does not really know whether he thought, at the time of the shooting, that he would have been robbed if he had not used the gun. But he also has a sense that the shooting represents deep feelings—resentment about an earlier victimization—beyond simply wanting to avoid a robbery. What he does know is that he has done a violent act totally different from anything he has ever done before. And somehow he has to come to terms with it, to explain it to himself.   In the course of doing that, he says things that represent a variety of conflicting images of himself. At one moment he will say that he did not feel threatened; at another time he will speak about the boys' "body language" that made him feel he was in danger; shortly thereafter he will say that he wanted to make the boys suffer.

To be sure, this last reconstruction of the thoughts of the participants in the Goetz incident is highly speculative, but it fits the facts as well as other more extreme moral suppositions. With all that has been written and said about the case, there has been little consideration given to the possibility of such moral ambiguity. Yet one might draw overall conclusions other than that Goetz is blameworthy and the boys blameless, or that the boys are blameworthy and Goetz a hero. One might conclude that both parties had a right to be where they were, doing what they were doing, or that both parties were asking for trouble, and if trouble came, they both deserved to suffer.

The Goetz case, then, serves as an illustration of the tendency (when the facts of actual criminal encounters enable one to make any one of several moral judgments about the principal parties in those incidents) for people to conclude that party A was altogether in the right and party B was altogether in the wrong, or that party B was altogether in the right and party A altogether in the wrong. Although the actors in those incidents might well have been affected by circumstances beyond their control, and might have harbored mixed, contradictory motives, when it comes to the dominant public reaction, it turns out to reflect what we shall call "moral polarization." Such polarization, as we have indicated above, is commonly recognized in fiction for young people, and in "trashy" and escapist literature for adults.   But there are complex processes—psychological processes, and processes related to the structure of the media and of the criminal justice system—that lead to morally polarized judgments of participants in real criminal incidents as well.

THE MORAL BASIS OF CRIME

Although we have suggested that polarized evaluations fail to do justice to the facts of criminal encounters, it does not follow that moral judgments in themselves should have no place in a society's approach to its crime problem. At the societal level, moral judgments are no more than the application of a society's values to particular objects and actions. What we recognize as criminal laws in modern societies are an outgrowth of informally applied rules that suffice to maintain peaceful relations in smaller, simpler societies. In tribal societies in which every individual is known to the entire community, social order can be maintained by means that seem gentle in comparison with criminal sanctions in modern societies. If one man takes an unfair share of the proceeds of a communal hunt, for example, it will not be long before everyone in the community knows about the transgression. Thereafter, he will be the subject of various forms of teasing, insults, exclusion from participation in group activities, and so forth. The result of these sanctions is not only that the offender will be discouraged from repeating the offense but that others, observing this example, will likewise learn to take no more game than they are entitled to.

As societies grow, individuals become more anonymous and therefore less susceptible to such informal measures of control, and yet the society needs as much as ever to have an effective way of dealing with threats to its welfare. It then formalizes the system of control. This is done in two ways: first, by specifying, usually in writing, the acts that are considered harmful, and second, by specifying the sanctions that will be imposed upon wrongdoers.

These two kinds of specifications, in themselves, buttress the system of moral values. To the extent that there is a lack of clarity in abstractly formulated values—for example, in a statement like "it is wrong to steal"—the process of working out, writing down, and applying the general precept to particular situations forces the society's members to consider a number of issues for which clarification serves the collective interest. Ultimately the prohibition against stealing will serve the group better, to the extent that it is expressed in specific rules—rules formulated after having reflected upon how ownership should be determined in the first place, what objects should be considered public and which private property, which forms of theft deserve greater punishment than others, and what other social costs and benefits might accompany measures designed to protect property rights.

Thus, as people are socialized into the ways of their groups, they become aware that a society's moral code defines certain acts as inconsiderate or degenerate, as bad manners, or as threatening to the social fabric. It serves the educational function of informing people about acceptable ways of conducting themselves. But it also serves a deterrent function: It ensures that, when people commit crimes, their fellows will respond in ways that render it less likely that the offender will repeat the act.

STEREOTYPING AS OVERGENERALIZATION

Although social expressions of moral judgment, insofar as they function as a mechanism for shaping behavior, may appear to be directed toward specific actions that are deemed "bad," in practice such pronouncements are extrapolated from actions to actors. Thus, we do not respond simply to autonomous acts as bad. Rather, we attribute badness to the author of the behavior. After all, sanctions are carried out against people, not against isolated bits of behavior. It is people who are fined, imprisoned, or beheaded; and so, if the punishment is to be directed toward the whole person, the tendency is to justify that action by characterizing the whole person as bad. If the opinion prevails among members of a community that appearing in public without clothes is inherently evil, and it becomes known that an actor has taken part in nude scenes on stage, it is but a short step to conclude that the actor must be a bad person, capable of other wrongful deeds as well. Thus, the people who have made such a negative judgment about the unclothed actor would not be surprised to learn that he is a drug user, a thief, or a child molester.

On the other hand, a person whose actions have been evaluated positively may be insulated, as it were, from evidence of wrongdoing, even to the extent that those making the judgments will deny reports of behavior that does not fit in with their expectations. A boy who has mastered the skills necessary to become an Eagle Scout is thought to possess an admirable character, so much so that if an accusation of wrongdoing is leveled against him, family and neighbors will insist that he could not have committed the offense; good people simply do not do things that are clearly evil.

This tendency to extend judgments from the act to the actor, therefore, tends to negate the likelihood that negative acts will be viewed as aberrations, that they are out of keeping with the offender's general character. Whereas it might be true that some people who have committed theft are generally considerate in their relationships with others—they may be conscientious taxpayers, valued employees, loyal patriots, or generous contributors to organized charity—the "bad guy" label uses evidence of one antisocial act to stigmatize the person as a whole. It is as though the community says that the person who commits a criminal act, no matter what else the person does that is praiseworthy, deserves to be generally condemned.

In more general terms, the process by which a limited amount of information about a person or group is used as the basis for attributing certain characteristics to that person or group is known as stereotyping. As Lippman (1922) has observed, there is economy and indeed often necessity in the propensity to view others in terms of a few selected attributes. There is always the danger, however, that the attributes selected are irrelevant or misleading. Whereas the ability to generalize from particular experiences often serves as a useful guide for future behavior, the most astute among us learn to be wary of the temptation to overgeneralize.

It is this distinction between generalization and overgeneralization in moral judgment that should be kept in mind as we proceed to examine the ways in which participants in criminal encounters are evaluated. To the extent that a moral judgment is based upon a wide range of information about the motivations, constraints, and opportunities of all actors in the encounter, it may be said to represent a valid generalization; to the extent that such considerations are not taken into account, it may be described as overgeneralized or stereotyped.

It is not always true that stereotypes reflect moral attitudes. For example, on the basis of having observed that virtually all members of a group of Japanese tourists carry cameras, one may harbor the stereotype that Japanese are fond of photography without judging that interest to be good or bad. Nevertheless, many stereotypes, even if not explicitly value laden, are readily expanded upon in judgmental terms. For example, the stereotype of black people as fond of watermelon is not inherently pejorative, but it is only a short step from that stereotype to the picture of a dark-skinned cartoon character gobbling ecstatically in the middle of a watermelon patch.

When it comes to stereotypes of criminal encounters, what naturally comes first to mind, as we have indicated previously, is the stereotype of the criminal as resolutely evil—a person essentially different from you and me, who harbors the basest of motives, and whose life style reflects a lack of the sensibilities shared by respectable members of society. The typical victim, in contrast, is seen as a respectable citizen who is unlucky enough to have been in the wrong place at the wrong time and whose suffering is undeserved.

There are, however, times when this picture is reversed. As shown in the second view of the Goetz case presented above, some "victims" may be viewed as having provoked a criminal act by means of their own threatening behavior. Other victims may be perceived as having "asked for it" in other ways—inviting rape through sexually seductive behavior, encouraging burglary by flaunting their wealth, provoking political terrorism through dictatorial government. In such cases the tables are turned. When the victim is a bad guy, that perception is taken as justification for the offender's act, and the latter is perceived as a good guy.

In still other criminal encounters the emphasis for moral responsibility is located not within the particular actors present but within the groups to which they belong. Just as an individual's personal characteristics or dispositions may be blamed for the role he plays in a criminal encounter, so too may the person's ethnic group, or social class, or gang, be endowed with characteristics, either desirable or undesirable, to explain the member's participation in the criminal encounter. Thus groups as well as individuals are thought of as either bad or good. Consequently, in the chapters that follow, we shall examine images of offenders, victims, and their groups, as each have been portrayed as good guys and bad guys.

CRIME AND POLITICAL RHETORIC

In an effort to explain the thinking, as well as the appeal, of President Ronald Reagan, the journalist Leslie Gelb observed that "he reduces complications to simple symbols and images of good and bad, American and un-American. That allows him to cut through the complexities that bewilder and hold no interest for the general public, putting him squarely on the public's wavelength" (Gelb, 1985: 113). For our purposes the point is not the limitations of Mr. Reagan's mental abilities, but rather the observation that the public is receptive toward issues couched in such simplistic terms. It is a commonplace of political wisdom that officeseekers and officeholders are most successful when they can associate themselves with the right side of simple issues and cast their opponents on the wrong side, and that they will drive away potential supporters if their speeches plumb the intricacies of complex issues (Putnam, 1971; Scheingold, 1984).

And it is but a short step from presenting issues to the public in simplistic terms of good and bad to actually formulating and implementing public policy on such a basis. For one thing, as Gelb suggests, the public may well elect people to high office who themselves tend to view the world in this way; for another, even those people in policy-making positions who can deal with finer nuances in their own minds are often inclined to support measures they can easily defend among their constituents.

One need not view the adult population as mentally incapable of considering ambiguities and complexities in public policy in order to explain a preference for simple explanations and solutions. Especially in the United States, that preference seems to be related to the strong tradition of anti-intellectualism within the dominant culture. Part of the popularity of political speakers with reputations as "great communicators," from Lincoln to the Roosevelts to Reagan, seems to derive from their ability to reduce complex problems to simple—and sometimes simplistic—matters, and to portray them to suggest that there is only one "right" solution, while at the same time implying that their opponents are presenting the issues as complex in order to confuse the simple truths that the speakers have just voiced.

Another cultural tradition that seems to play a part in the public's receptiveness to issues posed as morality plays is the American tendency not to be surprised when the holders of public office see politics as a game in which the dominant players are expected to be acting out of self-interest. The contradiction between this perception and the ideal—that ours is supposed to be a government, not only of and by the people, but for them as well—leads to cynicism, and ultimately to a tendency not to take politics too seriously.

The most visible part of the political process consists of the interplay among individuals who subscribe to the view that the public prefers to hear simple slogans rather than detailed proposals. It has become so commonplace to speak of the political arena that we tend to forget that arenas were originally places where Roman gladiators did battle, not to determine public policy, but simply to amuse the emperor and members of the public. The term "political arena" was originally a metaphor, suggesting that although the primary goal of political controversy is to produce policies that will be implemented in the public interest, it often appears as well to provide the same kind of satisfaction to onlookers as gladiatorial spectacles.

Indeed, it was a tradition during the golden age of American oratory in the nineteenth century for a carnival-like atmosphere to accompany the appearance of statesmen like Daniel Webster, Frederick Douglass, or William Jennings Bryan, and for their audiences to applaud orators who denounced the evils of states' rights, slavery, or the gold standard, as they might cheer the popular entertainers of the day. In the present century different styles of communicating with the public have been adapted to radio and television, and modern candidates since Dwight Eisenhower have been coached to regard the American public as people who like their messages in simple, black and white terms, conveyed in a folksy manner. Above all it is important to hold the attention of the mass audience, to speak sufficiently on its wavelength to keep its members from getting bored and changing the channel. Ronald Reagan has been widely regarded as master of the art.

Having noted the element of entertainment in political rhetoric, we, of course, recognize that there is more to political decisionmaking than oratorical style. On issues of importance to the public, its members are indeed concerned with substance. All politicians are keenly aware that their careers progress when they pay attention to matters of immediate concern to their constituents. When Communist aggression was perceived as a threat to national security, dovish legislators lost out to the hawks; when unemployment is widespread, it behooves the people's representatives to support job programs; and when crime is a matter of widespread public concern, there are benefits to be derived from condemning criminals as bad guys and acting to punish them.

In 1935 Thomas E. Dewey was appointed by Governor Herbert Lehman of New York as special prosecutor against organized crime. Dewey's subsequent reputation as a "racket-buster," enhanced by his success in persuading a jury to convict Lucky Luciano as kingpin of a large-scale prostitution enterprise, was an important factor in his election as governor in 1942, which led in turn to two nominations, in 1944 and 1948, as the Republican candidate for president (Dewey, 1974). He was of course required to address a broad range of issues as he climbed the ladder of political power, but it is interesting to note the kind of rhetoric that provided an impetus for his early successes. In a 1935 radio address, Dewey characterized the targets of his investigation as "those predatory vultures who traffic on a wholesale scale in the bodies of women and mere girls for profit" (Dewey, 1974: 14).

And more recently, in an analysis of the Arizona legislature's debate over a tough new criminal code, it was observed that characterizing criminals as villains served to enhance the legislators' status as heroes:

Essentially, the legislators feel compelled to adhere to the popular notion that all crime occurs basically the same way—violently by the crazed molester, the assailant poised behind the bush for the attack. . . . These the legislator identifies as "villains."

The legislator then overcompensates by glossing the new criminal laws with overboard and tough sounding language and creates impressive penalties to fit, in hopes that he or she will be identified as "hero" come election day (Adams, quoted in Levine, Musheno, and Palumbo, 1980: 49).

Although calls for cracking down on crime, supported by diatribes against evil perpetrators, have been a mainstay of political campaigns in large American cities for many decades, they became especially salient in the period beginning in the late 1960s. Riots following the assassination of Martin Luther King, Jr., in 1968 raised the general problem of crime in the streets to the level of a national issue. Just as the 1950s was a period in which the dominant threat to our society was seen to originate in the imperialistic intentions of a foreign power, so the late 1960s was the beginning of a period, continuing into the 1990s, in which conventional property crimes—street muggings, house and apartment burglaries, rape, and so forth—came to be seen as the greatest threat to established order in the United States. Toward the end of the 1960s respondents to public opinion polls, especially in large cities, mentioned crime more frequently than any other issue when asked about their major concerns. And it was during this period that Ronald Reagan was elected governor of California, and Richard Nixon was elected president of the United States, each in no small measure on the basis of a law-and-order campaign in which the "good-guy" voters were asked to support a crackdown on the "bad-guy" criminals (Brown, 1970: ch. 40; Elias, 1986: 19; Heinz, Jacob, and Lineberry, 1983; Levine, Musheno, and Palumbo, 1980: 48–49; Quinney, 1975: 23).

Barry Goldwater's unsuccessful presidential bid in 1964 was perhaps the first instance in which crime, and particularly the "law and order" approach to it, was an issue of top priority in a nationwide campaign. Since then it has been incumbent upon candidates of both major parties to address the issue. In the 1984 presidential campaign, for example, each party raised the issue as a matter of concern to potential victims; the Republicans in general terms of safety for citizens, the Democrats with emphasis on the special vulnerability of poor urban dwellers. The Republican platform, in calling for imprisonment "swiftly, surely, and long enough to insure public safety," supported its approach by asserting that criminals must be held accountable for their misdeeds. "Republicans believe that individuals are responsible for their actions" (Committee on Resolutions of the Republican National Convention, 1984: 36).

The Democrats tried to present a less ideological stance. "Neither a permissive liberalism nor a static conservatism is the answer to reducing crime." And yet, to avoid the appearance of being too soft on crime, they reassured potential supporters: "While we must eliminate those elements—like unemployment and poverty—that foster the criminal atmosphere, we must never let them be used as an excuse" (Democratic National Committee, 1984: 41).

Although moral postures are implied in these formal statements, the need for broad support in a presidential campaign precludes overt characterizations of even street criminals as good guys or bad guys, for fear that such rhetoric may be seen as tarring various ethnic groups with a broad brush. The need for broad support is often true in local politics as well, so that politicians' appeals to underlying polarized attitudes are more likely to be conveyed through subtle gestures or intonation when addressing a particular audience, rather than words that might be quoted to the candidate's disadvantage in other settings. There are situations, however, in which local politicians feel that they have enough support from some constituencies that they need not worry about alienating others. In such cases moral characterizations can be quite explicit.

There is no better example of this approach than the rhetoric employed by Frank Rizzo, who rose through the ranks of the Philadelphia police department to become police commissioner, and ultimately, two-term mayor of the city in the 1970s. Rizzo's election was generally attributed to his strength in "row-house Philadelphia" (Daughen and Binzen, 1977: 327), inhabited by white ethnic groups that had been a mainstay of the city's labor force for generations. His constituents increasingly saw themselves victimized by a rising black population, which was perceived as threatening the white groups' economic and political power as well as their property values, physical safety, and possessions. The law-and-order issue was central in Rizzo's campaign, which in turn reflected his tenure as a high-profile police commissioner who "saw cops as the white hats fighting the real enemy, criminals, and he was determined to deal with them in his own way" (Hamilton, 1973: 137). That way included arrests of people who offended Rizzo's moral sensibilities by wearing clothing and hair styles associated with the hippie culture of the 1960s and by frequenting coffee houses in the downtown area near high-priced businesses and apartment houses. He condemned these "weirdos" and "creeps" as a threat to traditional lifestyles in the city of brotherly love and showed so little sensitivity to their civil rights that he acquired a reputation throughout his tenure on the force as a police officer who, even when there was no basis for bringing criminal charges against "hippies" and other nonconformists, regularly harassed them. But he saved his strongest condemnation for those street criminals whom he perceived to be turning the streets into a jungle. These he reviled on various occasions as "hoodlums," "wild animals," "pukes," "barbarians," and "yellow dogs."

He was in turn condemned for his rhetoric by an official of the National Association for the Advancement of Colored People as a "promoter and exponent of black hatred" (Hamilton, 1973: 87). And Huey Newton, who was defense minister of the Black Panther Party at the time, vilified him as a "mad dog" and "some kind of savage" (Daughen and Binzen, 1977: 153). Rizzo, moreover, extended his moral judgments beyond the crime fighters and criminals themselves to the opinion-holding public. "If you were for Frank Rizzo," he let it be known, "you stood up for law and order; if you criticized him, you were a 'coddler of criminals' " (Daughen and Binzen, 1977: 83).

MORAL JUDGMENTS IN THE MASS MEDIA

In the early 1980s television station KABC in Los Angeles was inaugurating a "crimestoppers" hotline program, in which viewers were asked to telephone the station with any information they might have about unsolved crimes in the area. To stimulate interest, the station ran a spot advertisement for the program with the following voiceover: "Us. Them. Us. Them. Us. Them." Following an invitation to call the hotline, the announcer closed by saying, "It really has come down to this—it's either us or them. And at Channel Seven we think it's about time it started being us again" (Madlin, 1983: 33).

Anyone familiar with the history of journalism will recognize the language of this advertisement as simply a recent, skillful example of what newspaper people have known for a long time: that sensationalism attracts audiences, and that dramatizing the good-guys, bad-guys theme is a surefire technique in the arsenal of sensational reporting. In modern journalism expectations of objectivity impose some limits on the use of morally laden language in straight news stories, whereas editorial writers are freer to use creatively pejorative language in describing criminals than are regular reporters. For example, reporters for the *New York Daily News* described the white teenagers who attacked three black men in the Howard

Beach section of the city in 1986 simply as "a mob of white thugs" (Gearty and Gentile, 1986: 3), but two days later an editorial in the same paper described the same assailants as "a rabble of gutless imitations of men" ("And the cowardice of hate," 1986: 24). In a similar vein, a holdup in a Boston housing development provoked an editorial in a tenant newsletter describing area youth who threaten community safety as "gangs of rotten young degenerates . . . who congregate like vultures" (quoted in Lukas, 1985: 411).

Moral evaluations affect both the selection of crimes for news coverage and the mode of presentation. Selection occurs for a variety of reasons—space available, economic and political pressures, ideologies of particular editors—but above all communicators' impressions of what their audiences want. In large cities, for example, it often happens that even property offenses involving thousands of dollars worth of goods are so taken for granted that they are thought to be unworthy of media attention. To be worthy of any attention at all by the media in a large city, a crime must result in serious injury, death, or loss of property of very great value; involve a prominent person as offender or victim; or have some other unusual quality. Often that unusual quality has to do with the depravity of the offender or the innocence of the victim. Thus killings in which the offenders have cannibalized the corpses of their victims or sexual attacks upon very young children are more likely to be reported in detail by the metropolitan press than are more mundane homicides and rapes, on the assumption that the public is more interested in such crimes. It is not only true that papers employing a sensational approach to crime news tend to have the largest circulations, but it also turns out that the circulation for a given paper is greater for issues with sensational crimes in banner headlines (Bachmuth, Miller, and Rosen, 1960; Levine, Musheno, and Palumbo, 1980: 44).

Following an incident in which one of its delivery trucks was robbed of $125,000, the *New York Daily News* launched a "crimefighter" campaign. It was inaugurated in early 1982 with an announcement, on the day after the theft, that the paper would select a citizen "crimefighter of the week." During the three-month campaign, seventeen individuals were so designated and given one thousand dollar rewards, in each case for an act of courageous intervention or resistance in a mugging or similar crime. During this period the paper ran special articles, in addition to the usual crime news, suggesting solutions for the crime problem and inviting readers to submit their suggestions as well.

A content analysis of articles appearing during the campaign indicated that the war against crime was portrayed as "the forceful acts of 'good' individuals against the random acts of 'bad' individuals" (Gorelick, 1989: 432). Given the number of possible ways to depict the problem, the *Daily News* chose, according to the researcher who analyzed its presentation, to ignore any approach suggesting some alteration of the economic or social structure as a viable approach to crimefighting, and instead to favor the individual bad-guys–good-guys" approach.

Another study compared the *Chicago Tribune*'s attention to different categories of crime with police statistics. Graber (1980: 39) found mention of violent crimes—murder, rape, robbery, and assault—overrepresented in press reports, and lesser offenses underreported. For example, murders made up 26 percent of the offenses reported in the *Tribune* in 1976, but only two-tenths of 1 percent of the offenses known to the Chicago police during that period. Burglaries, on the other hand, constituted just 2 percent of crimes making it to the *Tribune*'s pages for the year, while they made up 12 percent of those in police files.

Graber found crime stories, for the most part, to "read like police blotter reports, peopled by remote, impersonal motiveless figures. One rarely encounters flesh-and-blood human beings who are involved in the drama of crime and victimization" (1980: 47). There seemed to be some sense of journalistic obligation to record ordinary street crimes without much embellishment.

On the other hand, Graber notes, reporting is less bloodless "when the crime is a freakish one or involves an unlikely victim or a socially prominent person" (1980: 47). Any peculiar twist of circumstance may make a particular crime newsworthy: Frequently the twist is an incongruity between the person's role in society and his or her role in the offense. A respected citizen who turns out to be an embezzler, a mild-mannered housewife who takes a knife to her unfaithful husband, a high school honor student raped on the way home from choir practice—it is such instances of criminal involvement for people who would seem to have no criminal associations that attract newspaper readers and television viewers, and therefore are selected by the media for intensive coverage.

Among the surest candidates for media attention are offenders who have committed a number of separate, serious offenses, especially serial killers. Widely publicized incidents of this type in the recent past include New York's "Son of Sam" killer David Berkowitz, who confessed in 1978 to six lover's-lane murders and seven murder attempts; Wayne B.

Williams, who was convicted in 1982 of murdering two black children in Atlanta, and is believed by police to have committed an additional twenty-three similar acts; and San Francisco's Black Muslim "Zebra" killers, who, although convicted in 1976 of murdering only three white victims, are thought by authorities to have been responsible for a total of more than a dozen such crimes. Part of media attention to a wave of similar offenses can of course be justified as a public service, to alert the community to danger and thus to take appropriate precautions. But beyond the public's interest based on motives of self-protection, the news value of such incidents, apparent in the huge amount of media attention to serial offenders, reflects a widely held view that the tendency to repeat serious crimes is itself an indication of an evil nature.

Among other distinguishing qualities of crimes that are singled out for media attention, Roshier (1973) has reported a tendency for newspapers to select criminal incidents for which offenders have been captured, perhaps because it enables them to write about motives for the crimes. And in the realm of television fiction it is found that dramas about crime deal more often with premeditated offenses—again, an indication of the offender's malevolent nature—than they would if they were representative of offense types as reflected in official statistics.

Likewise, the moral depravity of offenders may be established by evidence that their victims are especially innocent or vulnerable. It is thus newsworthy when victims are physically handicapped or young, as was true of Williams's victims in Atlanta. In cases of child molestation or rape the offender's badness is compounded because he has transgressed the special taboo against sexual innocence. Similarly, offenses against the elderly may be emphasized because of that group's vulnerability. A case in point is Fishman's (1978) study of an alleged "crime wave" against the elderly in New York City in 1976, as reported by tabloid newspapers and television. In fact, the author found no evidence that an unusual number of older people had been crime victims during the seven-week period of the supposed upsurge in such incidents; rather, he concluded, journalists selected incidents from the police wire—their primary source for such information—in such a way as to support the idea that there was a wave.

Notwithstanding the obvious fact that public perception of crime is to a great extent conditioned by the way it is reported in print and broadcast media, it would be an oversimplification to conclude that public stereotypes of crime as violent offenses committed by young, lower-class, nonwhite males derive from disproportionate media attention to these sorts of crimes. Even when a particular newspaper's crime reporting describes offenders more often than not as employed in middle-class occupations, white, and over the age of twenty-five, Graber's research indicates that the readers of that newspaper continue to hold images of criminals conforming to the popular stereotype.

Specifically, it is the public, rather than the media, that perceives both criminals and victims as largely flawed in character, nonwhite, and lower class. It is the public, rather than the media, that thinks of crime almost exclusively in terms of street rather than white-collar crime. These are the two types of images that, in the views of radical criminologists, most closely represent the stereotypes that capitalist ruling classes like to perpetuate. Inasmuch as the media do not closely hold to this stereotypical line, they are not the capitalist mouthpieces that radical criminologists charge them to be (Graber, 1980: 68).

Thus, while the media play to certain stereotypes in terms of the kinds of crimes they give greatest attention to, Graber's data support the contention that popular stereotypes of crime are deeply rooted in our culture, perhaps in human nature itself, and are not simply a creation of the institutions of mass communication.

MORAL CONNOTATIONS IN EXPERT ANALYSIS OF CRIME

Parallel to the polarized view that prevails at the level of political rhetoric and newspaper and broadcast journalism, one can discern within academic criminology a distinction between approaches to crime predicated on a bad-guys view and approaches taking a good-guys view of criminal offenders. Although more subtle than the images depicted in films and political speeches, general theories of human behavior vary according to the emphasis on laudable or base attributes of human nature and to the view of social institutions as contributing to or detracting from man's civilizing tendencies. Accordingly, among theories seeking to explain behavior that departs from established norms, some see a natural connection between crime and normal human propensities, while others see it as a departure from those propensities.

The so-called "positivist" school of criminology, which dominated scientific analysis of crime in the United States for more than a century, was inaugurated on a foundation of bad-guy assumptions. These assumptions have been subsequently modified but are still apparent in the writings of modern adherents of this approach. The prototypical positivist research study is a comparison between criminals and noncriminals in order to find attributes on which they differ, and then, having noted such differences, it provides a conclusion that these variations explain why criminals commit the offending acts and noncriminals abstain from them. The observed attributes associated with criminal conduct are taken to be outward indications of a person's evil nature.

Credit for bringing this approach to criminology belongs to the nineteenth-century Italian physician Cesare Lombroso and his students. Through primitive research techniques (which have been subsequently discredited), Lombroso identified what he thought were certain physical signs—facial characteristics, arm length, flat feet—associated with "an irresistible craving for evil for its own sake" among criminals (Lombroso, 1972: xxv). Followers of positivism have continued to examine criminals in efforts to uncover genetic, hormonal, neurological, chemical, and personality characteristics that explain propensities to commit crime. One of the most widely read recent books on crime (Wilson and Herrnstein, 1985) devotes considerable attention to evidence supporting the positivist dictum that "the antisocial tendencies of criminals are the result of their physical and psychic organization, which differs essentially from that of normal individuals" (Lombroso-Ferrero, 1972: 5).

Not surprisingly, given their view that criminals are bad guys, Lombrosians took a sympathetic view of victims. In fact, the term "social defense" is used to describe the early positivists' policy orientation, which, having ascribed much serious crime to unalterable elements in the criminal's constitution, supported the use of scientific measurement to diagnose such intractable offenders in order that they would be imprisoned for long periods of time, thus reducing the chance that normal members of society would become victims (Wolfgang, 1972: 277).

Adopting the basic assumption of the positivist method, the German criminologist Hans von Hentig (1948) extended his analysis of the distinctive physical, mental, and social characteristics of criminals to a similar analysis of victims. In his elaborate typology, Hentig includes categories of "good"—that is, innocent or blameless—victims, but he also includes categories for people who are subject to victimization because of their "bad" motives or dispositions. These include "wanton" victims, whose licentiousness tempts others to commit crimes against them; "acquisitive" victims, whose greediness for wealth renders them vulnerable to confidence operators and racketeers; and "tormentors," whose abusiveness over long periods of time in family situations culminates in criminal retaliation against them. These latter categories of victims, who seem to have "asked for" and "deserve" to be victimized, compose a substantial portion of what have come to be called "victim-precipitated" crimes—homicides or rapes in which the victim's behavior is responsible to a significant degree for the occurrence of the criminal act (Amir, 1971: chap. 15; Wolfgang, 1958: chap. 14).

A quite different set of assumptions underlay another approach to crime, identified with that group of social reformers whose larger agenda is known as the Progressive movement (Rothman, 1980). Rather than attribute crime to qualities within the individual, the Progressives sought to explain crime as a result of alien social influences. Focusing their attention on juvenile offenders, they blamed overcrowded slum conditions, lax moral standards among recent immigrant groups, and insufficient opportunity for inculcation of the values and goals of the middle class. Children who got in trouble were seen not as bad people but rather as virtuous souls who were driven by forces beyond their control. The solution to these problems, then, was to eradicate criminogenic social conditions, using the tools of modern social science.

It was within this context that the academic discipline of criminology took shape in the United States. Much of its development may be attributed to the preeminence of the Department of Sociology at the University of Chicago during the early 1900s, where Progressive assumptions about causes for social problems, including crime, were embraced. The Chicago approach investigated social tensions arising from poverty, culture conflict among generations, and other circumstances impinging upon residents of certain urban areas. Some of their investigations were carried out through intensive interaction with the subjects of study, like Shaw's (1966) classic biography of a gang boy. Others followed Lombroso's Positivist School in the use of quantitative measurement but, unlike the positivists, the Chicago studies were addressed to characteristics external to the offender (Short and Strodtbeck, 1965). This difference from Lombroso's school is crucial; for, while the early positivists attributed responsibility for crime to internal biological and psychological states, supporting the image of criminals as bad guys, the Chicago criminologists, by emphasizing forces beyond the individual's control, tended to counter the bad-guy image.

It is significant that this emphasis on external forces was associated with the University of Chicago, for it was also at Chicago that there had been a longstanding connection between scholarly and practical efforts. John Dewey had chaired the university's Department of Philosophy, Psychology, and Pedagogy around the turn of the century. His pragmatic philosophy was imprinted not only on the American education establishment but also, through his involvement in Jane Addams's Hull House, on the settlement house movement and its efforts to deal with problems of delinquency in urban slums (Hawes, 1971). The most enduring effort reflecting the applied orientation of Chicago social scientists has been the Chicago Area Project, consisting of a variety of attempts starting in the 1930s to arouse community concern and constructive involvement as a way of counteracting the negative influence of delinquent gangs, broken homes, and other symptoms of a pathological environment (Finestone, 1976; Schlossman, Zellman, and Shavelson, 1984).

At the federal level there have been intermittent instances in which crime has been addressed as a national problem. The Wickersham Commission, appointed during Herbert Hoover's presidential term, conducted a wide-ranging survey. It provided, among other kinds of evidence, frequently quoted documentation of the prevalence of the use of physical force to secure confessions from criminal suspects. But the most comprehensive such survey was not carried out until Lyndon Johnson's presidency. In response to heightened public sentiment for federal attention to the crime problem, the President's Commission on Law Enforcement and Administration of Justice was established in 1965. A number of prominent criminologists served as staff members and consultants to the commission, and the commission's report reflected much of what was considered state-of-the-art criminology at the time (U. S. President's Commission, 1967a). While the commission also paid considerable attention to the fear of crime and its impact on victims, its recommendations were clearly within the Progressive tradition. On preventing crime, it stated:

The prevention of crime covers a wide range of activities: Eliminating social conditions closely associated with crime; improving the ability of the criminal justice system to detect, apprehend, judge, and reintegrate into their communities those who commit crimes; and reducing the situations in which crimes are most likely to be committed (U. S. President's Commission, 1967a: vi).

And, in proposing "new ways of dealing with offenders," the Commission also articulated Progressive ideology:

The Commission's [recommendation for] the development of a far broader range of alternatives for dealing with offenders is based on the belief that, while there are some who must be completely segregated from society, there are many instances in which segregation does more harm than good. Furthermore, by concentrating the resources of the police, the courts, and correctional agencies on the smaller number of offenders who really need them, it should be possible to give all offenders more effective treatment (U. S. President's Commission, 1967a: vii).

As ways of implementing the recommendation for prevention, the commission advocated strengthening families, improving slum schools, and making available job training and counseling. In dealing with convicted offenders it concentrated on young people, for whom it proposed youth service bureaus, to operate much like voluntary social service agencies. It also stressed the use, whenever possible, of community-based corrections. In the statements quoted previously, the Commission seems to take for granted that the social science technology is available to prevent crime and reintegrate offenders into the community, while it gives scant attention to the need for protecting the public from incorrigibles. Indeed, in its volume on juvenile delinquency (U. S. President's Commission, 1967b) major emphasis is given to labeling theory, a theory that defines crime not in terms of an individual's acts in contravention of law but in terms of selective or arbitrary application of laws by powerful individuals or groups.

Based in part on recommendations of the President's Commission, Congress passed the Omnibus Crime Control and Safe Streets Act during the last year of Johnson's term. That legislation provided the basis for the Law Enforcement Assistance Administration (LEAA), a division of the Justice Department that lasted for fifteen years under five presidents and expended more than seven billion dollars during that time.. Conceived as an agency for reducing crime and improving the criminal justice system, its emphases varied, depending on the priorities of agency administrators and the political agendas of particular presidential administrations. It sponsored projects as diverse as nationwide surveys of criminal victimization, community treatment instead of institutionalization for juvenile runaways and truants, and a study of the extent to which the right to counsel is denied to indigent criminal defendants (Navasky and Paster, 1976: 36–37).

But the highest priority by far, as measured by the agency's own budget breakdowns, was for police functions—training programs, communications systems and equipment, and special vehicles for riot control; these were essentially reflections of Nixon's "law and order" stance, aimed at helping the law enforcement personnel who represent respectable citizens to win the war against the troublemakers in our midst.

LEAA wound down its activities in 1980 when the Carter Administration failed to ask Congress for further funding. With its formal abolition in 1982, some programs were simply abandoned and others transferred to other agencies. But the agency's elimination should be understood, not as an autonomous event hindering otherwise fruitful crime reduction efforts. It was, rather, a symptom of the wane of Progressive assumptions about the redeemability of criminal offenders—assumptions reflected in the report of the President's Commission a decade and a half earlier, which had provided the initial rationale for efforts like LEAA.

What had happened to diminish support for the Progressive approaches recommended by the President's Commission? In the first place, there were discrepancies of emphasis between the commission proposals published in 1967 and the Omnibus Crime Control Act as actually passed in 1968. Whereas the commission's recommendations included emphasis on overcoming criminogenic social conditions such as slum schools, family disorganization, and inadequate job training, the legislation that founded LEAA stressed support for established components of the criminal justice system—no doubt a reflection of differences in orientation between commission members and staff, who were relatively insulated from pressures from the criminal justice establishment, and the more susceptible elected officials who passed the law. Then too, the concern over crime that had provided the impetus for the President's Commission had escalated with the assassination of Martin Luther King Jr., and the rioting that followed.

The legislation was enacted against the background of the rise of black power, an increasing militant anti-Vietnam war movement, and a growing national polarization epitomized in the presidential election of 1968, when Richard Nixon ran as a law and order candidate and aimed much of his fire at the civil libertarian values and policies of the Attorney General of the United States, Ramsey Clark (Navasky and Paster, 1976: 40–41).

A second factor helping to explain the demise of LEAA was the apparent ineffectiveness of a wide range of programs, many of which had preceded the LEAA initiative. A byproduct of the specific LEAA research agenda was a more general concern with scientific evaluation of techniques purported to prevent crime or treat offenders. When evaluations of various types of group therapy or evaluations of the delinquency prevention results of components of Johnson's War on Poverty of the 1960s were scrutinized, the evidence was discouraging. Based upon evaluations of rehabilitation programs, LEAA itself had become imbued with pessimism about the potential effectiveness of the techniques of personality and behavior modification so highly touted in American society in the post-World War II years, These negative results supported the melancholy conclusion that crime was so deeply rooted—in individuals' personalities or various components of the social fabric—as to be impervious to the best efforts of practitioners of the social and psychological sciences (Lipton, Martinson, and Wilks, 1975).

In addition to these reasons, LEAA simply succumbed in a budgetary crunch, along with many other domestic social programs, as the Reagan administration sought simultaneously to increase military appropriations and lower taxes. However dear the law-and-order slogan was to the hearts of Reagan's conservative supporters, it was apparently less salient than the economic and national defense considerations forming the foundation of the Reagan agenda.

Along with the decline of the Progressive faith there emerged during the 1970s a criminal justice philosophy known as the "justice model." It emphasized the importance of proportionality—of punishment as an act of social condemnation proportional to the gravity of the offense, as determined by (a) by the degree of harm to the victim, and (b) the offender's culpability: whether the act was done, for example, with the intention to do harm (von Hirsch, 1985: chap. 6). This philosophy was originally expressed as a critique of unjust practices in the criminal justice system that cut two ways: unfairness to some suspected or convicted offenders because they were treated too harshly and unfairness because others were treated too leniently (von Hirsch, 1976). The justice model has been appropriated by many law and order advocates, however, who see due process guarantees, plea bargaining, community treatment, probation and parole, and challenges to the death penalty as mechanisms within the criminal justice system improperly aiding the bad guys and endangering the security of the good ones.

An alternative to the justice model, which has had a similar effect in supplanting Progressive ideology and buttressing the law and order approach, is the theory that the criminal justice system's primary function in dealing with criminals should be incapacitation. This approach represents a meeting ground between the assumption that convicted offenders are a different breed from the rest of us (Miller, 1988) and "social defense" concern for vulnerable targets in society. Researchers at the RAND Corporation, starting with extensive interviews with incarcerated repeat offenders, have extrapolated from their samples to estimate the amount of crime that might be prevented if individuals prone to commit frequent crimes could be identified early and incarcerated for the period of their lives in which further offenses are predicted (Greenwood, 1982).

Questions remain about the feasibility of identifying such individuals, as well as about the ethics of punishing people for what they might do in the future, as opposed to punishing them for what they have done in the past. But beyond these considerations, questions have been raised about one of the assumptions of incapacitation—the assumption that there are a finite number of people prone to commit crimes, such that their identification and removal from free society would directly reduce the incidence of crime by just the number of offenses that those individuals would carry out if they were free. These questions derive from the more sociological view of Lombroso's student Enrico Ferri, who, borrowing from Durkheim, formulated a "law of criminal saturation," stating that "in a given social environment with definite individual and physical conditions, a fixed number of delicts, no more and no less, can be committed" (Ferri, 1917: 209). Although acknowledging that the conditions he refers to can change over time, Ferri concludes that imposing legal punishment is not an effective way to reduce the crime rate in a given society.

Recent theorists have amplified Ferri's idea by noting the context of many criminal acts that are committed by groups. They note the likelihood that if one member of a juvenile gang or criminal syndicate is incarcerated, his place will be taken by someone else through an "illegitimate labor market" (National Research Council, 1978: 65). This view, then, might be understood as a more pessimistic approach than the incapacitation perspective: pessimistic both in terms of the prevalence of deviance-prone people and also in terms of the possibility of reducing crime. Incapacitation assumes a finite number of people who are inclined to crime and who in fact engage in it, whereas "replacement theory" sees the pool of candidates for criminal careers as infinite—inexhaustible numbers of individuals with all the desire and resources needed to step into readymade positions within existing organizations, awaiting only the departure of incumbents and a summons to replace them.

THESES UNDERLYING THE PRESENT WORK

Before proceeding to the following chapters, the reader may find it helpful to be introduced to the basic theses underlying this work. They may be summarized as follows.

1. Making moral judgments is a fundamental and often useful process in human thought. A tendency toward extreme—or "polarized"—moral judgment, however, distorts reality and leads to maladaptive action.
2. Conventional criminal events are likely to be the subject of extreme moral judgments, in which perpetrators are seen as very bad people and morally guilty, and victims are seen as very good and morally innocent. Certain criminal events, however, do not fit the conventional stereotype, and in such cases criminals may be seen as good and victims as bad.
3. Current criminal justice policy is affected by moral polarization, which leads to conflict, frustration, and often stalemate.
4. Effective criminal justice policy will take account of moral judgments but try to avoid the one-sided or exaggerated elements of polarization.

The present chapter has presented an overview of perceptions of the nature of criminal acts, offenders, and the situations under which crime is embarked upon or abstained from. Chapters 2 and 3 will deal respectively with images of offenders as evil, and as good. Chapter 4 will treat both good and bad images of victims. Chapter 5 will do the same for groups: groups actually involved in criminal activity, groups influencing individuals to act in antisocial or prosocial ways, community structures, whole societies, and institutions representing social authority, like the courts and prisons. Chapter 6 will consider the nature of polarized thinking and polarization processes at the group level. And the final chapter will discuss various policies based on nonpolarized views of the crime problem and indicate how abandoning polarized thinking may lead to more effective criminal justice policy.

2

Offenders As Bad Guys

Among bad-guy views of criminal offenders one may distinguish between two broadly different approaches. One approach takes as its starting point a cynical view of human nature as a whole. Adherents of this view are not surprised that someone who covets another's possessions simply steals them, or that people with greater physical strength use it against those who are weaker. Antisocial conduct is considered "normal," in the sense that the motives impelling such behavior are inherent in the average person. Given the prevalence of base instincts throughout the human race, one need not uncover any special attributes among criminal offenders to explain their misdeeds: What requires explanation is, rather, why everyone does not act with similar disregard for the welfare of others. The mystery, from this perspective, is how anyone comes to act beyond self-interest, how it is that a few human beings transcend their most basic nature and concern themselves with the well-being of other individuals, groups, or the human race as a whole.

The other bad-guy approach, by contrast, starts by accepting the proposition that basic human propensities include concern for the rights of others and that normal social development entails learning to control one's own impulses for the benefit of one's family or ethnic group or nation. The issue for proponents of this outlook is to account for the peculiar circumstances of those abnormal individuals who commit acts that harm their fellows. It is from this perspective that the "disease model" of crime arises (MacNamara, 1977). The criminologist's job is to locate the source of the pathological process, if possible to treat its host but if not, to isolate the diseased person in order to prevent the spread of the infection to healthy individuals.

Between these two positions may be discerned a middle-ground view, that there is a substantial but not overwhelming propensity among people to violate others' rights. For some people these propensities predominate over altruistic ones; for others they are subordinated to social values stressing cooperation and compromise in light of the interests of people with whom they interact. Whether bad qualities govern people's behavior depends partly on their biological endowment and partly on what they have experienced during the course of their lives.

Each of these views—that badness is fundamental in human nature, that it is a departure from normal human conduct, and that it is frequently present but not predominant—is held in one form or another by many people in contemporary society. Variations are expressed in academic theories of crime, and they may be discerned in approaches to crime as a practical problem.

THE DOCTRINE OF SIN

Explanations of bad behavior as emanating from an evil nature are rooted in the concept of sinfulness as a human quality. Early Christian theology, formulated by St. Augustine in the fourth century A.D., expounded the doctrine that immorality, or badness, is a consequence of original sin, as exemplified by Adam's failure to resist temptation in the Garden of Eden. The lesson is clear: If the ancestor of us all was unable to do what was righteous in the eyes of God, we must all have strong inclinations toward violating authoritative rules. The pervasiveness of sin has been most strongly insisted upon by certain orthodox Protestants who since the sixteenth century have regarded sin as basically a condition of the soul, which can be overcome only by means of a profound "transformation of being" (Tillich, 1968: 213). Having sinned, one may be redeemed from a state of sin, through God's grace, by acts of atonement but absolution is by no means guaranteed.

Given the difficulty and uncertainty of the transformation from a state of sin to one of grace, acts of greed, lust, and violence do not require any explanation in terms of special circumstances or abnormalities. Since such acts are simply expressions of deep-seated dispositions characteristic of the human race as a whole, special explanation is required only for the relatively rare individuals who through God's grace manage to escape the widespread affliction of sin.

As far as American policy toward offenders is concerned, this religious doctrine found its strongest expression in the New England Calvinist tradition with its emphasis on the doctrine of predestination. The Puritans believed that the Almighty determines even before birth whether a person will be among the select few for whom eternal salvation is preordained or among the multitudes destined for perdition. In practice the doctrine could be used to justify severe legal punishment.

If a culprit standing before the bench is scheduled to spend eternity in hell, it does not matter very much how severely the judges treat him, for all the hardships and sufferings in this world will be no more than a faint hint of the torments awaiting him in the hereafter (Erikson, 1966: 190).

UNRESTRAINED IMPULSES

To refer to mankind as dominated by violent and selfishly acquisitive sentiments is even today to be associated with the views of the seventeenth-century philosopher Thomas Hobbes. Hobbes took credit for having founded the science of politics, or as he called it, Civil Philosophy, predicated on his observation of mankind's selfish tendencies (Hobbes, 1968: 10). In the absence of powerful sovereigns to keep their subjects docile through fear, people are dominated by competitive motives, which in turn lead them to strive for glory, power or material possessions. "Competition of Riches, Honour, Command, or other power, enclineth to Contention, Enmity, and War: Because the way of one Competitor, to the attaining of his desire, is to kill, subdue, supplant, or repell the other" (Hobbes, 1968: 161).

It is these human propensities which Hobbes saw as propelling human societies toward the "Warre of every one against every one" (Hobbes, 1968: 189), a result that is inevitable unless the group's members, foreseeing that their own interests would ultimately be jeopardized by all-out civil strife, agree to surrender their natural rights—that is, the right to do whatever is necessary to satisfy their human needs—to a powerful sovereign. The society's members then incur an obligation to the sovereign, who in turn should respect the will of the majority of his subjects. Although Hobbes did recognize differences among people with respect to the strength of their "passions," or what we would now call motives, such as partiality, pride, and revenge, the emphasis of his writings is on the general tendencies of humans to act in their own interests and to disregard the interests of others.

Hobbes's position on natural egoism has been accepted by many people through the ages, down to and including the twentieth century Dutch Marxist Willem Bonger. Bonger writes of the young child as having "the tendency to monopolize everything that he desires (the prehensory instinct, Lafargue names it). It is just this instinct that must be combated to make a child honest. It would therefore be more correct to say that dishonesty is innate" (quoted in Rennie, 1978: 113).

Social Control Theory

Views like that of Hobbes, asserting the need for restraining mechanisms to counteract aggressive propensities in human nature, have come to be known in modern criminology as "social control" theory. The prototype for sociological explanation in this tradition is Émile Durkheim's classic work on suicide. Starting with the observation that acts of suicide violate the rules of religious, family, and governmental authority in Western society, Durkheim attributes high suicide rates to a weakening influence of these institutions on personal conduct (1951: 208–9).

With respect to crime as well, social control theory explains high rates as a consequence of society's failure to keep people from following their personal desires (Vold and Bernard, 1986: 232). In a well ordered society, pressure from religious and family leaders serves to check any tendencies on the part of their group members to violate rules of property ownership, or rules proscribing violence against others. In modern society, however, the force of these social pressures becomes attenuated—a situation described by Durkheim as *anomic*, or normless (1951: 246–57).

Present-day control theorists no longer consider human nature to be dominated by animal instincts, as suggested by Hobbes. Nor do they necessarily express moral condemnation of impulsive behavior. Nevertheless, their underlying assumption of the harmfulness of impulsive behavior explains their inclusion among the bad-guy theorists.

The fullest modern exposition of control theory is presented by Travis Hirschi in the course of interpreting findings from a research project designed to reveal those social and psychological variables that best distinguish delinquents from nondelinquents. Control, for Hirschi, is exercised through social bonds that take the form of attachment to parents, school, and peers; of belief in middle class values; and of involvement in conventional activities like going to school, working, and engaging in sports. Hirschi finds that nondelinquents are indeed more tightly bound to society in these ways than are delinquents, supporting the conclusion that the absence of controlling forces promotes delinquency. He provides a classic statement of the view that the inclination to offend is pervasive. "The question 'Why do they do it?' is simply not the question [social control] theory is designed to answer. The question is, 'Why don't we do it?' There is much evidence that we would if we dared" (Hirschi, 1969: 34).

AFFINITIES TOWARD CRIME

The foregoing explanations of crimes do not lend themselves well to direct scientific verification, inasmuch as they make assumptions about universal human characteristics that are not readily observed. By contrast, those theories that view criminal tendencies as an attribute of some but not all people are more easily subject to study through the methods of modern social science. As indicated in Chapter 1, positivist methods consist of efforts to uncover those relatively enduring attributes linked to criminal behavior. The attributes are bad because they are thought to produce crime, and insofar as these attributes refer to internal states of individuals, those individuals are thought to be bad people.

In early times evil acts were accounted for by saying that their perpetrators were possessed by the Devil, who was regarded as God's powerful adversary, a force that might invade the soul and while there, supplant the hosts' self-control and manipulate their behavior to serve the Devil's own purpose. Similarly, witchcraft was considered a phenomenon in which the Devil used witches as his human agents to manipulate others in diabolical conduct. More recently, secular science has redefined internal states predisposing people to immoral behavior in biological, psychological, and social terms. Thus, crime may be accounted for as acts of offenders who, depending upon the disciplinary orientation of the explainer, possess chromosomal abnormalities, psychopathic personalities, or values derived from a subculture of violence.

Such explanations have been classified as theories of *affinity*, implying an "attractive force" between the person and deviant behavior (Matza, 1969: 92). It is an approach allowing for at least some degree of free will on the part of the offender. Whatever the circumstances giving rise to the internal state, moral condemnation is justified to the extent that the offender is perceived as "choosing" to engage in illegal conduct.

THE CLASSICAL SCHOOL

Because a person's freedom to choose between one course of conduct and another is a fundamental precept of the the classical school of criminology, we may consider how that school's adherents explain the difference between criminals and law-abiding individuals. The school originated in the eighteenth century, as an application of the philosophical Age of Enlightenment to the problem of crime, with the publication of a famous essay by an Italian aristocrat, Cesare Beccaria. The essay, "Dei delitti e delle penne [On Crimes and Punishments]," was so timely that "almost at once, as if an exposed nerve had been touched, all Europe was stirred to excitement" (Paolucci, 1963: x). It was essentially a political document, a condemnation of legal systems then prevalent in Europe in which punishment for crime was harsh, often brutal, and administered so as to favor the powerful, wealthy, and titled members of society and discriminate against the poor and powerless.

The thrust of Beccaria's writing was to advocate more humanitarian laws for punishing crime, and especially application of punishments, by a system blind to the offender's station in society. Following the utilitarian premise that people do what they anticipate will bring pleasure and avoid what they expect to be painful, Beccaria advocated that punishments be "stronger in proportion as they are contrary to the public good, and of the public safety and happiness [and] as the inducements to commit them are stronger" (Beccaria, 1963: 62).

Jeremy Bentham expounded the classical approach in a more fully developed form. His major work on crime, *An Introduction to the Principles of Morals and Legislation*, spells out in far more detail than Beccaria's essay an elaborate rationale and specific guidelines for criminal legislation. Although classical theory attributes free will to human beings in general, Bentham's (1970: 203) proposal for punishment as an "artificial consequence" of offending acts implies that without such threats of punishment the average person would be disposed to commit crimes. But he also found it necessary to consider the possibility that punishment might affect different people differently. In fact, he includes in his book a chapter titled, "Of Circumstances Influencing Sensibility." There, among a catalog of circumstances such as knowledge, intellectual power, insanity, and religious biases, he considers attributes reflecting the moral dimensions that we are concerned with here. For one thing, Bentham asserts, people vary in the extent of their "moral sensibility," the degree to which they are susceptible or impervious to the opinions of others. He then distinguishes this from another variable, "moral biases," which differ from moral sensibilities by taking account of particular acts. That is, two people may be equally susceptible to public opinion in a general way, but the first may be particularly sensitive to morals governing professional conduct, for example, and the second more concerned with standards governing obligations to family members.

Aside from these factors, Bentham suggests that crime may be understood as the behavior of bad people when he writes of "bent of inclinations" as one of the circumstances affecting a person's response to pain and pleasure.

By the bent of a man's inclinations may be understood the propensity he has to expect pleasure or pain from certain objects rather than from others. A man's inclinations may be said to have such or such a bent, when, amongst the several sorts of objects which afford pleasure in some degree to all men, he is apt to expect more pleasure from one particular sort, than from another particular sort, or more from any given particular sort, than another man would from that sort (Bentham, 1970: 49).

As formulated by Beccaria and Bentham, classical theory reflects a view of the offender's blameworthiness to the extent that it identifies pleasure with illegal behavior. Individual differences are not a major emphasis of the classical school, but in recognizing that some people but not others are motivated to gratify their own needs at the expense of others' rights, the classical theorists recognize distinctions in moral sensibility. When offenders choose to do something illegal because they anticipate that it will outweigh the expected punishment, while law-abiding citizens abstain because for them the consequences are weighted differently, one may conclude that the offenders' antisocial motives, or destructive needs, or considerations of self-interest, are more powerful than their desire for cooperation or sympathy for the feelings of their fellow citizens.

THE POSITIVIST SCHOOL

If adherents of the classical school appear at times to have admitted moral judgments through the back door, Cesare Lombroso, the founder of the positivist school, seems to have ushered them in at the front. Positivism applies to living organisms the scientific methods of the physical sciences with their emphasis on careful observation, experimentation, and precise measurement. Having brought this approach to criminology, Lombroso deserves credit for having made the bad-guys approach scientific. His major research efforts, and those for which he is best known, consisted of investigating the biological attributes of born criminals, those who are "organically fitted for evil" (quoted by Wolfgang, 1972: 279). In these investigations, Lombroso and his associates sought out connections between bad character and scientifically observable traits, or signs. Lombroso referred to these signs as *stigmata*, the plural of the Greek word meaning a mark of shame.

Not all interpretations of the correlates of crime, to be sure, have been expressed in terms of opprobrium. Indeed, it would seem that the deterministic stance of positivism, in contrast with the assumptions of free-will theories, would preclude imposing negative moral judgments upon criminal offenders; insofar as criminal conduct is attributable to factors beyond a person's control, it would seem unreasonable to blame him for it. As we shall see in the next chapter, there have also been in recent years many proponents of the view that one should *not* hold criminal actors blameworthy but rather excuse them because they have been subjected to social discrimination and frustrations due to circumstances beyond their control.

Nevertheless it can be observed that, among individuals who grow up in broken families, live in deteriorated neighborhoods, and have suffered from poor schooling and lack of job training, some pursue criminal careers and others do not. On this basis some theorists infer the possibility of freedom of choice within a deterministic framework—a position Matza (1964) refers to as "soft determinism." Just as the religious doctrine of predestination seems not to have discouraged the moral condemnation of the damned, so too has determinism gone along with scientific depictions of criminal offenders as blameworthy for acting in accordance with their predilections.

Biological Signs

As the study of crime became scientific, it tended at first to focus on aspects of the physical world—on geographical and climatic influences on the crime rate, and subsequently on physical attributes of the human organism. This approach is nicely congruent with the public's desire to distinguish the good guys from the bad guys. "To believe that lawbreakers must be marked by defects that set them apart from those who conformed to the law was comforting. Evil actions had an evil source, a biological inferiority certified by science, and thus the moral world fell into an understandable pattern" (Sykes, 1978: 241).

The positivists' interest in biological correlates of crime was foreshadowed in the early nineteenth century by the scientifically popular theory of phrenology, an approach to explaining behavior by examining the human skull. The founder of phrenology, Franz Joseph Gall, based his approach on the supposition that human temperament comprises twenty-six separate faculties of mind, each of which is located in a particular area of the brain. People possess such faculties to the degree that the corresponding regions of the brain are highly developed. The size of a region of the brain reflects the extent to which the person possesses the trait located there. The shape of a person's skull, in turn, corresponds to the contours of the brain, so that one may ascertain the magnitude of a particular faculty by noting whether there is a bump or a depression on the corresponding area of the skull's surface. Charles Caldwell, who published the first American textbook on phrenology, linked some of these faculties to propensities for distinct types of crime: one person, with a surplus of the "acquisitive" faculty, is disposed to a career as a thief; another, highly possessed of the faculty of "combativeness," tends to commit criminal assault. The new science had a considerable vogue among prison administrators; New York's Sing Sing Prison was lauded in 1847 as a "phrenologically conducted institution" (Davies, 1955: 102), and the Eastern Penitentiary in Pennsylvania continued to employ a phrenological framework to explain the criminal propensities of prisoners there until the early 1900s (Fink, 1938: chap. 1; Vold, 1958: 45–48).

Lombroso's emphasis on biological determinants of crime, quite different from that of the phrenologists, was based on his medical training and background in neuropathology, This background led him to develop an "atavistic" theory of behavior—a theory postulating that criminals are a subspecies of what we know as the modern biological species of mankind. He describes how an incident early in his career as a student of psychiatry led to that theory.

I, therefore, began to study criminals in the Italian prisons, and, amongst others, I made the acquaintance of the famous brigand Vilella. This man possessed such extraordinary agility, that he had been known to scale steep mountain heights bearing a sheep on his shoulders. His cynical effrontery was such that he openly boasted of his crimes. On his death one cold grey November morning, I was deputed to make the *post mortem,* and on laying open the skull I found on the occipital part, exactly on the spot where a spine is found in the normal skull, a distinct depression which I named *median occipital fossa,* because of its situation precisely in the middle of the occiput as in inferior animals, especially rodents. This depression, as in the case of animals, was correlated with the hypertrophy of the *vermis,* known in birds as the middle cerebellum (Lombroso-Ferrero, 1972: xxiv).

Clearly, these observations of Lombroso's were not occurring in a theoretical vacuum. On the contrary, they were made only a few years after the publication in 1859 of Darwin's *Origin of Species.* Thus, the theory of human evolution provided a basis for Lombroso's contention that the criminal was something less than fully evolved *homo sapiens*; he was, rather, a throwback to a subspecies lacking modern mankind's moral sensibilities.

Darwin's theory, though presented by its author with great care to observe accepted rules for reporting scientific evidence, had a tremendous influence on popular thought. An important channel was through popular fiction, especially when it made use of Darwinian themes to explain human violence. Inherited degeneracy sometimes cropped up in fictional depictions of aristocratic society, but most often it appeared in the lower social orders. In the turn-of-the-century novel *McTeague,* the title character is presented as having a veneer of gentleness. But when a friendly wrestling match turns into a grudge contest and his ear is bitten by his opponent, McTeague's primitive nature impels him to break his opponent's arm through an act of unaccustomed brutality. The author explains the transformation thus:

The brute that in McTeague lay so close to the surface leaped instantly to life, monstrous, not to be resisted. He sprang to his feet with a shrill and meaningless clamor, totally unlike the ordinary bass of his speaking tones. It was the hideous yelling of a hurt beast, the squealing of a wounded elephant. He framed no words; in the rush of high-pitched sound that issued from his wide-open mouth there was nothing articulate. It was something no longer human; it was rather an echo from the jungle (Norris, 1981: 182).

The propensity for Lombroso's brand of positivism to take on moral overtones, in spite of its deterministic assumptions, may be accounted for to a great extent through its connections with Darwin. Evolutionary theory itself implies a kind of progress from lower-order to higher-order animals. When the process of biological evolution is reversed, so that physical characteristics of more primitive mankind appear in present-day humans, these people can be expected to act without due regard for established social rules. Lombroso observed such connections between stigmata and crime:

Twenty-eight percent of criminals have handle-shaped ears standing out from the face as in the chimpanzee; in other cases they are placed at different levels. . . . The nose . . . is frequently twisted, up-turned or of a flattened, negroid character in thieves; in murderers, on the contrary, it is often aquiline like the beak of a bird of prey (Lombroso-Ferrero, 1972: 14-15).

Other anomalies especially likely to be found among criminals were receding chins, excessively long arms, premature dental caries, and flat feet.

Such observations, which provided Lombroso with a foundation for the theory of crime as evolutionary atavism, have been long discredited, as attempts to replicate them using controlled sampling have failed to show the differences reported by Lombroso and his students. Nevertheless, along with continuing efforts to improve scientific methodology in studying the biology of crime, certain more recent investigators have reverted to moralistic language in summarizing their research.

Among the most prominent of these is the physical anthropologist Earnest Hooton. While often describing offenders in morally laden terms, Hooton at the same time urged scientific objectivity in the biological study of crime. He noted resistance to these endeavors among social scientists, whom he perceived as ideologically biased against his approach because it implied limitations upon efforts to treat crime through the amelioration of criminogenic social conditions. But he also recognized opposition to biological theories in more conservative quarters: Among advocates of punitive sanctions against criminals, he pointed out, there is a reluctance to acknowledge the impact of constitutional factors, for to the extent that a person's criminality is determined by organic factors beyond his control, it appears unjust to make him suffer for it.

In research carried out during the 1930s Hooton and his coworkers at Harvard studied more than 17,000 American men, about one eighth of whom were noncriminals included for purposes of comparison with the majority of subjects, who were convicted offenders. In presenting his findings in summary form Hooton makes strenuous efforts to conform to the canons of science. He describes his methods in detail; controls racial, ethnic, and social variables in comparisons between offenders and "civilians"; explains how those methods were designed to meet accepted standards for sampling and statistical analysis; and notes the practical considerations that limited his efforts to achieve an ideal research design. Moreover, although he is prone to indulge in some stereotyping in interpreting his results, he is as likely to apply them negatively to the majority group as to minorities. For example, in speaking of Chinese and Japanese, he notes that "very few of [them] appear to get into jail, a fact which seems to reflect the difficulty of Americanizing the Oriental" (Hooton, 1939: 21). Nevertheless, when it comes to the interpretation of crime, although acknowledging the interaction of biological with environmental forces, Hooton's view of biological inheritance embodies clear moral connotations.

So I think that inherently inferior organisms are, for the most part, those which succumb to the adversities or temptations of their social environment and fall into antisocial behavior, and that it is impossible to improve and correct environment to a point at which these flawed and degenerate human beings will be able to succeed in honest social competition. The bad organism sullies a good environment and transforms it into one which is evil. Of course, I should by no means argue that man should cease to attempt to ameliorate his social environment, but, when he entirely neglects the improvement of his own organism, he condemns his environmental efforts to futility (Hooton, 1939: 388).

In the years since Hooton's study was published, research on biological factors associated with crime has continued. For some years a major focus was the connection between certain body types and criminal tendencies (Cortés and Gatti, 1972; Glueck and Glueck, 1956; Sheldon et al.,

1949); recent investigations have considered genetic, psychophysiologi-
cal, neurological and biochemical components (Mednick, Moffitt, and
Stack, 1987). There have been continuing refinements in techniques, and
the significance of the work has been recognized by such mainstream
criminologists as Norval Morris of the University of Chicago School of
Law (Morris and Tonry, 1980), and Marvin Wolfgang (1977) of the
University of Pennsylvania. These studies support the proposition that,
among possible variables commonly proposed as causes of crime, a definite though small component is attributable to biological sources.

And yet, as several observers (Farrington, 1987; Jeffery, 1979;
Mednick, 1987; Sagarin, 1980) have noted, there continues to be resistance to biological explanations of crime among substantial numbers of
American criminologists. A number of reasons have been adduced to account for this resistance. One reason has to do with academic territorial-
ity. Scientific criminology in the United States has traditionally come under the purview of university departments of sociology, which have a
vested interest in explaining criminal phenomena in terms of variables that
they are accustomed to deal with. The members of these departments are
consequently reluctant to grant legitimacy to theories beyond their sphere
of expertise.

Another explanation for resistance to biological explanations of crime
is derived from failure to accept their deterministic premises. At the ideological level, it derives from the persistence among modern liberals of the
optimism of the Progressive tradition, as discussed in Chapter 1, which
clings to hopes, even in the face of discouraging experience, that some
techniques will emerge for rehabilitating criminal offenders or for recon-
structing a crime-resistant society. Since such hopes would be difficult to
sustain in the face of evidence that crime is caused by deep-seated biological tendencies, adherents of the liberal view tend to disparage biological
explanations out of hand without considering the validity of scientific
findings.

Instructively, Sagarin (1980) considers the biology of crime among
the major "taboos" in criminology. Taboo, in the Freudian sense, is defined as "a series of socialized rules given a mystical sanction to guard individuals from committing acts for which they had strong unconscious inclinations" (Firth, 1964). Is it too much to suppose that the Freudian dynamic is involved here, that resisting biological explanations of crime is a
way of avoiding the inherent attractiveness of the notion of the constitu-

tionally evil criminal? The vehemence with which biological explanations of crime are often attacked, I submit, may itself serve as evidence of the attackers' "strong unconscious inclinations" toward them.·

MORAL DEFECT

Although he is often overshadowed by Lombroso's fame, it would be a mistake to fail to recognize the distinctive contribution made to the positivist position by Raffaele Garofalo, a younger contemporary of Lombroso's, whose influential textbook *Criminology* was published in 1885. Garofalo was a practicing lawyer who also held positions as a magistrate and professor of criminal law and procedure at the University of Naples.

Even more than Lombroso, Garofalo deals with crime as a moral issue, and with the offender in terms of moral incapacity. His starting point is "natural crime," which is not simply behavior proscribed by law, but rather conduct that is offensive to the universal senses of "pity" and "probity"—the former expressed as concern for the physical suffering of others and the latter as respect for property rights. The criminal, he concludes, is one who lacks such sentiments. Although he finds Lombroso's theory of specific physical stigmata to be unproven, Garofalo nonetheless considers the true criminal's moral deficiency to rest on some as yet unclear hereditary basis (Allen, 1972).

From the view that certain offenders' criminal propensities are innate it follows that efforts to reform them would be futile. Lacking the capacity for altruistic sentiments, they pose an ever-present danger if left at liberty. Thus it is not surprising that Garofalo, Lombroso, and other positivists emphasize legal measures aimed at "social defense"—protection of the civilized members of society. Once a person has been diagnosed as lacking the ability to sympathize with others, the state is justified in doing whatever is necessary to incapacitate him from doing further harm. For offenders whose criminal propensities are not overpowering, efforts should be made to place them in an environment to which they might adapt, but for the most intractable of them the state must resort to life imprisonment, transportation to a penal colony, or, in cases where the offender is altogether lacking in moral sensibilities and therefore "forever incapable of social life" (Allen, 1972: 330), legal execution.

Even among reformers who did not share the skepticism of the Italian school toward rehabilitation there was a belief in some form of innate deficiency among serious offenders, although they were confident that such deficiencies could be overcome by the reforms they advocated. Zebulon Brockway, architect of the ambitious and innovative Elmira Reformatory, which was opened in in New York in 1876, subscribed to the theory of moral defect. He was of the opinion that "imprisoned felons are defective; their crimes show this. They were out of adjustment with their environment rather than that their environment was exceptionally unfavorable.for their good behavior" (quoted by Hawes, 1971: 152–53).

The legal system in the United States was similarly unforgiving of offenders who exhibited a lack of ethical standards. It followed English precedent in absolving of criminal responsibility offenders with defects of "reason," but did not excuse "moral insanity," described by Prichard in 1835 as :

a form of mental derangement in which the intellectual functions appear to have sustained little or no injury, while the disorder is manifested, principally or alone, in the state of the feelings, temper, or habits. In cases of this nature the moral and active principles of the mind are strongly perverted or depraved; the power of self-government is lost or greatly impaired, and the individual is found incapable, not of talking or reasoning upon any subject proposed to him, but of conducting himself with decency and propriety in the business of life (quoted by Glover, 1960: 120).

Other terms like monomania, moral paresis, moral idiocy, and moral imbecility have been used to identify offenders who were observed to be deficient in this way. That this syndrome was rejected by the legal system as an excuse for crime was illustrated in the famous trial of Charles Guiteau for the assassination of President James Garfield in 1881. "Moral insanity" was claimed as the principal argument in his defense, but since his lawyers were unable to convince the jury that he was incapable of distinguishing right from wrong, he was convicted and hung (Rosenberg, 1968). His conviction illustrates the prevalent legal rule in the United States that " depravity, viciousness, perversity, and all manner of 'queer' behavior, if not associated with irrationality, must be considered as the behavior of sane individuals subject to control by regular court punishments" (Vold, 1958: 113–14).

Psychopathic Personality

Whereas the notion of moral defect as a clinical type has been known since Hippocrates, the peculiar pattern known as psychopathic personality is of more recent origin. The term "constitutional psychopath," connoting an innate basis for the disorder, was introduced in 1905 by Adolf Meyer, a Swiss-born psychiatrist, and during the early part of this century the syndrome was thought by many to have a hereditary basis. It received wide public attention in a popular book (March, 1954), Broadway play, and film titled *The Bad Seed*, a story about an eight-year-old girl who first drowned another child who had won a penmanship medal that the girl thought she herself deserved, and subsequently committed another homicide, this time by arson, against a handyman who suspected her of the drowning and threatened to report his suspicions to the authorities. As the story develops, the girl's mother learns for the first time that the couple she had until then considered her own real parents had in fact adopted her when she was very young after the trial and electrocution of her mother (her daughter's grandmother), a notorious multiple murderer. The idea of psychopathy as a genetically transmitted disorder—which had skipped a generation in *The Bad Seed*—had been the subject of other works of fiction; the popularity of this story no doubt disseminated the idea further, but that popularity also indicates that the hereditary theory was accepted as plausible by the general public.

The psychiatrist Hervey Cleckley is responsible for the best known current formulation of the syndrome. In his book *The Mask of Sanity* he lists among the psychopath's characteristics unreliability, untruthfulness, lack of remorse and shame, and antisocial behavior. His work is reflected in the *Diagnostic and Statistical Manual* (known widely as the *DSM*) of the American Psychiatric Association, which serves as the standard reference for classifying patterns of mental disorder and uses terms similar to Cleckley's. The preferred name for the disorder has itself undergone changes. The word "constitutional" less frequently preceded the term "psychopath" from about 1940 on, reflecting lack of evidence for a biological basis. Subsequently, in the 1952 *DSM*, the term "sociopathic personality disturbance, antisocial reaction," replaced "psychopathic personality disorder," apparently from a sense that the syndrome ought to be understood more as a product of social learning than an intrapsychic disorder—only to be changed once again in the 1968 edition to "antisocial personality disorder."

Many professionals continue to use the term "psychopath," and it also continues to be in favor as a subject of basic psychological research (Hare, 1970) as well as clinical investigation (Guze, 1976; Yochelson and Samenow, 1976). Although considerable controversy about its meaning persists—some critics find the term too broad, while others suggest that it is a nonexistent phenomenon—one of the consistent elements in varying conceptions of psychopathy is the psychopath's lack of sensibility to conventional moral standards. This alleged lack of moral sensibility is the modern scientific counterpart of the Hobbesian view of mankind's innate badness. Twentieth-century psychiatry no longer considers all members of the human species to be bad, as did Hobbes; rather, it employs the category of psychopath to distinguish from the rest of us those individuals who are destined by something within them to do evil.

BAD WOMEN AND GIRLS

Our first thought of the criminal is as a bad *guy*, and thus as a male offender. If on second thought we think of female offenders, the picture that comes to mind may be just as morally objectionable as that of the male criminal, but it is a less threatening image. Bad girls are less likely than men to be thought of as endangering other people's physical safety or property; their infractions are more likely to be perceived as the kind that offend moral sensibilities or harm themselves, such as prostitution.

Moreover, judgments about the badness of behavior often depend upon the gender of the malefactor. In fact, a mode of conduct such as sexual promiscuity is often considered real *mis*conduct only when engaged in by a female; when carried out by a male, it is regarded as altogether acceptable or at worst a mere peccadillo. Heidensohn (1985) has addressed the question: Why have certain cases of female deviance, like Lizzie Borden's alleged ax murder of her father and stepmother, attracted so much attention? Part of the answer, no doubt, is the simple irony of a horrible crime being committed by a member of the "gentle" sex. But another basis for such fascination questions the assumption of the supposed gentleness of the female. After all, Eve, the biblical temptress, has come to represent all women who have lured men to violate the precepts of established authority.

A number of writers have sought to explain serious transgressions by females by attributing to them an unusually evil nature. Lombroso and

Ferrero (1903: 147) cite an Italian proverb: "Rarely is a woman wicked, but when she is she surpasses the man." Having studied biological "degeneration" among female offenders, they conclude that there are fewer "born criminals" among them, but that the degree of their abnormality is greater. "In short, we may assert that if female born criminals are fewer in number than the males, they are often much more ferocious" (Lombroso and Ferrero, 1903: 150). They classified 18 percent of the female criminals they studied as born criminals, compared with 31 percent for male offenders (Lombroso and Ferrero, 1903: 104). Among women whose crime was prostitution, however, the proportion of born criminals was higher. Based on several studies, anomalies appeared among 37 percent of the composite sample of prostitutes. This the authors interpret as evidence supporting the view that prostitution is the archetypal female dereliction. Since "the primitive woman was rarely a murderess; but she was always a prostitute" (Lombroso and Ferrero, 1903: 111), it seems natural that biological atavism in women would be associated with the form of offense prevailing in earliest times. Similarly, the novelist Charles Brockden Brown wrote of woman that "when she fell into criminal ways, . . . she fell from a greater height, and rescaling the slope was for her correspondingly more difficult. The gulf that separates men from insects is not wider than that which severs the polluted from the chaste among women" (Allen, 1981: 31).

Insofar as arrest statistics are an accurate reflection of offender characteristics, they support the conclusion that women are less prone to crime than men. Although the proportion of females among arrestees in the United States has increased over the past forty years, they still compose only 21 percent of those arrested for major crimes in 1989, and 17 percent of those arrested for lesser crimes (U. S. Department of Justice, 1990: 189). If we address the question whether the kinds of crimes for which women are most likely to be arrested provide any basis for moral judgment, no unequivocal answer emerges. With the assumption that serious crimes of violence (murder and nonnegligent manslaughter, aggravated assault, and robbery) are worse than such property offenses as burglary and larceny, women are less guilty, for men are disproportionately represented in the former category, making up almost 90 percent of arrestees when force or its threat is involved. In the realm of sexual offenses no overall gender differences emerge. Women accounted for two-thirds of arrests made in 1989 on charges of prostitution and commercialized vice, but men made up 99 percent of arrestees for forcible rape and 92 percent of arrestees for other sex offenses.

Only if one considers badness as determined by the commission of surreptitious forms of crime do females appear to approach males in immorality. The 1989 figures show females constituting 34 percent of arrested suspects for forgery and counterfeiting, 39 percent for embezzlement, and 46 percent for fraud. Even though men make up the majority of individuals arrested for these offenses, some observers have suggested that women are more successful at surreptitious crime, and so take these data to support their conclusion that women actually surpass men as deceitful offenders.

Not too many years ago Pollak (1950: 8-15) enumerated the distinguished criminologists, female as well as male, who consider deceit as the hallmark of the female criminal. Having noted as a historical curiosity a fifteenth-century explanation for women's deceitfulness as a result of Eve's creation from a *curved* rib of Adam's, Pollak went on to advance, as an idea that had theretofore received too little attention, the hypothesis that women exceed men in the inclination to be deceitful because of gender differences in sexual physiology. He noted that

man must achieve an erection in order to perform the sex act and will not be able to hide his failure. His lack of positive emotion in the sexual sphere must become overt to the partner and pretense of sexual response is impossible for him, if it is lacking. Woman's body, however, permits such pretense to a certain degree and lack of orgasm does not prevent her ability to participate in the sex act. It cannot be denied that this basic physiological difference may well have a great influence on the degree of confidence which the two sexes have in the possible success of concealment and thus on their character pattern in this respect (Pollak, 1950: 10).

Pollak supplemented this conclusion by referring to social norms requiring women to use deceit to conceal their menstrual periods, to conceal information about sex from young children, and to ensnare men as husbands while professing to be merely passive recipients of their advances. These observations served to explain both the character of crimes committed by women, and also the tendency for the proportion of crime committed by females to be greatly underestimated by official statistics—a major thesis of his work. In elaborating his arguments Pollak takes as proven the characterization of women criminals as deceitful; in his view it is problematic only to determine how this state of affairs has come about.

In contrast with Pollak's reliance on social and biological explanations for the criminality of women, generations of observers have simply attributed it to supernatural forces. The witch often serves as the archetype of the female criminal, feared both for the magnitude of her powers and for the mysteries behind them. As Heidensohn (1985: 92) has pointed out, conviction for witchcraft was not so much a question of connecting the accused with a particular act as of establishing that she was believed to be possessed of evil powers. No doubt it helped to prove a woman to be a witch if her appearance fit the witch's stereotype. Lombroso and Ferrero themselves seem to attribute supernatural powers based on such a stereotype when they describe a sculpted bust of an old woman of Palermo, who had poisoned many people "simply for love of lucre," as "so full of virile angularities, and above all so deeply wrinkled, with its Satanic leer, [which] suffices of itself to prove that the woman in question was born to do evil" (1903: 72–73). And, lest we suppose that we have outgrown such nonsense, there is a case of a young woman convicted of arson in Italy in 1983 who, because of certain allegedly bizarre aspects of her case, was dubbed a witch by the media in a number of European countries and was so perceived by people she encountered upon her return to Scotland (cited in Heidensohn, 1985: 92–93).

BADNESS AS THE OFFENDER'S SELF IMAGE

Most writers who provide useful insights into the crime phenomenon are themselves more or less solid, law-abiding citizens. From time to time, however, people who have been chronic lawbreakers will, in the course of describing their escapades, also shed light on the forces that shaped their illegal careers. Typically such accounts have a deterministic flavor. The writers explain their criminality as an inevitable result of their parental upbringing (or its lack), exposure to violent gang influences, poverty and lack of legitimate economic opportunity, or antisocial values reinforced through experiences in early prison confinement (see for example Abbott, 1981).

Jean Genet is an exception. A brilliant writer acclaimed for plays and poetry as well as novels based largely on thirty-years experience as a member of the underworld—and prison inmate—in France, Spain, and numerous other European countries, Genet sets forth what has been called a "criminal manifesto" (Shoham and Rahav, 1982: 162–91)—a perverse world view that he has chosen as a personal code precisely because it is opposed to conventional morality. Although Genet perceives roots of his badness in being rejected as an illegitimate child in the village where he grew up, the self-image as a bad person was fully developed only as a result of conscious effort. He describes the mechanism as it evolved, in response to the pain of being imprisoned in a reformatory as a sixteen-year-old.

I worked out, without meaning to, a rigorous discipline. . . . To every charge brought against me, unjust though it be, from the bottom of my heart I shall answer yes. Hardly had I uttered the word—or the phrase signifying it—than I felt within me the need to become what I had been accused of being. . . . I kept no place in my heart where the feeling of my innocence might take shelter. . . . I owned to being the coward, traitor, thief, and fairy they saw in me (Genet, 1964: 176).

From that point on Genet's life was dedicated to fulfilling his image of himself as a bad person. If a man is expected to have sex with women, he would have sex with men. If a person is expected to be truthful, he would be deceitful. If a person is expected to earn a living by honest labor, he would be a thief. Indeed, he describes the discomfort he felt during a three-month stay in Nazi Germany. Because Germany was perceived as an outlaw nation, in which "the brain of the most scrupulous bourgeois concealed treasures of duplicity, hatred, meanness, cruelty, and lust" (Genet, 1964: 123), he found a lack of fulfillment in theft.

"It's a race of thieves," I thought to myself. "If I steal here, I perform no singular deed that might fulfill me. I obey the customary order: I do not destroy it. I am not committing evil. I am not upsetting anything. The outrageous is impossible. I am stealing in the void."

Genet's writings are unusual in the explicitness with which he formulates his crimes as motivated with consciously evil intent and in the enthusiasm with which he fulfills his role as a doer of evil. We cannot confidently impute the same kind of motivation to other criminals. But the basic process, in which some deviants accept rather than reject a deviant identity, has been observed in a variety of settings (Covington, 1984; Schur, 1971:

69–73). Edwin Lemert (1951) presents a scenario in which an individual, usually a juvenile without a history of deep involvement in criminal activities, happens to commit a deviant act that comes to the attention of the police, certain private citizens, or the public, and results in the actor being *labeled* as a criminal. If the actor accepts the label and then as a result proceeds to act according to the criminal role definition, that behavior is what Lemert refers to as *secondary deviance*. Tannenbaum earlier described the process as "the "dramatization of evil," which is "a process of tagging, defining, identifying, segregating, describing, emphasizing, making conscious and self-conscious; it becomes a way of stimulating, suggesting, emphasizing, and evoking the very traits that are complained of" (Tannenbaum, 1938: 19–20). Like other labeling theorists who emphasize the responsibility of external agents in creating the delinquent, Tannenbaum would suggest that most deviants do not share Genet's self-proclaimed culpability for his violations of the community's moral codes. But for those who do not believe in the strict determinism implied by labeling theory, Genet's example as a criminal whose evil acts emerge from a freely chosen self-image has wide applicability.

THE "NEW PUNITIVENESS"

Up to now this chapter has emphasized instances of moral condemnation of criminals that either actually took place in previous centuries or appeared more recently as holdovers from earlier times. For the twentieth century is recognized as an epoch in which, perhaps for the first time in history, civilized societies became imbued with the idea that crimes are not necessarily the actions of bad people, an epoch which has more than any previous period sought to lift moral culpability for criminal actions from the agents of those actions.

This outlook will be explored in some detail in Chapter 3 in connection with our consideration of offenders as good guys. At this point, however, we need to consider the departures that have become apparent since the late 1960s from the more benign images of criminals that prevailed a few years earlier. It is not now clear whether this departure represents a long-term reversal of the earlier twentieth-century trend toward less moral condemnation of criminals, or whether the progressive trend will continue in spite of the current outcropping of what we may call "the new punitiveness."

Increased Crime and Increased Fear

Allen (1981) has trenchantly analyzed the background and current forces giving rise to disenchantment with "the rehabilitative ideal" of the earlier part of the century. He notes that undercurrents of pessimism have deep roots in our culture.

One needs only to recall the names of Hawthorne and Melville to demonstrate that a vibrant optimism about the perfectibility of human beings is an incomplete description of antebellum tendencies. Even in the areas of criminal justice skepticism about the rehabilitative potential of the new penitentiaries was frequently expressed, and among some actually involved in administration of the systems, hopes for inmate reform were almost wholly rejected (Allen, 1981: 15-16).

Subsequently, even when training schools for juveniles and reformatories for young adults were established, doubts about their efficacy were reflected in failure to assign competent personnel to run them and failure to appropriate anything approaching the amount of funds necessary to put rehabilitative programs into operation. Thus, even as the rehabilitative idea was propounded down through the post-World War II period, a residue of contrary opinion could be heard.

Focusing on the period between the 1960s and 1981, the year in which his book was published, Allen considers reasons for the rehabilitative ideal's decline during those years. Having observed that the rehabilitative ideal flourishes only in a society with a high degree of consensus about social goals and confidence in the ability of its institutions to achieve those goals, he sees the 1970s as a period in which "modern America reveals a radical loss of confidence in its political and social institutions and a significant diminishment in its sense of public purpose" (Allen, 1981: 18). He then proceeds to show the relationship between this loss of purpose and the public's lack of confidence in such institutions as the schools, the family, the disciplines of psychiatry and psychology, the legal system, prisons, and the political system in general.

Clearly, the most significant phenomenon causing rehabilitative ideology to be supplanted by a more punitive public attitude toward criminals was an increasing public concern about crime. This concern was reinforced by well-publicized statistics from the Uniform Crime Reports showing an increase in crimes known to the police for the United States as a whole. Between 1960 and 1980 the murder rate doubled, from 5.1 to

10.2 per 100,000 population; for the same period the rate for burglary tripled, aggravated assault quadrupled, and robbery increased almost five-fold (Federal Bureau of Investigation 1961; 1981). Although criminologists have been critical of some of these statistics, especially if they are interpreted as totally accurate reflections of actual criminal behavior, there is little doubt that there is a real basis for the trends they suggest.

The effect of these changes on public attitudes has been profound. There is little doubt that, if the period in which confidence in the rehabilitative ideal was strong had been accompanied by a lessening of the crime rate, it would have been difficult to muster opposition to measures associated with the ideal. But the rising incidence of conventional crimes—which ordinary citizens experience when they find their cars have been broken into while left in a shopping center in broad daylight, their purses snatched on a street corner, or their houses burglarized while they were at work—does in fact lead those citizens to be apprehensive about the safety of their persons and property to a far greater degree than during the period prior to World War II. The increase in such fear, albeit to a lesser degree than the Uniform Crime Reports rates just mentioned, may be observed in responses to a survey administered to national samples in 1967, 1975, and 1979. To the question, "Is there any area right around here—that is, within a mile—where you would be afraid to walk alone at night?" 31 percent of a national sample responded affirmatively in 1967. By 1975 the figure increased to 42 percent, rose in 1975 to 45 percent, and fell back only slightly to 42 percent in 1979. And the increase was not limited to residents of large cities. In fact the greatest percentage increase in response to the question was not in cities with population of 500,000 or greater nor in those with populations between 50,000 and 500,000, but in towns and cities with 2,500 to 49,999 inhabitants, where the increase was from 22 percent in 1967 to 45 percent expressing fear in 1975 (U. S. Department of Justice. *Sourcebook*, 1981: 182).

The new punitiveness has also been reinforced by a lack of public confidence in observable results of correctional systems that had supposedly been influenced by the rehabilitative ideal. The perception is widespread that a high proportion of convicted criminals who have served time in prisons end up returning to them. Generalization about the overall rate of recidivism—that is, of relapse into criminal conduct— is tricky; the proportion depends greatly on the offender population surveyed, length of follow-up period, and the severity of the offense taken as an indicator of relapse. One team of authors with extensive experience as correctional practitioners and researchers has estimated, "out of a random cohort of 1,000 men released from prison in a given year, about 500 of them will return to prison or be sentenced to a jail term of three months or more within the following five years" (Carter, McGee, and Nelson, 1975: 118).

As for the other 50 percent who do not recidivate, people rarely give credit to implementation of the rehabilitative ideal in prisons. For one thing, when released convicts do not recidivate, it is seldom clear that their decision to forego further criminal activity is a result of anything particular about their prison experience. Very likely, they have simply passed beyond the age at which the motivations and norms conducive to many forms of illegal conduct prevail. For another, the ordinary correctional program reflects vary little of this ideal. Therapeutic correctional approaches are sometimes given only lip service, sometimes overtly sabotaged, and sometimes simply overwhelmed by the force of a hostile inmate social system. Therefore it is not surprising when such programs appear to have little impact.

One very influential survey (Lipton, Martinson, and Wilks, 1975) summarized 231 studies of offender rehabilitation that were published between 1945 and 1967. The widely publicized conclusion was that "with few and isolated exceptions, the rehabilitative efforts that have been reported so far have had no appreciable effect on recidivism" (Martinson, 1974: 25). Martinson and his coworkers appeared on the nationally televised news program *60 Minutes* and presented their findings at numerous professional meetings. Their so-called "nothing works" doctrine was cited in a number of newspaper editorials. Their study was subject to criticism from defenders of rehabilitation (Martinson, Palmer, and Adams, 1976), and Martinson (1979) himself acknowledged, on the basis of a follow-up survey including a broader range of studies, that the earlier conclusion had been too pessimistic, that some treatment programs do seem to lead to an appreciable reduction in recidivism. However, his modified conclusion never won the wide attention that the more dramatic "nothing works" verdict received.[1]

But even if rehabilitation as a whole has shown mixed results at best, defenders of the rehabilitative ideal might hope to find support in the outcomes of the very best programs, those that appear to be most successful in incorporating rehabilitative principles. There are indeed a number of programs which have been touted as exemplary of various treatment principles. Some of these have been staffed with counselors well-trained in psychology, social work, and other disciplines that have developed mandates for implementing the rehabilitative ideal. Others, such as the Federal Prison at Butner, North Carolina, or the Visionquest program for juvenile offenders, have placed great emphasis on evoking the latent impulses within offenders to make their own choices in the direction of prosocial lifestyles.

Unfortunately, a number of these very programs, launched with the greatest hopes and most enthusiastic support, have failed, when subject to carefully controlled evaluation, to live up to those hopes with which they were inaugurated. Lerman's study (1975) cast considerable doubt on the efficacy of the very ambitious Community Treatment Program of the California Youth Authority. Prisoners who had participated in the Butner program recidivated in the same proportion after release as a comparable group discharged from other prisons ("Inside Prisons," n.d.). And San Diego authorities, following up the first 100 youngsters from their jurisdiction who had gone through the Visionquest program, discovered that 92 percent had been rearrested within three years following their return to the community ("Visionquest," 1988).

These evaluations are typical of the maxim: the more careful the evaluation research, the less likely the finding that an intervention is effective. And the skepticism of disinterested professionals has pervaded the public consciousness. Just as cancer is at present considered a disease without a cure, in spite of evidence for a substantial proportion of remissions when certain forms of the disease are treated, so too is crime considered essentially a malady for which proven treatment methods are lacking. Although there are isolated instances of success, the institutions charged with encouraging lawful conduct and rehabilitating those who violate the criminal law—schools, families, police, courts, so-called correctional institutions—are widely regarded as having fallen down on the job.

Thus, one important element in the new punitiveness is a result of coupling, in the public mind, the lack of confidence in institutions intended to modify the behavior of wrongdoers on the one hand, with concern about the increasing incidence of crime on the other. Having made some efforts at treatment and then having observed the failure of those efforts, ordinary citizens simply throw up their hands and attribute the failure, not to some deficiencies in the techniques, which might be remedied through greater effort, but to unregenerate evil among the treatment failures. It is an attitude of desperation. In the public mind, the failure to control crime reinforces the view that many criminals are very bad guys indeed.

Less Eligibility

Another element in the new punitiveness is not really not new. It may be observed in O. Henry's story of the ne'er-do-well Soapy (Porter, 1953). Winter was coming on, and Soapy wanted to be committed to jail and thus be assured of bed and board for the coldest months of the year. And so he committed a number of minor crimes —breaking a shop window, eating a restaurant meal without paying, stealing an umbrella—in efforts to get the comfort he desired.

Soapy's perception of the situation—as one in which he would be better off committing a crime in order to reap the rewards of Blackwell's Island than remaining an upright observer of the law and suffering from the cold—illustrates the problem with any public policies that violate the principle of "less eligibility." The term may be traced to Jeremy Bentham, who advanced the principle that "the ordinary condition of a convict ought not to be made more eligible than that of the poorest class of subjects in a state of innocence and liberty" (quoted by Morris, 1966: 635).

The usual rationale for the principle, Morris notes, is "the reverse side of the coin of deterrence" (1966: 635). If criminal behavior leads to greater benefits than those available when one abides by the law, there will be an inducement for people to leave the ranks of the good guys and enter the ranks of the bad guys. But the principle can be observed in penal policies not so much as part of a rational design to make crime unattractive; rather, its power becomes evident in the popular consciousness whenever proposals are being considered for even minimal changes toward more humane treatment for criminal offenders. Even as the public has developed sympathy for the poor, the disabled, the orphaned—and supported measures to alleviate their distress—it has been at best indifferent to barbarities that seem naturally to accompany prison life. Sir Samuel Romilly, a friend of Bentham's and a stalwart supporter of Bentham's proposals for penal reform, consoled his friend when their efforts seemed to be at a standstill that the English people do not at any time care tuppence for prisons and prisoners and that when their attention was given to critical events like the wars with France they cared even less (Mack, 1969: 192).

For purposes of understanding "less eligibility," the public may be divided into those who see themselves as benefactors and those who see themselves as potential recipients of public services. The former group is made up of taxpayers who may be willing to help support elderly people whose contributions to social security now yield insufficient revenues to pay their current medical bills, or children whose parents cannot provide them with basic necessities. Help for these people, the taxpayers reason, is justified on the assumption that their problems arise from circumstances beyond their control. But these same taxpayers are often resentful at the thought that they are providing any support at all for convicted criminals. Even though recognizing the social necessity of prisons, taxpayers tend to feel that, beyond what is necessary to provide for security, expenditures for such institutions should be kept to an absolute minimum on the grounds that inmates deserve nothing better. And, if it should become apparent that any special rewards from public coffers are conferred on criminals, objections are bound to arise. For example, when a former English professor and accomplished poet, who happened to be serving life imprisonment for having murdered his wife, was awarded a grant of $7,500 from the National Endowment for the Arts, strong objections were raised, presumably on the grounds that the crime he had committed should render him ineligible for any kind of positive recognition ("Notes on people," 1977: C2).

A similar response was evoked by a *New York Daily News* story that revealed that Social Security disability benefits were being paid to David Berkowitz, the notorious "Son of Sam" killer, and to Jean Harris, who was convicted of murdering her lover, the prominent physician and diet-book author Herman Tarnower. Two *News* readers wrote to the editor to express their outrage, in light of their own experiences of being deprived of disability benefits to which they felt entitled ("Does crime pay?" 1981: 29). The issue here is one of competition for limited resources. To members of the public who see themselves in need of public assistance in one form or another—financial help to meet basic physical needs, or medical care, or job training, or psychological counseling—the claims of convicted offenders appear without merit. Since resources are finite, people "in a state of innocence and liberty" who lack good housing, for example, are indignant when they hear of prisons that look like campuses of expensive private colleges. If public resources are to be used to increase the quality of life for anyone, why should their needs not be met first? Their good behavior would seem to give them higher priority for living conditions that meet minimal standards, so that until all the slums inhabited by good people are transformed, bad guys deserve nothing better.

Both of these constituencies—taxpayers and law-abiding people who consider themselves candidates for social services—are better able to justify their claims to the extent that they adopt, in their own minds and in their views as expressed to others, an image of criminals as bad guys. Indeed, it serves their interests to portray criminals as the worst guys possible. When taxpayers regard criminals in the most negative moral terms, it becomes defensible to provide as little money as possible for their upkeep. Likewise for those people who might be considered as competitors with adjudicated offenders for allocations from the public treasury. They are likely to receive a larger share of the public pie to the extent that they are regarded as good guys who deserve such benefits, and their status as good guys is likely to be enhanced to the extent that they can contrast themselves with a group regarded as highly undeserving—the "bad guy" criminals who willfully exploit society for their own benefit.

Bad Guys Contrasted with Victims

A similar process occurs when the rights of crime victims are being considered. Our present system of criminal justice is often accused of paying too little attention to people who have suffered because their houses were burglarized, their cars stolen, their handbags snatched, or their heads beaten in one of the thousands of conventional crimes befalling blameless citizens every day. The system is called to task for a variety of reasons. It does too little to catch and punish the offenders, and even when it is successful in prosecuting and sanctioning them, it is insensitive to the needs of victims as complainants, and it does little or nothing to make up for the damage done by the crime.

The usual stereotype of the good, innocent victim will be considered in Chapter 5. Here we shall only point out that such an image is dramatized in proportion as the criminal is portrayed as a bad guy. The issue arises especially with respect to certain kinds of crimes in which victims are sometimes alleged to have some degree of responsibility for their victimization—for example, because they have been careless in frequenting dangerous places or forgetting to lock their houses. To make the case for the rights of victims as good guys, who are not responsible for what happened to them, it is advantageous to depict the perpetrators of offenses against them as bad guys who have a choice and who have exercised that choice to do wrong.

BADNESS AS A RATIONALE FOR LEGAL PUNISHMENT

The Crime Control Model

J. Edgar Hoover, the imperious Director of the Federal Bureau of Investigation for nearly fifty years, was a well-known exponent of the good-guys–bad-guys view. His was a selective vision. He considered virtually all people identified with the political left as dangerous bad guys, but not the right-wing conservatives who resisted lawful court orders for racial desegregation. Noted for his ability to foster a favorable public image of his agency, thereby providing support for the policies he pursued as the Bureau's director, he enhanced the FBI's image as good guys by picturing criminals as profoundly evil. The colorful terms he employed to describe various kinds of lawbreakers seem well designed to convey such images: "scum from the boiling pot of the underworld," "public rats," "lowest dregs of society," "scuttling rats in the ship of politics," and "vermin in human form" (Barnes and Teeters, 1951: 454).

Behind this kind of rhetoric is a view of the criminal justice system that Herbert Packer has termed the *crime control model.* Underlying the model he sees a "value system . . . based on the proposition that the repression of criminal conduct is by far the most important function to be performed by the criminal process" (Packer, 1968: 158). The model is concerned with processing suspects efficiently, relying when necessary on informal procedures, because formalities—such civil rights as protection of suspects against unwarranted searches and arrests, and privileges against self-incrimination and for representation by counsel in criminal proceedings—are considered impediments to the repressive function. It is based not on the traditional presumption of innocence, but on a presumption of guilt—the assumption, prior to formal consideration of the evidence, that a criminal suspect is a bad and dangerous person, whom it is necessary to remove from circulation in order to protect the rights of the respectable majority.

Dangerousness

Whereas the crime control model assumes that any criminal suspect is dangerous, a recently emphasized variant of that approach seeks to distinguish those offenders who are serious threats to society from those whose offenses are slight or infrequent enough so that draconian measures against them are unnecessary. The latter approach grew out of strategic decisions in the war on crime of the 1970s, based on an awareness that resources for the criminal justice system are finite and that priorities have to be established.

Dangerousness is usually equated with the potential to commit crimes involving threats to personal safety. In fact the Dangerous Offender Project, an extensive research undertaking of the Academy of Contemporary Problems in Columbus, Ohio, defined a dangerous offender for its purposes as one likely to commit a criminal act in which bodily harm is inflicted or threatened (Conrad, 1985: 7–8).

The issue of dangerousness is one that mental health professionals, especially those who work in correctional settings, have to face regularly. Suppose a psychiatric ward houses twenty people, all of whom have a similar background of abusive behavior toward family and neighbors but no documented instances of serious criminal assaults. Each of them has at one time or another threatened serious bodily harm against someone on the outside, but on the basis of experience the ward psychiatrist predicts that each of the patients has only a 5 percent chance of actually committing such an act if released. Put otherwise, it is likely that if all the patients are set free, nineteen will not carry out their threats, and one will. But the psychiatrist does not know which one it will be.

If no patients are discharged, the doctor does not risk being held responsible for any crime that any of them might commit, but nineteen people remain confined who might have been at liberty without harming anyone. If all are discharged, and the prediction is correct, the doctor will be held responsible for the crimes committed by the one patient. Very likely the risk involved in releasing the group will be perceived as too great; thus, all twenty end up being treated as dangerous.

A good deal of effort has gone into attempts to predict criminal violence. Monahan (1981) has compared clinical prediction, based on personality tests and individual case histories, with statistical prediction, based to a considerable extent on such demographic variables as age, sex, marital status, race, and socioeconomic status. Statistical predictions of violent behavior can be made with an accuracy considerably better than chance, for groups of subjects with similar background characteristics. When it comes to making predictions for individuals eligible for probation or parole, however, or in the mental hospital situation described above, the "false negative" cases—those in which violence is not predicted, but occurs nevertheless—provide grounds for applying the tar of dangerousness with sweeping strokes.

But the term "dangerous offender" is not limited to violence-prone individuals; it is also used to refer to those who may limit themselves to property crimes but who are expected to commit many such offenses. Considerable research attention (and funds) have been directed in recent years toward answering questions about these "career criminals." First, is there in fact a circumscribed population responsible for a significant proportion of crime? If so, how much crime, and particularly, how much violent crime can be accounted for by this population? And finally, can one therefore identify these dangerous individuals and get them out of the way—incapacitate them—early in their careers, for the time when they would be committing such acts, and thus save the larger society from the harm that would be done if they were at liberty for that period?

These questions have been addressed in retrospective studies of adult offenders, and in prospective studies of children. It has been observed that delinquent adolescents frequently outgrow their youthful deviance to become solid citizens as adults. But if one examines the backgrounds of career criminals, one almost invariably finds that the pattern of law-breaking has begun very early; criminal careers are seldom embarked upon by adults who have been model law-abiding youngsters.

The most extensive systematic study of patterns in early delinquency involvement was carried out at the Center for Studies in Criminology and Criminal Law at the University of Pennsylvania (Wolfgang, Figlio, and Sellin, 1972). Using school and police records, the investigators endeavored to study delinquency rates for all boys born in 1945 who were living in Philadelphia on their tenth birthday and who continued living there until they were eighteen. They considered the problems of using police records as a measure of delinquency. On the one hand, there are many acts of delinquency that do not come to police attention; on the other, not all offenders are in fact guilty of the offenses charged by police. A compromise was reached for purposes of this research: to study "police contacts with juveniles resulting in their being taken into custody, no matter what disposition the police made of their cases" (Wolfgang, Figlio, and Sellin, 1972: 22). Given the number of cases that had to be dealt with and the problems with alternative measures, it seems a sensible compromise.

Usable records were obtained for 9,945 individuals; taken together, they were responsible for 10, 214 offenses, or an average of about one apiece. But the distribution of offenses among youngsters was far from even. The boys were classified into four groups: nondelinquents, one-time offenders, non-chronic recidivists (two to four offenses), and chronic recidivists (five or more offenses). Sixty-five percent of the cohort had no recorded offenses. One-time offenders made up 16 percent of the cohort and were responsible for 16 percent of the offenses. Twelve percent of the boys were non-chronic recidivists, accounting for 32 percent of the police contacts. And the chronic offenders, only 6 percent of the cohort, committed 52 percent of the offenses. Moreover, when "seriousness scores"—based on the gravity of physical injury done or value of property stolen or damaged—were computed for the offenses charged, the average for chronic offenders' delinquencies was 127, compared with 81 for one-time offenders. This study is frequently cited in support of the view that, even before reaching adulthood, harmful acts are concentrated within a rather small segment of the population. One boy in three is bad enough to get into trouble with the police at least once before he turns eighteen, but only one in sixteen is bad enough to merit their repeated attention. (A subsequent study reports on a sample of the Philadelphia cohort followed until age thirty. See Wolfgang, Thornberry, and Figlio, 1987.)

The Dangerous Offender Project mentioned previously included a similar study of 1,222 boys and girls in the Columbus, Ohio, metropolitan area, born between 1956 and 1960, who had at least one arrest for a violent offense. This study differed from the Philadelphia study by including girls as well as boys, and by excluding nonoffenders as well as offenders who restricted themselves to nonviolent crimes. In concentrating on violence, the investigators were apparently pursuing an interest of the Lilly Endowment, which supported the research, in the phenomenon of the "young monster," an interest stimulated by the case of a notorious fourteen-year-old multiple rapist in Indianapolis. Conrad and his coworkers identified forty-two boys (and apparently no girls) in their cohort who had committed more than one offense of "aggravated violence [in which] serious physical harm was inflicted or threatened" (Conrad, 1985: 41). These boys had been arrested eighty-four times for violence as juveniles, including four murder charges and eight for forcible rape.

When last followed up as adults in 1983, seventeen of the forty-two were serving terms of imprisonment. Nonetheless, these forty-two youngsters made up only 3 percent of the total cohort of violent offenders. Considering that the cohort accounted for only 2 percent of their age mates in the study area, these "young monsters" represent only .0006 of the population of boys and girls in their age group in Franklin County. Conrad concludes, "Young monsters are rare birds requiring individual study rather than the statistical computation of their frequency" (1985: 42).

As another component of the Dangerous Offender Project, Conrad and his coworkers carried out a retrospective analysis of the official records of 1,591 "career thugs." Conrad notes the absence of qualities in that sample that he would consider necessary for special opprobrium at the same time that he acknowledges that offenders with such qualities do exist. "From time to time mysterious circumstance produces a criminal monster, a man or woman whose violence is so persistent and so cruel that it grossly exceeds the criminality of the ordinary thug." He notes, however, "No such person was found in our sample" (Conrad, 1985: 75). If we are concerned about our ability to deal with criminals who present substantial threats to society, either because of the violent nature of their acts or because of the frequency with which they commit them, the Philadelphia and Columbus studies document the presence of such individuals in our midst, but show that, even among the population of persons with criminal records, they make up only a small portion.

A different approach to the problem has been taken by the RAND Corporation, a private organization that has carried out research on criminal justice under contracts with the federal government. The RAND approach consists of using in-depth interviews to study more intensively the histories of adult criminal careers. While the Philadelphia study has the advantage of representativeness because of its large cohort, encouraging confidence in the generalizability of its findings to other populations, and the Columbus studies zero in on violence, the advantage of the RAND approach is to seek information on "hidden crime"—offenses that have not been officially recorded by the authorities—as well as officially recorded violations of the law, and to provide clearer insight into the processes involved in committing oneself to a life of crime as opposed to conventional alternatives.

Forty-nine inmates of a California prison for men, all of whom were serving their present sentences for armed robbery, participated in face-to-face, private interviews with the researchers in sessions lasting about two hours and covering their criminal histories from the time of the first juvenile arrest to the time of the interview session (Petersilia, Greenwood, and Lavin, 1978). Questions covered such topics as family background and employment but emphasized criminal activity and contact with the criminal justice system. An effort was made to document each criminal incident, whether known to the police or not, that the individual had committed.

Each offender's frequency of committing nine major offenses, including auto theft, aggravated assault, drug sales, burglary, and robbery, was tabulated. Results showed that the forty-nine men had committed a total of 10,505 offenses, or an average of 214 per offender. The average career was about twenty years long, but the typical offender had spent half that time in prison, so that he had committed about twenty crimes per year of street time. Had it been possible to identify such an individual and keep him incarcerated for the whole twenty-year period, the study implies, society would have been spared those 200-odd victimizations.

Implications like the foregoing are reminiscent of the social defense considerations of Lombroso and his followers. In recent years there have been a number of research studies (Chaiken and Chaiken, 1982; Cohen, 1978; Greenwood, 1982) aimed at assessing the precise effects of what Bentham called "disablement" (Mack, 1969: 120), and what is now commonly referred to as "incapacitation"—locking potential offenders away from free society to keep them from carrying out criminal activity there. Most recently these studies have been concerned with "selective incapacitation." Such studies begin by constructing a scale, based on attributes that distinguish particularly dangerous offenders from others—for example, conviction and remand to a training school before the age of sixteen, or drug use. Individuals at the high end of the scale are then identified as potential candidates for incapacitation, and estimates are made of the number of crimes that might have been prevented if these individuals had been incarcerated when the telltale signs of future criminality first became apparent. These estimates at best indicate only a modest reduction in overall crime rates, and even so, they have been widely criticized as overstating the predictive power of the scales (Blackmore and Welsh, 1983; von Hirsch, 1985: 103–46). It is not as easy to cure crime by identifying and isolating the most dangerous offenders as the public would like to believe.

The Justice Model

The idea of hurting those who have hurt us—the "urge to punish"—is deeply rooted in human psychology (Weihofen, 1956; Zilboorg, 1954). There is satisfaction in retaliating ourselves, but also satisfaction if someone else inflicts the punishment. When it is the community's well-being that is endangered by a criminal in its presence, feelings of security are restored when its members collectively drive the malefactor into the wilderness.

Criminal law is often explained as an outgrowth of the instinct for vengeance. Indeed, the Victorian jurist Sir James Stephen advocated the retention of this motive in the penology of his day: "I think it highly desirable that criminals should be hated, that the punishment inflicted on them should be so contrived as to give expression to that hatred, and to justify it so far as the public provision of means for expressing and gratifying a healthy natural sentiment can justify and encourage it" (quoted in Weihofen, 1956: 137).

What is missing in this view of criminal law, however, is the moral component. Legal systems cannot be based on vague notions that certain acts affront the community. Rather, they must be based on an abstract set of communal values, a set of standards of human rights or propriety from which may be derived laws forbidding specific acts or omissions. This assumption of a morality encompassing definitions of good and evil is basic to the concept of retribution as reflected in "the justice model," as it is used to rationalize modern criminal justice policy.

The basic tenet of the justice model is not new. "Of all the justifications for punishment, the idea that the commission of a crime throws the moral world out of a balance that is then restored by punishing the wrongdoer is perhaps one of the oldest" (Sykes, 1978: 481). "Punishment as reprobation" (Cohen, 1961: 60–61) is based on the view that groups have established standards of behavior, and that they properly affirm these rules when they punish people who violate them. When the group undertakes to reprobate—to "condemn as unworthy or evil" (Webster's Seventh New Collegiate Dictionary, 1971: 728)—one of its members, the pain inflicted is defensible simply on the basis that the offender *deserves* it.

This "just deserts" theory has been embraced as a revival of concern for the moral responsibility of lawbreakers, or more precisely, as a refutation of the rehabilitation model's propensity to absolve criminals of such responsibility. It was brought to the fore more than a dozen years ago by Andrew von Hirsch (1976), who had been the executive director of the Committee for the Study of Incarceration, an entity convened with support from private foundations having a membership of liberal academics and other people with a professional interest in the criminal justice system. In a report titled *Doing Justice*, von Hirsch begins by surveying four justifications that have been advanced for incarcerating criminal offenders—incapacitation, deterrence, rehabilitation, and just deserts, which he calls simply "desert." After pointing out the inadequacies of the first three justifications, he proceeds to defend the fourth. He cites Kant's argument that legal punishment is a "categorical imperative," or fundamental ethical principle not derived from other principles, to be applied because offenders have done wrong. Kant defends punishment even in circumstances when it would have no deterrent effect on future misconduct.

Even if a Civil Society resolved to dissolve itself with the consent of all its members—as might be supposed in the case of a People inhabiting an island resolving to separate and scatter themselves throughout the whole world—the last Murderer lying in the prison ought to be executed before the resolution was carried out. This ought to be done in order that everyone may realize the desert of his deeds, and that bloodguiltiness may not remain upon the people; for otherwise they might all be regarded as participators in the murder as a public violation of Justice (Kant, 1974: 198).

Von Hirsch subscribes to Kant's reasoning: that in a group of free individuals bound by reciprocal obligations to respect one another's rights, criminal acts bring an unfair advantage to some parties at the expense of others. Punishment, then, properly imposes suffering on offenders to offset the gains derived from their crimes, at the same time that it provides some satisfaction for the victims to make up for their losses, thus restoring an appropriate balance among relationships within the group.

The justice model has been prominent in debates about criminal justice policy in recent years as a basis for sentencing reform. A number of writers (Fogel, 1979; American Friends Service Committee Working Party, 1971) who embraced the model early in its present incarnation did so primarily out of concern that many individuals who had been convicted of conventional street crimes were suffering as a result of sentencing laws that granted wide discretion to judges and parole boards. In practice, that discretion favored criminals who already had such advantages as education and higher social status. In comparison with them, minority-group offenders, those who looked disreputable or appeared inarticulate and those who were not bright enough or skilled enough at feigning repentance, tended to be sentenced to incarceration rather than probation or to longer rather than shorter terms of imprisonment.

An illustration of the kind of problem addressed by some advocates of the justice model is reflected in an analysis of plea bargaining (Rosett and Cressey, 1976; Cressey, 1982), which challenges accepted wisdom about the way in which criminal justice policy is carried out. It is normally assumed that courts decide first, as a matter of fact, whether accused people are guilty of the offenses charged against them, and then as a matter of policy how to deal with them. Actually, according to this analysis, it is the other way around. "Put simply, defense attorneys, prosecutors, and judges first agree on what the sentence should be for an individual defendant. The agreement stems from negotiations about the defendant's character and the circumstances of the offense." That is to say, one of the first issues dealt with is whether the defendant on a burglary charge is a "bad guy" who should be given a prison term, or a "good guy" who deserves nothing worse than a fine or a short stay in the county jail. Only after having made this judgement "the trio [prosecutor, defense attorney, and judge], acting in concert, selects from the statute books a crime whose stipulated punishment is consistent with what has been decided upon as appropriate for the defendant at the bar" (Cressey, 1982: xiii–xiv).

Both Fogel and the American Friends Service Committee Working Party were also strongly critical of the tendency to use the treatment model as justification for depriving offenders of their liberty for longer periods than could be justified on the basis of the harm caused by the criminal act. As described by one member of the Working Party, its proposal to punish the perpetrators of criminal acts to a degree commensurate with their social harmfulness "would direct law enforcement toward the crimes of the corporation and the state, reduce penalties for crimes commonly committed by the lower classes, and in the case of 'victimless' crimes and some of the lesser offenses against property and public order, lead to decriminalization" (Greenberg and Humphries, 1981: 369).

Inspired by the justice model, a number of states have undertaken to reform their sentencing practices in recent years. One such effort, the Minnesota Sentencing Guidelines, was first implemented in 1981. A study of early results of that effort indicates a rate of imprisonment slightly lower than the figure for 1978, the preguidelines year selected for purposes of comparison, but slightly longer sentences being served after implementation of the guidelines (Knapp, 1982). The justice model is attractive to legislators who enact statutes providing for determinate sentencing, closely tied to offense seriousness, as a rebuff to judges who are perceived as using sentencing discretion to impose lenient sentences on serious offenders. At the same time, a state like California, having returned to the use of determinate sentencing in 1976, in subsequent years modified its statutes to lengthen terms and restore judicial discretion. Apparently the longer terms were a response to political pressure, and the return to discretion a pragmatic measure to take account of limited prison space.

There are many voters who fear crime and criminals, and few convicted offenders who do (or even may) vote, making it tempting for legislators to adopt posturing stances of toughness. Under the traditional indeterminate sentence, such posturing did not make much difference: legislators inflated maximum sentences during election years, but these did not determine the times actually served by prisoners. However, the politics of legislative sentencing do matter when a legislature undertakes to prescribe actual durations of confinement (von Hirsch, 1982: 167–68).

Whereas cracking down on the bad-guy criminal has always been a useful ploy for political candidates, sentencing discretion has provided a way of avoiding the economic costs of such practices in the past; if the justice model is to be truly implemented, society will in the future have to pay the cost of maintaining its bad-guy stereotype.

The justice model, then, although designed to overcome the inequities of moral judgment institutionalized as judicial discretion, provides in its own way a rationale for a bad-guys approach to criminal justice policy. The notion of calibrating the harm of a criminal offense, and then proportioning punishment to that harm, is not inherently conducive to an exaggerated view of offenders as morally repugnant people. One should not minimize the real basis of the vulnerability to crime felt by many law-abiding citizens, particularly in metropolitan areas of the United States today. But when the public demands punishments for ordinary crime that require offenders to spend very substantial portions of their lives deprived of the liberties that most of us take for granted, closely confined in the violent milieu of present-day prisons, it seems reasonable to conclude that the underlying process is not very different from the impulses that in the past led those who were regarded as servants of Satan to be burned at the stake.

NOTE

1. For a summary of issues in evaluating rehabilitation, and some recent examples, see Wilson (1983: chap. 9).

3

Offenders As Good Guys

In a recent issue of a scholarly journal there appears a vignette of a twenty-year-old man who has beaten his eighteen-year-old wife into unconsciousness. What the reader is told about him emphasizes not his crime, but the life circumstances that seem to have doomed him to an existence beyond the pale of respectable society. We are informed that his intelligence is subnormal, that he was raised in poverty, that he was brutalized by his father, and that he was first committed to reform school at the age of twelve. Life for him has always been a matter of sheer survival in a hostile world. That survival has been made possible through shoplifting and breaking into cars to steal their contents. Any legitimate jobs he has ever held were lost as a result of violent outbursts on his part, seemingly a recapitulation of the violence his father had carried out against him, his siblings, and his mother. In the vignette he is referred to simply as "the runner"—running from the police, who are pursuing him because of the beating he has inflicted upon his wife.

He is out there somewhere, suffering the alienating punishment of a society that has no compassion for its own mistakes. . . . The wounds will heal on those he has beaten, and their lives will move on once they separate themselves from him. . . . But not for him, because he is still the victim of violence that began before he can remember, suffering from wounds that are too deep to bleed, and too long standing to cure with band-aid therapy. Or with more punishment (Clark, 1984: 15).

In this sketch the harm done by "the runner" to others is minimized at the same time that society is castigated for failing to show compassion toward him. Strikingly, there is no hint that he is himself blameworthy.

The portrayal, though extreme, reflects a point of view held by some professionals who deal directly with lawbreakers, by some social scientists who study them, and by some members of the general public. In this view, offenders whom others would hold responsible for serious criminal behavior are in effect absolved of that responsibility; rather than being objects of obloquy, they are treated with sympathy because of the forces that have driven them to that behavior. They are virtually exempted from inclusion among the ranks of the truly bad guys and instead regarded as fundamentally good guys who could do no other than engage in bad behavior.

The example of "the runner" illustrates one of the most common situations in which criminals are depicted without moral condemnation—a situation of environmental deprivation. But, as we shall see in this chapter, faulty upbringing is not the only justification for exempting malefactors from moral stigmatization and permitting them to retain good-guy status. Other factors—such as an intention to protest some grave social injustice, or to end the life of a beloved spouse suffering from an incurable and agonizingly painful disease—can lead to the same result.

Before proceeding further, we should note that the term "good guy" as employed in common usage—and in the present work—is not a polar opposite of the term "bad guy." Bad guys are sinners, but good guys need not be saints. One is accorded good-guy status simply in the absence of evidence of willfully bad behavior, while the bad guy has to *do* something to earn the label. Most people think of themselves and their friends as good guys just because they usually earn their pay and treat their families with affection and adhere to society's most important rules—and they routinely preserve these perceptions by using certain justifications for instances of harmful behavior, whether carried out by themselves or by others.

LEGAL EXCUSES FOR ACTS CONTRAVENING THE CRIMINAL LAW

At the simplest level, the criminal law accepts certain excuses as justification for behavior that would otherwise be treated as criminal. Acts may correspond to the law's definition of assault but their perpetrators not held legally accountable if they did the acts under a reasonable belief that their actions were necessary to defend themselves from attack by another actor. Similarly, the law recognizes defenses of necessity and duress. Necessity is a legal excuse when someone violates the criminal law in order to prevent a greater harm that would ensue were the law not broken—for example, driving a car without a license in order to escape a fire (Siegel, 1989: 41). And duress justifies actions violating criminal statutes when one person is threatened by another with serious injury or death unless the first person complies with the other's demand that he do the illegal act. These legally recognized excuses take account of the possibility that situations may arise in which a person is forced to choose between two evils, and the law exonerates actors when they choose the lesser one. If the evil done is unquestionably a lesser one than the evil avoided, there is little difficulty in regarding the person who chooses it as a good guy.

More problematic, however, is another form of legal and moral defense, which takes into account the element of crime known as *mens rea,* or "guilty mind." Most crimes are defined in such a way that, in order to convict a person of the offense, it is necessary to prove not only that the accused has done an act proscribed by law, but that it was done in a state of mind deserving moral condemnation. A murder conviction, for example, requires proof that the accused intended to cause the death of another, as well as proof that he actually did the killing. Or for a larceny conviction, it is necessary to prove that a theft of someone else's property was done with the knowledge that the property belonged to the other person. Other acts may be criminal if they are done with a reckless mental state, or a state of mind exhibiting criminal negligence.

The purpose of including such states of mind among required elements for criminal conviction is to distinguish and punish those harms that are results of the actor's bad intentions or gross imprudence from those that occur by accident, as a result of forces beyond ordinary human control. Suppose I am hunting with proper authorization in an area well posted and fenced off as a private hunting preserve. I fire my rifle at a deer in plain sight and at proper range, but the bullet misses the deer and strikes and kills a trespasser asleep and hidden under a nearby bush. Even though the harm is great, the law, taking into account that I did not wish to kill the victim, did not know he was nearby, and had made sure to hunt in an area where the likelihood of my bullet's striking another person was extremely small, would very likely hold me blameless and preserve my good-guy reputation.

In practice, issues of *mens rea* are problematic because most cases are not as clear cut as the example just provided. Since it is strictly speaking impossible to observe a person's mental state directly, one must rely on indirect evidence—the subject's reports, witnesses' observations of the subject's demeanor, and so forth. Given the ambiguities of this kind of evidence, it is not surprising that a courtroom defense based on lack of *mens rea* is often suspect, if circumstances suggest even the remote possibility of an evil motive. The beautiful young wife, having shot her wealthy, elderly husband to death, claims that she mistook him for an intruder. A jury finds her not guilty of murder, for there is not enough evidence that she actually intended to kill him to overcome her claim that it was accidental. Nevertheless she is accorded less than total good-guy status on her return to the community. In general, when an act is done but *mens rea* not proven, public opinion is often harsher than the law; despite the legal outcome, a stigma similar to that applied to convicted offenders persists.

Apart from those cases in which the necessary mental state for a particular type of offense has not been established, lack of *mens rea* may negate criminal culpability in another situation—that in which the forbidden act is committed by someone who was insane at the time. In an extreme case, one person may kill another under a delusion that if he were to refrain from doing so, the other person would kill him first. In these circumstances we are reluctant to treat the offender as though he were driven by some evil impulse, and so we allow him to employ the so-called insanity defense. Insanity is determined differently in different jurisdictions, but the most common test is based on the "M'Naghten rule." The rule was originally established to justify the acquittal of a man who thought he was killing Sir Robert Peel, the Prime Minister of England, in 1843 but mistakenly killed Peel's private secretary instead. According to the rule as formulated at that time,

To establish a defense on the ground of insanity, it must be clearly proved that, at the time of committing the act, the party accused was labouring under such a defect of reason, from disease of the mind, as not to know the nature and quality of the act he was doing, or if he did know it . . . he did not know he was doing what was wrong (Glueck, 1962: 44–45).

Commonly known as the "right-wrong" test, the M'Naghten rule has remained influential over the years because it gives expression to the popular sentiment that consciousness of wrongdoing is essential for the imputation of criminal responsibility. For many years an important role in the determination has been given over, at least formally, to psychiatrists. These medical experts interview defendants who have chosen the insanity defense and then offer their expert opinions in court as to whether or not they meet its legal criteria. But in a typical case there are some psychiatrists testifying for the defense who offer their professional judgment that the accused did not know right from wrong at the time of committing the act, and other psychiatrists testifying for the prosecution who conceive of legal insanity more narrowly and express the opinion that the accused was able to apprehend the wrongfulness of the act at the time of committing it. The jury is then free to make its own assessment of the defendant's mental condition, in which process it may also express its own moral judgment of him or her.

The question of whether a person accused of crime knew right from wrong does not routinely arise in legal proceedings. The law presumes that the accused can make the distinction unless the defense asserts otherwise, in which case the determination must be made by the jury, taking into account the experts' testimony or, if the right to a jury trial has been waived, by a judge. In other cases involving the question of *mens rea*, however, the issue is resolved by means of an arbitrary dividing line— those cases in which "infancy," referring not only to babyhood but extending through later childhood years, is thought to negate the "guilty mind" element. Faced with the problem of deciding at what point to hold young people responsible for criminal acts, the Anglo-American legal system relied at least in part on arbitrary cutting points. The classic formulation of the traditional common law was set forth by the great English jurist Blackstone in the eighteenth century (Tappan, 1949: 167–69). Before its fourteenth birthday, any child who had committed a felony was presumed to be *doli incapax*, that is, incapable of evil. A further distinction was made between children under the age of seven and those from seven through thirteen. The presumption of non-evil intent was said to be "irrebuttable" for those in the younger age group; in effect, the youngster under seven was automatically exempt from punishment. For those between seven and fourteen, the *doli incapax* presumption was "rebuttable": The prosecutor could introduce evidence to show that the accused was capable of having evil intentions, and if that evidence was convincing the child would be convicted and sentenced as an adult. The further the youth was from having reached his fourteenth birthday, the less likely a successful prosecution. Upon conviction imprisonment with adult offenders could be imposed, although youth was often considered as a mitigating factor, and reports suggesting regular application of the death penalty to children appear to be exaggerated (Platt, 1969: appendix).

At present most states in the United States deal with youngsters up to the age of seventeen or eighteen within a separate legal structure, the juvenile court system, with certain exceptions for very serious offenses. These exceptions apart, young people who violate criminal statutes, just like the mentally deluded, are treated as lacking the capacity to form fully the evil intent that would justify imposing on them the punishments prescribed for adults.

We shall return later to a discussion of the juvenile court. At this point however, having called attention to some of the provisions by which the law maintains good-guy standing for people who have transgressed criminal laws, we shall examine some of the philosophical viewpoints that provide a basis for positive attitudes toward criminal offenders.

OFFENDERS AS SHARERS IN THE GOODNESS OF ALL MANKIND

Just as the New England Calvinists' perception of criminals as evil was rooted in their view of the human condition as pervaded by sin, the Quakers were able to see the good in criminals because their teachings emphasized the essential goodness of all humankind. In the Quaker view, there is an inner light, the spirit of God, which dwells in every person. Although circumstances may lead a person to do wrong, the possibility of human perfectibility remains; even the worst of criminals is not beyond redemption. Indeed the thrust of the Quaker approach is optimistic—to emphasize the possibility of approximation to a society of heaven on earth (West, 1962).

Quakers have been in the vanguard of efforts since the eighteenth century to abolish the death penalty and to reform prisons. Their position on capital punishment follows from the belief in perfectibility, as well as from the Biblical injunction against killing and the Quaker abhorrence of any kind of violent act. As for the attention to prison reform, it has been suggested that the Quaker concern has in part come about because of the numerous members of the Society of Friends who have themselves been imprisoned in matters of conscience and thus know prison life from first-hand experience. Quaker compassion for criminals may also be understood as sympathy stemming from Quakers' own frequent experiences of having been treated as outcasts within free communities.

John Bellers, a Quaker whose writing spanned the late seventeenth and early eighteenth centuries, is said to have been the first proponent of the revolutionary idea that the whole end of justice should be reform of the criminal. By providing prisons where inmates would have the opportunity to contemplate in silence—very like a Quaker meeting—the indwelling spirit of God may come to the fore and direct the person toward a life free from sin. Thus, Bellers took as his special mission the amelioration of the welfare of prisoners. His calling was based on the Quaker view of the equal position of all mankind in the sight of God. "Consider the nobility of your nature," he urged in a pamphlet addressed to imprisoned offenders, "being of the same species with other Men, and therefore capable by a thoro' reformation to become Saints on Earth, and as Angels in Heaven to reign with our Saviour there" (Newman, 1972: 195).

This view led Bellers to advocate improvement of the living conditions for prisoners in England—better food, housing, and sanitation. His concerns were reflected in the famous endeavors of Elizabeth Fry in Newgate Prison a hundred years later, which included separation of men and women prisoners, and segregation of hardened criminals from first offenders. Mrs. Fry went beyond inducing prison officials to make better provision for the basic needs of prison inmates. She was concerned with providing within the prison opportunities for education, exercise, and meaningful work. Her Quaker faith in every person's perfectibility led her to believe that even the worst offenders might, given the proper opportunity for reflection on their past misdeeds, exposure to Bible reading, and uplifting moral exhortation, relinquish their former sinfulness and be released from prison as useful members of their community.

Similarly in the United States the Quaker influence was reflected in the influential Pennsylvania prison system, established at the beginning of the nineteenth century. In Philadelphia inmates of the Walnut Street Jail, and later the Eastern and Western Penitentiaries in Pennsylvania, were confined in individual cells and not permitted to speak to anyone other than the prison staff, certain public officials, and members of the Philadelphia Society for Alleviating the Misery of Public Prisons, which society reflected a strong Quaker influence (Teeters, 1937). The purpose of this isolation was to prevent the impact of any corrupting influences upon the prisoners, under the assumption that they would then have an opportunity to reflect upon their evil habits and to see the way toward a more virtuous life. In their report for the year 1854 state inspectors rhapsodized about the system's effect on the typical prisoner at Western Penitentiary in the following terms:

Shut out from a tumultuous world, and separated from those equally guilty with himself, he can indulge his remorse unseen, and find ample opportunity for reflection and reformation. His daily intercourse is with good men, who in administering to his necessities, animate his crushed hopes, and pour into his ear the oil of joy and consolation . . . and weekly he enjoys the privilege of hearing God's holy word expounded by a faithful and zealous Christian minister. . . . The system has disappointed the anticipation of its enemies and surpassed the confident expectations of its friends (Barnes, 1972: 131).

YOUNG OFFENDERS AS REDEEMABLE

The Quakers were unique among Christian denominations in their devotion to rehabilitation of criminals; but there were other people, some inspired by religious precepts, some by more secular humanitarian impulses, who were optimistic about the possibilities for criminals to become good citizens. Not all of them shared the Quakers' belief in mankind's fundamental goodness; some subscribed to the view that human nature is susceptible to change for either better or worse, especially among young offenders. From this perspective young people with proper guidance could become saintly, but under corrupt influence, sinful. A report of the Philadelphia House of Refuge expresses the view that "youth is particularly susceptible of reform. . . . It has not yet felt the long continued pressure, which distorts its natural growth. . . . No habit can be rooted so firmly as to refuse a cure." Similarly, the Boston Children's Friend Society addressed the task of rehabilitating those "whose plastic natures may be molded into images of perfect beauty, or as perfect repulsiveness" (Rothman, 1971: 213).

Yet the weight of opinion seems to have been that young people were amenable to correction even if they had shown early signs of lawbreaking. An indication of this emphasis is the composition of populations in early facilities for young offenders. In such facilities, the modern distinction was blurred, if it existed at all, between youngsters who had committed crimes and those who were dependent or neglected. Descended from orphanages established in the 1700s, they became known as "houses of refuge" for children who had been denied proper parental care and guidance, whether or not this neglect had culminated in delinquent behavior. One of the earliest was the Magdalen Society, founded in Philadelphia in 1800 to care for girls who "in an unguarded hour have been robbed of their innocence and sunk into wretchedness and guilt" (Teeters, 1959: 672).

The first House of Refuge in New York City was organized by John Griscom, a Quaker schoolteacher who raised $18,000 through the Society for the Reformation of Juvenile Delinquents in the City of New York, and leased a barracks from the government on Madison Square. The House of Refuge was to be a "manufactory, prison, and school," to which the courts might send not only children convicted of crimes, but also those who were vagrant, homeless, or neglected and considered by a judge to be proper objects for such treatment (Hawes, 1971: chap. 10). It was opened on January 1, 1825, its first residents six boys and three girls gathered from the streets. The Society's view of its charges and its aspirations for them are reflected in a speech delivered to the waifs by one of its founders, the Reverend John Stanford.

You are to look on these walls which surround the building, not so much as a prison, but as an hospitable dwelling, in which you enjoy comfort and safety from those who led you astray. And, I may venture to say, that in all probability, this is the best home any of you ever enjoyed. You have no need for me to tell you, that the consideration of all these favors should stimulate you to submission, industry, and gratitude. You are not placed here for punishment, [but rather] to produce your moral development (Teeters, 1959: 673).

There were differences of opinion about the age of transition at which wayward children, considered good at heart in spite of wrongful behavior, would develop a hardening of bad moral character so that they would no longer be amenable to the gentle guidance envisioned in the early houses of refuge. The Massachusetts State Reform School for Boys was created by law in 1847 as the first fully state-supported institution for juvenile delinquents. Although it was recognized that punishment would be part of the disciplinary structure of the school, emphasis was also placed on "manual labor," under the assumption that instilling habits of hard work in the boys would discourage them from continuing their lives of vagrancy and petty crime when they were released. The institution was obliged by law to accept boys up to the age of sixteen, but Theodore Lyman, a wealthy ship owner who provided substantial financial support to the school (in spite of the fact that it was a public institution), had sought to restrict its population to youngsters under fourteen, because he had observed that fourteen- and fifteen-year olds "are difficult to manage. . . . If they have been for some time in a vicious course, they become by 14 or 15 hardened, bad themselves, and very fit to make others bad" (Hawes, 1971: 82-83). Nonetheless, most of the state institutions that were subsequently established rejected the common law precedent setting fourteen as the age of moral responsibility and followed the Massachusetts example by separating offenders under sixteen from "real" adult criminals.

THE JUVENILE COURT AND THE MEDICAL MODEL

Assigning young offenders to houses of refuge rather than adult prisons was a practice that evolved in the nineteenth century out of concern for their tender sensibilities. Even so, the legal system to which young suspects were exposed throughout this period—the body of law and the tribunal responsible for applying it—was no different from that which applied to mature individuals accused of crime. That situation changed very quickly in the early part of the twentieth century with the development of juvenile courts, which met separately from adult courts, with special judges and special laws suited to the age of the offenders who appeared before them. The prototype was formally inaugurated by an act of the Illinois legislature in 1899, which established the first separate tribunal for young offenders in Cook County (Chicago). The innovation was rapidly taken up elsewhere: twenty-one additional states had juvenile courts by 1912, and by 1925 the total number of states with such courts reached forty-six (Tappan, 1949: 172). Juvenile courts were enjoined, not to punish delinquents brought before them, but rather to act, as the Illinois statute put it, in "the best interests of the child." This injunction was based on the premise that children under juvenile jurisdiction are not so much dangerous to society as they are themselves in danger of not being able to participate fully in the benefits that society confers on its respectable members.

The juvenile court was a high point of the Progressive movement, which emerged in the early decades of the twentieth century as an expression of dissatisfaction with the correctional institutions of the 1800s and advocated as substitutes for the institutional approach rehabilitative measures based on an assessment of individual needs and circumstances (Rothman, 1980). The term "Progressive" denotes an almost boundless faith in progress. In this view juvenile delinquency is a problem of *troubled* rather than *troubling* children. Thomas Mott Osborne, an important exponent of the Progressive movement who sought to apply his perspective during a short period as warden of Sing Sing Prison, is described by one student of the period as a man who "viewed life as a morality play with virtue and vice struggling for the soul of mankind. Human nature was inherently good, he believed, evil and corruption being the products of environment and association" (Holl, 1971: 24). Such faith was not an innovation of the period; Americans have been known as optimists from the beginning. This new optimism acknowledged shortcomings in American life—poverty, immorality, ignorance, crime—but put its faith in science to overcome those shortcomings.

And the model for applying science to human problems was medicine. In dealing with crime, the medical model required examining the individual, diagnosing the nature of the malady, ascertaining its cause, and prescribing a treatment to counteract the infecting agent. From this perspective criminals were no more to be blamed for the harm they caused than were others who suffered from physical maladies.

Bernard Glueck typifies the exponents of the "medical model" as applied to crime. Glueck was a psychiatrist who carried out a study of the inmates at Sing Sing Prison during the early part of this century. He criticized the criminal justice system as a whole for its lack of clear purpose in dealing with the problem of crime but noted an exception in the field of probation. There, he noted with approval, criminals are dealt with just like any other patients. "The offender who is selected for this type of management could, theoretically at any rate, at once become identified with any other maladjusted individual requiring scientific and purposeful understanding and help, irrespective of the fact that his particular maladjustment expressed itself, among other things, in criminal conduct" (Glueck, 1959: 92). The problem of security was acknowledged by Glueck as making one difference between noncriminal patients and some criminal ones, but he tended to minimize it and held out hope that improved psychiatric techniques would in time obviate the need to confine criminals who are being treated.

Another noted psychiatrist who began studying offenders at about the time of Glueck's Sing Sing research was William Healy—in this case, at the Juvenile Psychopathic Institute in Chicago. Healy found weaknesses in earlier scientific studies of criminals, like those of Lombroso, and he expressed skepticism about efforts to construct theories of crime from the weak research evidence then available. Healy;s data on persistent juvenile offenders provided little support for hereditary explanations of crime, nor did they indicate particular physical stigmata associated with delinquent behavior. As for the concepts "moral imbecility" and "moral insanity," he concluded that few if any cases could be found in which there is a moral incapacity separable from feeblemindedness or emotional disorder. Although Healy gave credit to Lombroso and his followers for electing to study individual offenders in order to come to a scientific understanding of crime, he indicated that they were led to invalid conclusions about moral incapacity because their methods were not adequate to show that moral insensitivity could in turn be explained by the "accident of environment" or intellectual incapacity: "The statistics that we are offered concerning criminals, whether about their deeds, their ears, their religious faith, or what not, are presented without knowledge of essential facts, such as whether or not they were mentally defective; and thus lead us nowhere for purposes of practical treatment" (Healy, 1915: 17).

Healy was an early advocate of psychological testing, and he combined the results of such tests, along with data about an offender's medical history and social environment, in detailed case histories that he presented to illustrate the interplay of many factors in accounting for the delinquency of an individual. It is interesting that Healy, as a psychiatrist, has been given major credit for shifting the emphasis in American criminology from biological and moral defects innate in the individual to external sociological factors (Radzinowicz, 1966). His early writings eschewed imposing any theoretical assumptions on the data, which led some critics to charge him with "crass empiricism," although in his later work, in collaboration with Augusta Bronner, he found Freudian psychodynamics a useful interpretive scheme.

Understanding "mental conflicts" was for Healy the clue to explaining the legal infractions committed by many of the youngsters he examined, first in Chicago and later at the Judge Baker Guidance Center in Boston. They were not bad children who derived pleasure from harming others. The motives that led them to delinquent acts seemed at times to be alien to their total selves—like a parasite that insinuates itself into a healthy organism and disrupts its normal functions. Here the connection between the medical model and the image of the good offender is most apparent.

We find that some misdoers do not, in their misconduct, appear to be carrying out their keenest desires. Their actions are forced, as it were, by something in themselves, not of themselves. . . . So far as we can learn, the impulse arising from mental conflict has no penumbra of delightfulness; on the contrary, it seems as if one of its most noteworthy characteristics is the curious absence of any idea of pleasure to be derived from following it. We have heard the expression from not a few misdoers, "I don't know what makes me do it. I don't want to do it, and I feel sorry afterwards" (Healy, 1917: 17).

SOCIAL WORK IDEOLOGY AND CRIME

Although psychiatrists like Glueck and Healy were responsible for the initial use of the medical model to explain and guide the treatment of criminal offenders, the discipline that has borne the major share of responsibility for such treatment is social work. The development of social work as a profession is closely linked to the Progressive movement. Settlement houses, the earliest base of operations for the new profession, were established in areas of first settlement for immigrants from Europe to large American cities. Their mission was to help the newcomers adjust to their new environment, teaching everything from hygiene and job skills to English and sculpture. Of the problems of the immigrant ghettos, delinquency and crime were among the most visible to the outside world, so that efforts to prevent the onset of delinquency and to nip it in the bud before it could develop into full-blown criminality were given high priority.

Thus the settlement houses developed programs aimed at bringing youngsters in off the streets and providing wholesome outlets for their energies in the form of athletics, hobby clubs, and trips to parks or beaches, as alternatives to hanging out on street corners and getting into trouble. Initially it was anticipated that they would welcome the opportunity to engage in such beneficial pursuits. However, it shortly became apparent that for most of them, the promise of rewards for participation in activities supervised by middle-class settlement house workers was insufficient to counter the attraction of gang membership and street life. It turned out that the children who did take advantage of the settlement house programs were those least in danger of becoming involved in delinquent activities.

In order to have access to hard-to-reach delinquents or pre-delinquents, social workers shifted their base of operations from the settlement house to the juvenile court—in particular, to the probation division, which was mentioned with approval, as noted previously, by the psychiatrist Bernard Glueck. There are two components of probation. First, after it has been established, either by plea or judicial determination, that a suspect is guilty of delinquency, a probation officer attached to the court carries out a pre-sentence investigation. The information gathered in this process goes far beyond what is admissible in court to prove innocence or guilt; it emphasizes the social adjustment of the individual in the family, work, school, and so forth. Such information is presented in the pre-sentence report, often with a recommendation as to whether the person should be sent to prison or a training school, or released on probation.

If the judge chooses the latter disposition, then the second component of probation, probation supervision, comes into play. The individual is not incarcerated, but allowed to return home, or to a community residence, provided that certain conditions of probation are fulfilled—attending school, holding a steady job, reporting regularly to the probation officer, or staying away from company and places likely to tempt the probationer to do wrong, such as specific former accomplices in crime, bars, and gambling places. Pressure to adhere to the conditions is applied by the threat that violations may be reported to the court, subjecting probationers to the imprisonment that they were initially spared.

The legal structure of probation is thus a coercive one, but especially as interpreted in the juvenile courts, the underlying assumptions are benign. The investigative process aims at discovering the strengths of the candidates for probation and the external forces that compelled them to engage in delinquency. To the extent that some good qualities are uncovered and the misconduct attributed to forces beyond the person's control, a recommendation can be made to keep such youngsters in the community and to counteract the forces leading them astray by referral to an appropriate social agency or other treatment program.

In the early juvenile courts probation officers were unlikely to be professionally qualified as social workers, a situation that persists in some courts even now. But very quickly the probation officer who had a master's degree from a school of social work became the role model in prestigious probation departments. As a result the "old school" probation officers—those who perceived themselves as law-enforcement agents not very different from police officers, and who expressed stereotypically negative moral judgments about lawbreakers—found themselves being supplanted by officers who either had graduate training in social work hemselves or were trained, supervised, and evaluated by superiors with such training. As a result the ideology of social work, with its emphasis on finding and working with the good within each person, has become the most influential dogma in the philosophy of probation. Consequently, probation agencies have come to represent the most visible element of the good offender approach within criminal justice systems.

THERAPIES BASED ON THE GOOD-GUYS MODEL

Much of the framework for group as well as individual methods in treating offenders is based on theories of personality. The "good-guys" approach in personality has developed largely as a reaction to the Freudians' emphasis on socially unacceptable aspects of erotic and aggressive drives. "When working with troublesome youth we all too often see only their limitations and not their strengths" (Vorrath and Brendtro, 1974: 13). Part of the reaction has been to affirm the positive side of these drives, particularly of sexual impulses; another form, significant for the present discussion, is to stress the presence of natural inclinations toward socially desirable behavior.

Insofar as the treatment of offenders is concerned, this approach explains illegal behavior as an expression of antisocial drives that have become temporarily dominant, and advocates therapy that stresses the client's "strengths" or "prosocial" tendencies. As evidence for the existence of such cooperative tendencies, two familiar criteria have been used. One is the presence of these attributes in lower animals. Cooperation, for example, as observed in species ranging from ants to subhuman primates, is cited to support the evolutionary basis for prosocial behavior among humans (Montagu, 1976: 43–44). A second type of evidence comes from anthropological studies of primitive societies, in some of which, contrary to the popular stereotype, war is unknown and overt violence of any kind is rare (Montagu, 1978: 4–5). The therapist working with offenders may take these observations as evidence that prosocial proclivities are at least as much a part of the human mental apparatus as antisocial ones, so that the task of treatment emerges as an effort to bring these positive drives to the surface and to encourage and reinforce behavior reflecting these drives as a substitute for antisocial conduct.

This approach to offender therapy reflects the orientation of humanistic psychology. As opposed to the pessimism of the Freudian school with its emphasis on the struggle between Eros and Death in modern society (Freud, 1961: 77), humanistic psychology stresses that aspect of the human organism which "embraces and prizes others in an atmosphere of caring and love" (Tageson, 1982: 38).   Humanistic psychologists like Carl Rogers, Abraham Maslow, and Rollo May explain antisocial behavior as the result of faulty socialization which alienates some people from their deepest altruistic nature.   Therapy consists of helping the patient—or client, as humanistic therapists prefer to call those they treat—to be attuned to the full range of their "personal data"; to the extent that this is achieved, the client will be "a generally caring person who will safeguard the best interests of humanity in general" (Tageson, 1982: 39).

Among therapists who deal with delinquents and criminals, William Glasser is notable for having formulated a treatment approach which assumes that offenders are at bottom no different from social conformists. Originally trained in traditional psychoanalytic therapy, Glasser rejected the Freudian approach to therapy as unworkable for offenders and developed a technique to which he gave the name "reality therapy." Reality therapy is based on the proposition that social deviants are like others in that they possess as their most basic strivings the need to love and be loved, and the need for self-respect—"to feel worthwhile"—and for respect from others. Glasser cites the case of an adolescent girl whom he treated while she was confined in an institution in California as a convicted shoplifter. Jeri's initial approach to the psychiatrist was manipulative, with no sign of remorse for her illegal behavior, only regret that it had resulted in her confinement. Glasser's treatment plan was based on the assumption that Jeri's bravado was merely a façade masking feelings of insecurity and guilt. Eventually the façade was penetrated, enabling Jeri to face her needs for respect and affection and paving the way for her apparently successful rehabilitation (Glasser, 1975: 91–97).   Glasser does not claim that reality therapy can be successful with all offenders, but lack of success in his view does not indicate an absence of essentially positive basic needs but only an inability to uncover them.

INMATE SELF-GOVERNMENT

A curious twist on the notion of moral character was expressed by William R. George, founder of the George Junior Republic, a privately sponsored residential institution for boys that has been in existence since 1895.   George's view might be characterized as the "badness as goodness" doctrine: a belief that bad behavior is not a direct reflection of an underlying evil nature but that it is, on the contrary, a sign of potential. "There are bad boys," he said, "mighty bad ones, too, and the badder they are the better I like to get them in the Republic" (Hawes, 1971: 155). This was so, he explained, because:

The boy who has sufficient energy and impetus to be aggressively bad has in him the stuff from which good public citizens are made. We take the misspent energy and transform it to serve some useful end, by means of the boy being responsible for his own badness, and the gradual training of his moral nature to the ideas of Democracy (Hawes, 1971: 155–56).

Unlike some other Progressives, George did not adhere to the view that all children were good, but rather that the great majority of them had the capacity to develop good moral character with proper training. "The benevolent person who assumes that all normal boys are good," he observed, "makes as great a mistake as the vindictive person who assumes that they are all bad. . . . The term 'angelic savages' aptly describes them" (Holl, 1971: 242).

Responsibility for "moral training" rests with the residents of the Republic, which accepts youngsters between the ages of sixteen and twenty-one referred by the courts or private social agencies. Organized along political lines, it is administered by a president, senate, house of representatives, and various administrative officials—all offices occupied by residents who are elected by their peers. The youngsters are responsible for making the laws, adjudicating infractions through a court system, and imposing punishments. Although its admission procedures no longer adhere to George's notion that the children whose behavior is worst are the best candidates for the Republic (if indeed they ever did), the Republic's operating philosophy has continued to embrace an attitude of confidence in human nature that underlies every institution governed by democratic procedures.

The George Junior Republic is significant because it pioneered the idea of self-government in correctional institutions, which was but one component of the Progressive opposition to autocratic control of all institutions and support for self-government in schools, colleges, labor unions, and businesses. Modified forms of self-government had been experimented with as early as 1824 at the House of Refuge for juvenile delinquents in New York City, and in 1826 at the Boston House of Refuge. The children in both facilities were apparently allowed a significant voice in disciplinary matters. And, contrary to the expectation that offenders would simply recreate the law of the jungle among themselves if given autonomy to govern their own affairs, such experiments purported to demonstrate that within an environment in which adult authorities are perceived as genuinely committed to assist the inmates in their own reform, young residents can formulate rules designed to promote the common good and apply them in a way that is accepted as fair by their peers.

Even among those responsible for administering traditional prisons, with sizable numbers of older and hardened career offenders, there are advocates of a degree of self-government (Baker, 1977), or what Bloomberg (1977) has called "participatory management." This approach asserts the legitimacy of inmates' rights to have control over what happens to them, but it also expresses faith that they are capable of exercising a degree of that control in a responsible way. It is an approach with a long and not particularly successful history. For one thing, it has often been used in a manipulative way by administrators who seize upon it as a way of appeasing inmates' demands. Such administrators establish Inmate Advisory Councils, through which inmate representatives decide among narrowly limited options in selected areas of prison life, for example, movies and menu preferences. For another, such renowned reform-oriented prison administrators as Alexander Maconochie, Howard B. Gill, Thomas Mott Osborne, and Tom Murton—who have allowed inmates a more fully collaborative role in prison affairs—have ended up by being dismissed for their efforts, even though they appeared to be successful in reducing assaults, escapes, and recidivism (Baunach, in Bloomberg, 1977: 159). Nonetheless, in spite of the failure of past experiments in inmate self-government to gain wide support, the persistence of the idea testifies to the durability of faith that a capacity to exercise responsibility on their own behalf is present even among the hardened criminals who compose the majority of the population in traditional prisons.

Of proposals espousing a measure of voluntary choice for prison inmates, Professor Norval Morris has advanced the best-known recent variant. Like other critics of the rehabilitative ideal as proposed (if not actually implemented) during the post-World War II period, Morris finds fault with the coercive element: If not actually required to participate in therapy sessions, inmates were often manipulated to take part because, it was made clear to them, satisfactory participation in therapeutic sessions would count strongly in their favor when the time came to consider them for release on parole. Morris is concerned not only with the ethical problem of this kind of coercion, but also with the practical results. Referring to this kind of program as a "coerced cure," he rejects it because of the likelihood that prisoners will only go through the motions of being involved in programs in order to obtain early release. "They must present a façade of being involved in their own 'rehabilitation' and building that façade may preclude the reality of reformative effort" (Morris, 1974: 17). As an alternative to "coerced cure," Morris advocates what he calls "facilitated change." The essential difference is that the latter model, which might offer a range of therapies, education, and employment opportunities similar to traditional rehabilitation programs, would make participation in them purely voluntary. If an inmate's sentence provided for the possibility of parole, the date would be determined, the inmate so informed within the first few weeks of serving time, and only a serious infraction of prison rules would delay that date. Thus free of the need to present a façade of involvement in rehabilitation, inmates would be free to choose participation or nonparticipation, and if participation, for no other reason than that they see it as having real benefit for themselves. Morris's proposal seems to reflect less optimism about criminals as a group than the self-government model. But it does suggest that many of them do as individuals have the capacity to choose prison programs that will contribute to their resocialization, and that the absence of coercion will encourage them to make that choice.

Like Bentham, Morris proceeds from his theoretical assumptions to propose a model institution. Morris's ideal is a prison for 200 violent recidivists between the ages of eighteen and thirty-five who have served time in other prisons and are within one to three years of a date for release on parole. Among a wide range of available programs, attendance would be compulsory only at small inmate-staff discussion group meetings. After being oriented to the program, inmates would be able to choose whether they wished to stay in this experimental institution or return to their original institutions. For those who stay there is nothing to gain in terms of early release by involvement in therapeutic activities; in fact, for some prisoners choosing the experimental program would entail a release date later than the time of discharge they would have had if they had stayed at their original institutions.

In fact, Morris's model has been implemented at the federal prison at Butner, North Carolina, for "deep-end" offenders—prisoners selected because of indications that they would be especially likely to engage in violence or be troublesome in other ways in a typically structured institution. The Butner prison is a highly secure facility, but the physical arrangements differ markedly from those in traditional prisons. For example, instead of cells inmates have small individual dormitory-like rooms which they themselves can lock and unlock. A wide variety of educational, vocational training, and therapeutic activities are available; a major feature is the voluntariness of inmate participation in them. Evaluation of the Butner experiment shows positive effects in terms of markedly less tension and violence than would be expected of these inmates in a traditional prison setting, but unhappily recidivism rates do not appear to be lowered as a result of this innovative program. The apparent bad guys may act like good guys in the ideal environment of the Butner prison, but whatever the circumstances enabling them to respect the rights of one another in the prison community, those conditions do not seem to prevail on the outside ("Inside Prisons," n.d.; Trotter, 1976).

The Progressive approach persists among many professionals who deal with offenders, pre-delinquents, or simply normal law-abiding people with antisocial impulses. Although it has been challenged within the past fifteen or twenty years by those who are optimistic about the value of deterrence and incapacitation in controlling crime as well as by those who are simply pessimistic about rehabilitation, until the early 1970s rehabilitation was generally accepted as the policy of choice for dealing with the vast majority of criminals—all but the few whose minds were so warped that they were viewed as beyond redemption. Stanton Wheeler, a sociologist whose earliest work examined attitude changes over the course of serving time in a traditional prison, expressed this consensus in 1968. He described agencies of delinquency control—police, probation, courts, and correctional institutions—as "part of the general movement toward a more humanitarian, professional, and scientific approach to problems of deviant behavior: a movement which is reflected in changed criminal law and procedure, in new forms of treatment for mental illness, in an effort to provide greater public understanding and tolerance for the criminal and the sick" (Wheeler, 1968: 317). The thrust toward more humanitarian treatment of offenders has been in decline in the years since Wheeler's observations were made, but there remains a core of clinical workers, academic criminologists, policy makers, and members of the public who stay faithful to the concept of the criminal mind as a repository of the basic stuff needed to heal itself.

THE GOOD OFFENDER AND THE REFORMATORY

The Houses of Refuge, mentioned earlier in this chapter, represented the best thinking of the period during which they emerged, during the second quarter of the nineteenth century—the notion that good behavior or bad behavior is no more than a manifestation of the underlying moral character of the individual so that crime reflects a failure of the spirit rather than a rational choice. In order to effect a change in behavior, it was therefore thought necessary for reformers to induce those who were accustomed to breaking the law to undergo a spiritual transformation, usually implying a healthy dose of divine intervention. The religious foundations gradually gave way to the more secular orientation of the Progressive movement, which combined faith in the underlying goodness of lawbreakers with optimism about the power of the emerging sciences of human behavior to bring that goodness to the fore. This combination was apparent in the thinking of administrators like William George, psychiatric proponents of the medical model like Glueck and Healy, and the social reformers whose ideas were institutionalized in the juvenile court and probation systems.

Faith in science, at its most optimistic, hinted at the possibility of redemption for a great majority of criminal offenders, if not all of them. But for the most part the new scientific thinking served to temper the optimistic excesses of good-guy morality. There were differences between those who thought of evil as the natural endowment of all humankind, and those who saw it as characteristic of some portion of the species, as noted in Chapter 2. In the same way, observers of human goodness differed as to whether they felt it dominated all or only some people. And just as science had been used to single out incorrigibly evil offenders for harsh treatment, it came to be used to select those whose innate goodness made them candidates for more benign handling.

The institution that first embodied this view—that certain individuals ought to be set apart from the general population of convicted offenders for special correctional effort because they possessed traits indicating their suitability for such treatment—was the reformatory. And the man most responsible for the reformatory movement in the United States was Zebulon Brockway. Brockway, who later became famous as the superintendent of the New York State Reformatory at Elmira, entered prison work as a guard in Connecticut and by 1864, at the age of twenty-seven, had worked his way up to the position of superintendent of the penitentiary at Rochester, New York. He was profoundly discouraged by the apparent futility of an approach aimed at spiritual transformation. At that time, he later recalled, the "belief was prevalent that every good must come mysteriously and directly from the supernatural source. More and more the chaplain preached and prayed and redoubled his persuasiveness; yet no miraculous changes were manifested" (Brockway, 1969: 66).

Brockway subsequently headed the Detroit House of Correction and then, in 1876, was called to the position of superintendent of the New York State Reformatory at Elmira, a newly constructed institution for first felony offenders between the ages of sixteen and thirty. The term "reformatory" was used to designate an institution midway between the comparatively benign houses of refuge for children and the purely punitive penitentiaries for adult offenders. The program established by Brockway—especially the idea of the indeterminate sentence—bears striking resemblances to the short-lived effort by Alexander Maconochie, a correctional pioneer at one of the British penal colonies in Australia in the 1840s, although Brockway's system was developed on the basis of his own experiences. Maconochie developed a "mark system," by which prisoners' good conduct and hard work were rewarded with favorable consideration for early release as well as privileges while still in confinement. That approach was adopted in turn by Sir Walter Crofton, chairman of the Board of Directors of the Irish Prisons in the 1850s, but it was many years later when Brockway became aware of these innovations. The Elmira system emphasized trade training and academic education more than traditional prisons, but it is indeterminate sentencing with a maximum fixed by the court but no minimum for which Elmira is best known. Release of inmates prior to the expiration of their maximum sentences— parole—was conditional on their good behavior.

An important ingredient of the reformatory approach was a classification system.

All reformatory inmates were graded into three classes according to achievement and conduct: new prisoners were entered in the second grade for the first 6 months and were demoted to the third grade for bad conduct, or promoted to the first grade as they earned their "marks"; only prisoners who were in the first grade were eligible for parole (Attorney General's Survey of Release Procedures, 1973: 42–43).

This system was actually foreshadowed by a more complex classification system at the Boston House of Reformation, founded in 1826, where a six-class system prevailed: three good levels, with privileges extending to unsupervised excursions away from the institution at the highest level, and three bad grades, which might entail restrictions even on speaking (Hawes, 1971: 53).

The classification system at Elmira was a departure from the moral suasion that Brockway had found unsuccessful in his early career. It was a reflection of a newly developing scientific orientation emphasizing behavioral rather than spiritual change. Brockway explained the new principle, "that the state shall not judge the heart's intentions, and not judging or knowing, shall not designedly trespass on the mystical field of the soul's moral relations, but instead shall remain devoted to the regulation of the prisoner's conduct with sole regard to the public security" (Hawes, 1971: 150). Offenders were thus no longer to be judged on the basis of their internal moral condition, nor simply on the basis of external conduct, which may be deceiving. Their "reclamation" was ascertained by an assessment of their character, "which is found in resisting evil and in triumphing over its influence" (Brockway, 1969: 406).

The reformatory, as Brockway conceived it, represents a philosophy that Rothman has identified as characteristic of the nineteenth-century approach to the problem of crime. Criminality was primarily the result of young people's exposure to "a community pervaded with vice" (Rothman, 1971); the solution was to remove them from criminogenic surroundings and place them in institutions which might be thought of as people-changing factories. Brockway discusses the goal of the reformatory as an auto manufacturer might discuss the prerequisites for turning out a quality product (perhaps some of his experience rubbed off from two years he spent in private business between his superintendency of the Detroit House of Correction and his assumption of that role at Elmira). "A high standard of behavior is essential," he said, "which can only be maintained by most minute regulations, very complete supervision, with wise and vigorous management" (Hawes, 1971: 149). The notion that inmates are individuals with unique potentialities and limitations was not a part of his conception of the Reformatory's task. In Brockway's view they were, rather, raw materials which might be turned into useful products by the application of appropriate technology.

In his writing Brockway does classify prisoners as "difficult," "average," and "better" types, the great majority falling into the intermediate category. The difficult prisoners were in large measure suffering from constitutional abnormalities, in Brockway's view, and might never be confidently judged so little threatening to public safety as to warrant their release from confinement. At the other extreme were a number of the "better" prisoners, regarded as "criminals of occasion" who had made but one misstep, quickly repented, and gone on to lead exemplary lives. The average prisoners, although demonstrably weaker of body, intellect, and character than members of the general population, were so amenable to reclamation that Brockway was able to cite statistics to the effect that 81.9 percent of the 3,723 parolees released from Elmira between 1876 and 1893 had not returned to crime (Brockway, 1969: 325). In contrast with a bad-guy view, in which the evil element stays with the criminal and exerts its influence throughout his life, Brockway sees the stigma of crime as something that cannot be totally extirpated from one's past, but that for the average criminal can nevertheless be annulled through exposure to proper reformative influences. When successful, the criminal's reformation may be regarded thus: "As a gunshot embedded in the flesh may become encysted, the wound healed, the injury unobserved and unconsciously borne, so the injury of a criminal act and conviction may be covered with the cloak of constant good behavior and fade from the discharged prisoners' habitual remembrance, in its cyst of conscious social rectitude" (Brockway, 1969: 78).

CLASSIFICATION OF OFFENDERS IN PRISON SYSTEMS

In modern correctional institutions good-guy stereotypes are most apparent in procedures used to assign inmates to one or another facility or program. Sometimes the process is begun by the courts as part of sentencing following determination of guilt. The judge, guided by a probation department recommendation, not only imposes sentence of a particular length, but also may send the accused to a facility with very few restrictions if his attitude toward the offender is favorable. More commonly the environment in which a prisoner will be serving time is determined during a period of residence in a special classification center separate from a custodial prison or in a classification unit attached to a prison.

Although classification is typically rationalized in terms of rehabilitative as well as management goals, in practice the most important concern is security: whether the inmate shall be placed in a maximum-security, medium-security, or minimum-security institution or unit (Hippchen,

1978: 6). The more an inmate is perceived as a good guy, who basically accepts and internalizes institutional restrictions, the more likely he is to be selected for minimum custody or "special placement" in a camp or halfway house (Bennett, 1986: 251). Considerable efforts have been made in recent years to develop scientific, objective classification techniques (Alexander, 1986). More sophisticated forms of classification based on assessment by clinical psychologists have been used as a part of psychosocial treatment strategies. Noteworthy is the I-level scheme developed by Warren (1976) and her coworkers, which has been influential in rehabilitation programs for young offenders in California. I-levels correspond to levels of psychological maturity: Delinquents with lower I-levels are greatly dependent on adults and fixated on gratification of their own needs, while those at higher levels are capable of greater independence and responsibility for meeting social obligations. The implication is obvious that the higher the maturity level, the better. The system is organized around the expectation that clients in treatment will move from lower to higher levels of maturity, ultimately reaching a degree of maturity that will justify discharge from the treatment program. A somewhat similar scheme of psychological classification has been combined with a "class-level system" at the Robert F. Kennedy Center, a residential center for delinquents who have violated federal laws, in Morgantown, West Virginia (Gerard, 1973). Boys are designated Trainees on entry. Typically, they advance by proper conduct to Apprentice status in three to five months, and from Apprentice to Honor class in five to eight months. As a beneficiary of the Progressives' benign view of young offenders, and in keeping with the Kennedy Center's emphasis on positive reinforcement, all of the class names—Trainee, Apprentice, and Honor—have positive connotations. Apparently there are no bad guys here. There are good guys, better guys, and best guys—an attenuation of the polarization process.

In the foregoing examples inmate classification refers to a formal process—indeed usually a highly bureaucratized one—for categorizing offenders according to whether they are good guys who can be trusted not to abscond and who may profit from some form of therapeutic intervention, or whether they are bad guys for whom incarceration can be no more than a "holding operation." Beyond the formal classification schemes, however, many observers have noted the tendency for staff members in criminal justice agencies to develop informal classificatory schemes with moral overtones. The results of a study by McCleary (1978: chap. 4) do not demonstrate moral *polarization*, strictly speaking, since all offenders are not classified at the extremes, but those results do indicate different ways of handling criminals who are located at opposite ends of the moral continuum. In this study of parole officers, McCleary has shown how they divide parolees into three groups. One group, the bulk of the case load, is informally classified as the "paper men": clients regarded as neither particularly dangerous nor particularly good candidates for rehabilitation. The term indicates that they are carried as members of the case load on paper but in fact get little attention from the parole officer. A second group comprises the "troublemakers," those parolees who, even if they do not pose a real threat to the society at large, cause problems for their parole officers by making it difficult for the officers to insure that all the bureaucratic demands of the agency are complied with. The few "good guys" within the case load are known as "sincere " clients, those who have shown themselves willing to accept the parole officer as a therapist. They report regularly for scheduled appointments, face up to their problems candidly, make a real effort at rehabilitation, and pose no threat to the parole contract by violating conditions of parole or committing additional offenses.

These categories determine the amount of attention a client gets from his parole officer. The paper men, as indicated above, get minimal attention. However, the dangerous parolees must be followed closely in an effort to control their behavior, for the parole agency as a whole and the assigned officer in particular are held responsible when convicted offenders commit additional crimes while under parole supervision. The sincere clients also get special attention: They may have weekly appointments, in contrast with the paper men, who may be seen as infrequently as every six months. And favored treatment for the sincere clients means not only that they benefit from whatever advice or insights result from their meetings with their parole officers; being included in this category means also that, should the parolee make a misstep during his term on parole, he can count on his officer to defend him.

STATUS OFFENDERS AS GOOD GUYS

Within juvenile courts in recent years there has emerged a classification category that singles out certain young offenders for "good guy" status. It is a legal distinction aimed at differentiating those youngsters whose misconduct is at the level of adult crime from those who come to the law's attention for lesser misdeeds. The distinction had been blurred in the early juvenile courts. Because of their attention to the delinquents' best interests, those courts had cast a broader net than the criminal law; they were authorized to deal not only with youths who had broken the criminal law but also with those who had done things, like drinking alcoholic beverages, which are not illegal for older people. In their zeal to help any young people who showed signs of social maladjustment, the framers of juvenile justice statutes made it possible for all of them to be labeled juvenile delinquents and treated accordingly.

Around 1970, however, a new kind of polarization emerged, as American society came to see itself as increasingly threatened by the misconduct of some juveniles, while there persisted a concern among juvenile justice experts that others guilty of only minor transgressions might be dealt with too harshly. On the one hand, a number of states passed "transfer statutes" (Sussman, 1978), so called because they provided for the transfer of juveniles who had committed specified serious criminal offenses like murder or armed robbery to the adult court system, where they could be given prison sentences far more severe than those prescribed for ordinary delinquents. Meanwhile, in a number of states juveniles who had formerly been treated as delinquents although they had not broken any criminal laws were no longer classified as real delinquents but rather as "status offenders"—people whose acts are legal infractions only by virtue of their youthful status. The New York Family Court Act of 1962, for example, uses the term "person in need of supervision" (PINS) to refer to youths under the age of sixteen who are "incorrigible, ungovernable or habitually disobedient and beyond the lawful control of parent or other lawful authority." Whereas delinquents may have some degree of responsibility for the behavior bringing them to the court's attention, the PINS category seems to imply that fault may lie with the inadequacy of supervising authorities rather than with the youngsters themselves—thus exempting them from the bad-guy label.

GOOD PEOPLE WHO HAVE BROKEN THE LAW

The reputation that a person enjoys within a community may serve as a kind of counterforce, protecting the person from the stigma that would ordinarily attach to violation of the criminal law. William Chambliss carried out a study of two gangs of boys, the Saints and the Roughnecks, residing in the same community and attending the same high school. The gangs were similar in that both engaged in illegal drinking and small-scale theft, but they were perceived differently by residents of the community. The Roughnecks had a reputation as troublemakers for whom the townspeople predicted a bad end, whereas the Saints' offenses were dismissed as youthful peccadillos that would be outgrown as they went on to college and eventually fulfilled their roles as members of respected families.

It comes as little surprise that the Saints and Roughnecks came from different social strata. The Saints were from upper middle-class families; they dressed neatly and were observed to treat adults with respect. In spite of their delinquencies, they did well in school and were active in extracurricular activities. The Roughnecks came from lower-class families and had a slovenly appearance. Rather than take part in extracurricular school activities, they spent nearly all their spare time hanging around the corner drugstore, drinking and getting into fights.

There were several explanations for the different response by the community. In part, the Saints' access to cars made it possible for them to carry on some of their illegal activities in places that were not as public as the street corner where the Roughnecks hung out. But it was also true that the Saints' deviance, when observed, was minimized; their family backgrounds, appearance, and demeanor were inconsistent with public stereotypes of delinquency, while the Roughnecks were regarded as troublesome because they fit the image of the delinquent. This discrepancy in images existed in spite of acts of vandalism committed by the Saints, which Chambliss estimated to cause greater financial loss to the community than the property losses occasioned by the Roughnecks' behavior, and the Saints' reckless driving, which posed a greater threat to the physical safety of the community. Still, the Saints' respectable backgrounds led the community to rationalize their delinquency as "sowing wild oats," while the Roughnecks bore the full brunt of community disapproval for their deviant conduct (Chambliss, 1973).

Chambliss's study calls attention to a perceptual process in which certain individuals, even if thought to have committed criminal offenses, continue to be regarded as good people by virtue of their association with prestigious families, social groups, business enterprises, or religious and charitable activities. Such immunity is not always granted, of course, but under certain circumstances a person's high social status or record of personal achievement may simply lead people to disbelieve that the person committed the alleged crime, even in the face of otherwise compelling evidence.

In fact, the law provides a mechanism—the testimony of "character witnesses"—by which being known as a "good guy" can benefit someone on trial for any crime.

It is well settled that in a criminal prosecution, the defendant may introduce reputation evidence as to his own good character for the purpose of raising an inference that he would not be likely to commit the offense charged. . . . This he does by calling a qualified witness or witnesses to testify to his good reputation in the community for the particular trait involved in the crime charged (Prince, 1973: 121–22).

If half a dozen respectable character witnesses, appearing on behalf of someone accused of embezzlement, testify with deep conviction that they are intimately familiar with the reputation of the accused in the community, and that that reputation consists of a unanimous view that he is a thoroughly honest individual, such testimony may indeed cause a jury to have sufficient "reasonable doubt" about the charges to render a not guilty verdict.

More often than denying the accusation, however, a person's social standing may result in minimizing the criminal character of an offense. Family social position had much to do with the good reputations that members of the Saints' gang managed to maintain, as indicated in the Chambliss study. And it has until recently been conventional wisdom among criminologists that a similar process explains the lenient treatment traditionally accorded such upperworld offenders as stock traders who buy and sell based on insider information, and legislators whose votes are influenced by campaign contributions or personal gifts from constituents.

Most of the evidence for this tolerance is provided by studies of the relative leniency with which the criminal justice system treats high-status criminals (Clinard and Yeager, 1980), but there is also some direct evidence from attitude surveys. Aubert (1952) studied attitudes toward violation of price-control and rationing regulations by businesses. Among Norwegian businessmen surveyed, a distinction was made between such offenses committed by "outsiders"—new firms, small firms, and disreputable firms—and offenses committed by "the good established firms." Violations committed by the "outsiders" were regarded as real crimes but those committed by the established firms tended to be rationalized as harmless, or mere technical violations.

On the other hand, recent surveys seem to indicate that the American public regards the seriousness of white-collar offenses as equal to or greater than that of ordinary crimes. In one study illegal retail price fixing was judged slightly more serious than the crime of robbing a victim of $1,000 by threatening assault with a lead pipe; also, pollution of a city's water supply by a factory and thereby making one person ill was adjudged much more serious than a house burglary of $100 (Clinard and Yaeger, 1980: 5–6; see also Conklin, 1977: 20–27).

How can one explain this apparent discrepancy—between the lenient treatment meted out to white-collar criminals by the criminal justice system, and the public attitude that their transgressions are far from trivial? Conklin has enumerated a number of reasons for the lenient treatment of business offenders, including the reluctance of victims to prosecute, political influence, and the difficulty of pinpointing responsibility within an organizational framework. Prominent among reasons cited is social status. Indeed, it sometimes seems that the magnitude of an offense is itself an indicator of status and therefore a basis for exculpation. As a character in Eugene O'Neill's play *The Emperor Jones* puts it, "For de little stealin dey gits you in jail soon or late. For de big stealin' dey makes you emperor and puts you in de Hall o' Fame when you croaks" (Mars, 1983). And it is of course significant that "dey" themselves enjoy high status. "Because businessmen, lawmakers, and judges come from similar social backgrounds, are of similar age, have often been educated at the same universities, associate with the same people, and have similar outlooks on the world, it is not surprising that legislators and judges are unwilling to treat business offenders harshly" (Conklin, 1977: 112). Moreover, social reputation and lack of criminal conviction operate in an interactive way: "Lawmakers and judges see businessmen as respectable because they have rarely been convicted of crimes; however, they have rarely been convicted of crimes because they are regarded as respectable" (Conklin, 1977: 113).

Conklin makes an interesting comparison between the legal system's treatment of business offenders and its treatment of juvenile delinquents. In each case, he suggests, there is a tendency to provide special treatment: in the case of delinquents, through a special juvenile court to avoid the stigma of criminal prosecution, and in the case of business offenders, by opting to pursue civil action when criminal prosecution is an alternative possibility. Seemingly, the special treatment is chosen because both business offenders and delinquents are perceived as fundamentally good guys—that is, they fail to meet the test of intentional wrongdoing that would qualify them for bad-guy status. In support of this analogy Conklin quotes a lawyer who portrays a corporation he is defending in much the same way as one might defend a client before the juvenile court as a way-ward innocent: "I know I represent a corporation, and a rather young cor-poration, if Your Honor please, which I am afraid lost its way. It was or-ganized to build a pipeline from Texas to New Jersey and got lost around Woodbridge, sadly enough" (Conklin, 1977: 121).

Whatever the attitude of the general public toward high-status offend-ers, there are abundant instances in which their convictions have not caused them to lose esteem among their peers. In a feature article on cor-porate crime in 1982, *U. S. News and World Report* examined the after-math of criminal convictions of top executives for offenses ranging from tax evasion to discharging dangerous pollutants into public waterways. Typically, court-imposed penalties were lenient, and the offenders were in no way impeded in advancing their careers. When the Fruehauf Corpo-ration was convicted in 1975 of tax evasion, the board chairman of the manufacturer of truck trailers was allowed to do community service in-stead of serving time in prison, while the company continued to provide him with all fringe benefits, and restored him to the chairmanship of its executive committee six months later. The company president received a similar sentence from the court and benefits from the company, in addition to 100-dollar-an-hour consultant fees. The president was also reinstated in his earlier position, and subsequently, upon his colleague's retirement, promoted to the board chairmanship at a salary of more than $300,000.

Another case followed up by the magazine was the widely publicized conviction of David Begelman, who had been president of Columbia Pictures, for converting $40,000 of company funds to his personal use. Begelman resigned his position, pleaded guilty, and was given probation. And shortly thereafter he became head of another studio. Concerning his standing in the community, the *U. S. News* article quotes the *Los Angeles Times*: "Begelman came to be viewed in Hollywood as more a charming rogue than a convicted embezzler, the scandal a sort of corporate dueling scar that added a touch of character" (Kelly, 1982: 28–29).

The sports world is another community that appears to excuse its im-portant members when they commit certain crimes. The University of New Mexico's head basketball coach in the 1970s was charged in connec-tion with a recruiting scandal. He had been dismissed from his post, and in 1981 was convicted by a jury on twenty-one of twenty-two counts, for filing false travel vouchers and receiving reimbursement for trips he never took. The judge in the case, in sentencing him to probation rather than prison, noted that the coach had not used the money for his own benefit; rather, it was spent on illegal recruiting and support for basketball players. In justifying his decision not to impose a prison sentence, the judge said, "I'm being asked to sentence a man because he got caught, not because his conduct was unacceptable. The question is how fair is it to incarcerate a man for doing what almost everyone in the community wanted him to do—namely, win basketball games at whatever cost" ("Ellenberger avoids a prison sentence," 1981).

In some cases one's reputation within a particular segment of the larger community may provide the basis for a positive moral judgment strong enough to overcome the negative image associated with a criminal act. A literary reputation can serve this function. Even a law-and order advocate like William F. Buckley, Jr., could defend a murderer with literary credentials, and the support of Norman Mailer for Jack Henry Abbott, author of *In the Belly of the Beast*, is well known. It is said that the French are especially inclined to forgive intellectuals who happen to engage in ordinary crimes. Several years ago a convicted robber named Roger Knobelspiess came to the attention of the French literati because of two books he had written on "the horrors of prison life in a non-Marxist state." With the support of celebrities such as the film stars Yves Montand and Simone Signoret and the historian Michel Foucault, Knobelspiess was granted a pardon by President François Mitterand, a pardon justified, in the words of the historian Claude Manceron, on the basis that "France must not deprive itself of this natural resource" (Goodman, 1983).

CRIMES AS GOOD DEEDS

At the beginning of this chapter we noted that it was ordinarily not necessary for people to engage in exceptionally praiseworthy acts in order to merit being considered by others as "good guys"; one can have a "good-guy" reputation simply by not being bad. So far, the examples of offenders as good guys considered here are instances in which, for reasons mentioned above, harmful acts do not confer moral opprobrium on the people who commit them, and so these people may continue to be regarded as good guys.

However, we can also speak of the good offender in a stronger sense—in the sense that the act done, though apparently in violation of the criminal law, is nevertheless regarded as praiseworthy. Here too, as in the cases noted earlier when lack of *mens rea* serves as a defense, the law exonerates people who carry out some of these actions. The police officer who shoots a bank robber, the passerby coming to the aid of a mugging victim who uses a karate chop to fight off the assailant, a mother slapping her child for telling a lie —each of these people has committed a physical action that is ordinarily criminal, but because of special circumstances may be deemed legal. The actual behavior fits precisely with what the law has proscribed, but an exception is made on legal grounds of justification. Parents disciplining their children, public officials performing their duties, and good samaritans coming to the defense of their fellow citizens whose physical safety or property are in jeopardy, are all given freedom to carry out praiseworthy activities, which activities under more usual circumstances would be subject to criminal penalties.

In each of these cases the law's exception may be defended on both subjective and objective grounds. From the actors' subjective point of view they were doing something commendable—bringing up a child properly, fulfilling an obligation as an officer of the law, coming to the aid of a victim in distress—all of these are respected sentiments. Correspondingly, at the objective level, society benefits when its servants do their jobs, its citizens help one another, its parents raise their children properly. In these cases there appears to be a correspondence between good intentions and good results.

Actually, to the extent that the law excuses the kind of behaviors mentioned above, one might question the appropriateness of treating these instances as offenses at all, since their circumstances effectively make them non-offenses. But there are other offenses, done for what many people regard as commendable motives, which are still treated by the law as crimes. In taking account of good intentions the law does not always correspond to public opinion.

Pure cases of mercy killing are the best example of a discrepancy between legal codes and popular sentiment. Even when the victim is suffering greatly from a disease, when the chances of remission are nonexistent, and when there can be no alternative motive for the offender than an altruistic desire to end the suffering, the law, at least in the United States, is unshakable: no legal justification. A widely publicized case in point was that of Roswell Gilbert, a seventy-five-year-old retired engineer whose wife was suffering greatly from Alzheimer's disease and osteoporosis. Moved by her pleas to "Please, let me die," Gilbert ended her life with two bullets to the head as she lay on a sofa in their Florida condominium. He was convicted of first-degree murder and sentenced to life in prison, with no possibility of parole for twenty-five years.

What made the case unusual was the fact that so severe a penalty was imposed in what seemed a typical instance of euthanasia, for in most known cases there is not even a short term of imprisonment. A similarly lenient attitude tends to prevail in those cases where life support systems for permanently comatose patients are disconnected without legal authorization. Whether death is caused by injection or other active means, or by termination of artificial supports, such cases are often simply hushed up by informal agreement among those who are aware of the circumstances. Seldom are any formal legal steps taken against such perpetrators unless there is reason to doubt the purity of their motives. And even if legal action is initiated, prosecutors go out of their way to find some basis to dismiss the charges, grand juries refuse to indict, judges dismiss charges or accept a guilty plea with the understanding that the person will be placed on probation. And in those instances when such cases go to a jury trial, it is not uncommon for the jury to find in favor of such defendants. In spite of instruction from the judge to the jurors that they may not legally consider the defendant's motive, however pure, to end the victim's suffering, the jury is very likely to render a verdict of acquittal. Even with strong evidence indicating that the act was done by the accused and with no legal basis for exoneration, the jury's "not guilty" verdict ratifies its good guy perception of the accused by simply asserting that he didn't do it (Ain and Gentile, 1985; Givens, 1985; "Merciless jury," 1985; Schmidt, 1990; Vaux, 1988).

THE GOOD GANGSTER

Miguel Otero, a former governor of New Mexico, recalled that in a peaceful encounter with Billy the Kid he had found the famous bandit "pleasant to meet" and remarked on the Kid's reputation as "always being kind and considerate to the old, the young, and the poor; he was loyal to his friends and, above all, loved his mother devotedly" (Kooistra, 1989: 8).

"Social bandit" is the term coined by Eric Hobsbawm, a British social historian, to refer to outlaws in rural societies who are regarded as criminals by the official government, but are "considered by their people as heroes, as champions, avengers, fighters for justice, perhaps even leaders of liberation, and in any case as men to be admired, helped, and supported" (1969: 13). What makes certain kinds of banditry "social" is that such bandits, themselves of peasant stock, act only against landowners who exploit the peasantry, and so are perceived as supporting the interests of their own people. Citing examples throughout Europe and in Asia, Australia, North Africa, and the Americas, Hobsbawm sees social banditry as a phenomenon associated with a society's transition from a tribal or kinship-based system to industrial capitalism.

In twelfth-century England, it was Robin Hood and his merry men whose exploits in stealing from the wealthy and giving to the needy were extolled in legend. In the nineteenth century it was Billy the Kid who was glorified for stealing from people who had more wealth than they needed and turning the proceeds over to poor Mexicans in the American Southwest. These "noble robbers" (to use another of Hobsbawm's terms) were as much heroes as the daredevils of history who have prevailed over superior power on military battlefields.

Most celebrated among the robbers of the American frontier was the James-Younger gang. Jesse and Frank James and the Younger brothers led a group of outlaws that appealed to the American public not only for the daring and success of their robberies, but because they were directed against the symbol of forces that threatened the free spirits of the Wild West—the railroads. To envision the great steam engines belching black smoke and despoiling the serenity of the great prairies, and then to see a handful of men on horseback cause the engineer to bring his machine to a grinding halt, so that the freight cars carrying bullion and the wealthy passengers would yield money and jewelry to the ragged, hard-riding bunch: Of such images are the reputations of heroes made.

Less important than reality is the image constructed of the bandits by their admirers. And it was often necessary to build upon the known facts to make "the people's champion . . . not only . . . honest and respectable, but entirely admirable" (Hobsbawm, 1969: 40). There is no historical record suggesting that the members of the James gang, for example, were more morally fastidious than other common criminals in their choice of victims. Yet the myth was widely accepted that Jesse never robbed preachers, widows, orphans, or ex-Confederates. And if these credentials were insufficient to establish his good-guy status, some of his admirers were even willing to accept the assertion that he was "a devout Baptist who taught in a church singing school" (Hobsbawm, 1969: 42)!

The myths of the Wild West heroes were initially recorded and embroidered by contemporary writers. And in turn, with the advent of radio, movies, and eventually television, they were endowed with many of the virtues of modern superheroes. "The Western movies were tales of open space, fables of solitude and masculinity where marshal and bandit were free to roam, to endure, and to survive by perpetual courage and rapacious instinct" (Inciardi, 1975: 170). This is not to say that all Western outlaws were regarded as good. In fact the public was well aware of the distinction between the good outlaws—like Jesse James, Billy the Kid, and Joaquin Murrieta (the subject of a book titled *The Robin Hood of El Dorado*)—and those who were described in terms of "evil" and wickedness, like the Dalton gang.

In the early part of the twentieth century the names were different—Bonnie Parker and Clyde Barrow, John Dillinger, "Ma" Barker, "Baby-Face" Nelson, and others—and the targets tended to be banks rather than stagecoaches and trains, but the public's fascination—even reverence—for the bandits was the same. And the connection is not simply in the public mind; a chain of personal influence has in fact been traced from fifteen-year-old Jesse James as a member of Quantrill's Raiders during the Civil War to the career of "Pretty Boy" Floyd in the 1920s (Inciardi, 1975: 96–97).

The modern counterpart is the organized crime syndicate of the twentieth century, and its members too are glamorized in the public mind. Aside from that part of the attraction based on romanticism and identification with the rebel, modern gangsters are spoken of in terms of respect by solid citizens outside the underworld. Some such expressions result from quite conscious public relations campaigns; charitable organizations like the Salvation Army and Knights of Columbus benefit from the generosity of Italian syndicate members, as has Brandeis University from occasional "small gifts" from Meyer Lansky (Cressey, 1969: 275). But much good opinion is spontaneous rather than orchestrated. William F. Whyte, in his classic study of Boston's Italian North End during the 1930s, quotes a respectable young businessman on the subject of T. S., the leading racketeer in Cornerville and an influential member of the syndicate in Boston, and his associates:

These gangsters are the finest fellows you want to meet. They'll do a lot for you, Bill. You go up to them and say, "I haven't eaten for four days, and I haven't got a place to sleep," and they'll give you something. Now you go up to a businessman, one of the respected members of the community, and ask him. He throws you right out of the office (Whyte, 1981: 142).

Even when engaging in illegal activities gangsters' conduct often reflects niceties recognized by the general norms. It is not uncommon to read about ordinary criminals who abort their intended crimes when they discover that their victims are physically handicapped, ill, or destitute, and similar norms prevail among members of organized crime in a form derived from the "rustic chivalry" of a peasant society (Ianni, 1972: 21). Loyalty, honor, respect for legitimate authority and obedience to it, honesty, not revealing confidences: These central values of the Cosa Nostra organization are also central in American culture. Mike Giovanni, a subject in Whyte's study who was paid as a strong-arm man in labor disputes, showed an admirable sense of class loyalty by limiting his services to the union and refusing offers to fight for employers (Whyte, 1981: 10). Similarly, at around the time of World War I the New York gang leader "Dopey Benny" Fein, who had earlier sold the services of his toughs to the highest bidder, underwent an apparent change of heart.

For some three years there was scarcely a strike in New York in which these gangsters were not employed, and during this period Dopey Benny's annual income averaged between fifteen and twenty thousand dollars. So widely feared was he that a group of employers once offered him fifteen thousand dollars if he would remain neutral during a threatened strike. But Dopey Benny indignantly refused, saying that his heart was naturally with the working man, and that he would continue to hold himself and his gangsters at the disposal of the union officials (Asbury, 1970: 363).

INSTRUMENTAL CRIMINALS

A variant on the genre of criminals who are seen as good guys because of their kindness to others is that class of offenders whose transgressions benefit, not their fellow man, but needs of their own that are considered legitimate. Whether a particular need is legitimate or not is of course open to controversy. Theft of bread to survive in the face of starvation is widely tolerated; of caviar to satisfy a craving for that delicacy, generally frowned upon. In between there is room for considerable difference of opinion. Poor boys from ghetto areas have been known to steal expensive Adidas sneakers because they were not accepted as gang members when they wore less expensive ones, the best their parents could afford to buy for them. Are they wrong to do so? Some opinion holders would assert that they should get part time jobs to buy better sneakers for themselves, but others would deny the availability of such jobs, and further point out that in some areas membership in a tough gang is not simply a matter of personal preference but is in reality important to insure one's physical safety.

A number of academic criminologists have emphasized the "instrumental" quality of criminal behavior—that the conduct is not considered desirable or undesirable in itself by offenders but is instead engaged in to achieve some external purpose (Schwendinger and Schwendinger, 1967). Such purposes may be congruent with values accepted by the larger society. In a study of "hustling" in the black ghetto, Lewis compares it with legitimate business and concludes that "while much of the behavior I am discussing is illegal it is also within the range of that which is normatively valued in the cultural mainstream of contemporary society" (1970: 177). In another study of hustling, Krisberg recognizes the discrepancy between hustlers' activities and the norms of the larger community, but he emphasizes "the psychology of survival": the hustlers' perceptions that they are the victims of circumstances that leave them no alternative but crime in order to satisfy the requirements of material existence (1974: 243).

It is not only the offenders who consider themselves blameless because of the pressures on them to commit crime. As will be seen in Chapter 4, much of the strong criticism of contemporary society and many of the calls for government intervention to reduce inequities stem from arguments that emphasize the blameworthiness of the society at large, and the consequent blamelessness of individuals who have no choice but to commit crimes as a way of adapting to that immoral structure.

Indeed, the instrumental focus has been extended beyond being applied only to criminal acts justified as necessary to meet basic sustenance needs. It has been stretched to define, as rational criminality, the activities of a wide range of skilled offenders whose gains provide them with a style of life going well beyond sheer survival. There has recently been considerable emphasis on one variant of the instrumental approach known as criminal opportunity theory. It is grounded in research which has shown decreases in crime rates when potential offenders know that various security measures have been taken—for example, marking household possessions with identification numbers, instituting an exact fare system on city buses, beefing up airport security, or equipping automobiles with ignition locks. The theory explains crime occurrences as outcomes of a process in which the amount of payoff, the likelihood of encountering resistance from victims or bystanders, and the chance of eventual apprehension by the authorities are rationally calculated, using techniques developed for explaining legitimate economic decisionmaking—and implying no discontinuity between motives for criminal and noncriminal behavior. Cook, an economist, has made the assumption explicit in reviewing criminal opportunity theory and research evidence bearing on it.

In summary, an increase in the net payoff per unit of effort on the part of the criminal will, other things being equal, increase the overall volume of property crime. Denial of this proposition is tantamount to claiming that potential criminals as a group are unresponsive to economic incentives—that they are fundamentally different from everyone else, if indeed there is anyone who can be excluded from the "potential criminal" category (1986: 18).

It would be an exaggeration to say that public opinion always supports the view that the end justifies the means, when the means are criminal behavior. Yet some people are considerably influenced by the knowledge that an act was committed for an instrumental purpose rather than as a "senseless" act. A pilot study of public opinion about sentencing has shown that people would choose less severe punishments for an offender if he said that he had carried out a larceny or a robbery to buy clothes necessary for peer group status, than if he said he did it simply out of a personal dislike for the victim (Claster, 1978).

THE OFFENDER AS VIGILANTE

The scene is the American frontier in the third quarter of the nineteenth century. The notorious James gang has just robbed a bank in Gory Gulch, murdered two bank clerks and three innocent bystanders, and is fleeing into the hills. Not far behind is a quickly assembled posse. The gang members, more experienced riders, are increasing the distance between themselves and their pursuers, but the horse of one gang member—say, Jesse's brother, Frank—stumbles, and horse and rider fall to the ground. By the time Frank gets to his feet the posse has ridden up and taken him into custody, while the rest of the gang is too far ahead to be overtaken.

With Frank locked up in the ramshackle Gory Gulch jail, the towns-people must decide how to proceed. There is no resident judge; legally, all court business must wait until the circuit judge arrives for a two-week period every three months. But he has just been in Gory Gulch a week before, and the townspeople fear that between now and his next visit the gang will return and carry out a jailbreak. Therefore, in this prototype of countless film scripts, a kangaroo court convicts him and he is hanged in a ceremony for which the whole town turns out, including small children whose parents use the opportunity to indicate what happens to anyone who thinks he can live beyond the rules of recognized authority.

Here our concern is not with the gang's crimes but with the lynching, as a prototype of vigilantism. Vigilantes act in situations in which there is a perception that deviant behavior is beyond the bounds of informal controls, and legal mechanisms are either absent or inadequate to the task. These conditions were present on the American frontier, with its vast, sparsely settled territory and lack of established institutions. Vigilantism was encouraged not only by the rudimentary nature of frontier legal systems, but also by the lack of informal mechanisms of deterrence, like developed religious and family groupings.

Similarities between the Wild West and present-day cities have often been noted—anonymity, rivalries among groups, acceptance of violent solutions for perceived problems—so that it is not surprising to find a vigilantist rationale invoked to support the good-guy image of city dwellers who commit illegal acts against those whom they see as threats to their community. The Bernhard Goetz incident discussed in Chapter 1 is a prime example, but it is only the most widely publicized among many. A number of other examples of vigilantism in the recent past are recounted in a book written by a *New York Times* reporter (Burrows, 1976: ch. 10), and such incidents continue to occur (Gest, 1987).

It is perhaps not surprising to find a recent instance of group vigilantism in the New West, where the spirit of good-guy vigilantes of the Old West may have inspired a campaign directed against the current threat of drugs instead of the old threat of cattle rustling. A group of high-school students calling themselves the Legion of Doom came to public attention in Fort Worth, Texas in 1985. Mostly honor students and athletes, these students launched a campaign which included bombing one auto and shooting at another one driven by other students who Legion members thought were responsible for dealing drugs and other criminal activities at their school ("Eight youths accused ," 1985; "Honor students," 1985; "Student group," 1985).

A more spontaneous form of retaliation broke out on an East Harlem street in 1988, when about a dozen people chased a man who had snatched a twenty-dollar bill from a bakery customer about to purchase a birthday cake. The vigilantes caught up with him a block away from the site of the theft, and beat him with sticks and fists. Finally one of the avengers hit him repeatedly with a garbage can while he was lying on the sidewalk, causing his death. Eight people were charged in the assault. Subsequently charges against seven of them were dropped, and the remaining defendant was allowed to plead guilty to second-degree manslaughter with the promise of only three to six years imprisonment. The lenient sentence was consistent with public perception of the assailants as good guys and the court's awareness of evidence of the dead man's bad character, based not only on the theft but also on his reputation as a drug addict and the presence of needle tracks covering both arms ("Defendant in beating death," 1988; Hays, 1988; McQuiston, 1988).

A fictional counterpart of the Goetz case is presented in the book *Death Wish* (Garfield, 1972), which was subsequently made into a popular movie. The book's hero (played by Charles Bronson in the film version) is a New York accountant whose lifelong political stance might be described as conventionally liberal. A robbery attempt results in the death of his wife and the transformation of his daughter from a well-functioning young married woman into a sufferer from severe catatonic psychosis. The hero is obsessed with fear and rage. Upon learning that he cannot obtain a permit to own a pistol legally in New York, he purchases one on a business trip to Arizona. Then, returning home, he wanders the city looking for street criminals about to commit or in the process of committing their crimes. Within a period of a few days he kills eight people in five separate incidents involving victims engaging in offenses of varying severity, and the media publicize the presence of a single vigilante responsible for all the killings.

In the last scene in the book the hero has just shot three boys who were throwing bricks at a passing train. He walks half a block away from the scene, then looks back to see a policeman quietly facing him. The officer is aware that he is facing the vigilante described in the publicity, but he simply turns his back. The hero then resumes his walk away from the scene until he finds a taxi to take him home.

While the policeman in this scene is officially required to arrest the hero, by failing to do so he demonstrates that he adheres, rather, to the informal norm that an urban vigilante is a good guy doing justice in compensation for the inadequacies of the official agencies. Just as the circuit-riding judges in the Old West were seen as few and far between, and not unlikely corrupt to boot, so too is the criminal justice system in a number of American cities regarded as too slow, too lenient, and too uncertain. And so there is respect for the person who has the courage to stand up to attackers, who does not take victimization lying down. It is more than acceptance, for the person who retaliates is seen as serving not only his or her interests, but those of society as well.

THE POLITICAL CRIMINAL

Among the most praised criminal acts are those motivated by a political doctrine embodying high principles of freedom, equality, and justice. When, for example, an assault threatens the life of a high government official, it is often done in a situation in which the assailants are very likely to be caught and punished. In such cases the expectation of punishment itself suggests the absence of a simple selfish motive and therefore the presence of a higher one. On November 1, 1950, at a time when President Harry S. Truman was temporarily residing at Blair House because the White House was being renovated, two representatives of a movement for Puerto Rican independence shot and killed one security officer guarding the residence and wounded two others. The fatally wounded guard had managed to get off one shot killing his assailant, Griselio Torresola, before he himself died, and the other assailant was also wounded in the interchange of gunfire. The president, who was taking an afternoon nap in an upstairs bedroom at the time, came to the window at the sound of shots, and the incident is often remembered as an attempt on his life. But there is no evidence that it was aimed at his assassination. Rather, according to newspaper reports, which include testimony from the surviving assailant, Oscar Collazo, the pair had been primarily concerned with staging an attention-getting demonstration at the president's residence and had concluded that the best way to insure the publicity they desired was to provoke their own deaths.

Although the fatal shots had been fired by his partner, Collazo was convicted of homicide and sentenced to die for his part in the incident.

Truman commuted the sentence to life imprisonment, and in 1979, President Jimmy Carter commuted further, to time served, the sentence of Collazo, as well as the sentences of four other Puerto Rican Nationalists who had been responsible for wounding four Congressmen on the house floor in a demonstration in 1954. Following their release Collazo and the other Nationalists came to New York, where they spoke before crowds of cheering Puerto Ricans and appeared at a news conference at the United Nations before returning to Puerto Rico. Back home, their plane was greeted by a crowd estimated at five thousand supporters.

Collazo and Torresola are prototypes of the criminal who is respected as a person acting on behalf of a struggle to gain a valued end—in this case the independence of territory annexed by a powerful nation and exploited for economic benefit by the larger state. There is ample evidence that these criminals were indeed prompted by political ideology: their involvement with a political party that had been responsible for similar incidents of violence elsewhere, the risks taken, the apparently rational method in which the act was carried out, the fact that the publicity desired did in fact result from the act, and statements made by them and their associates confirming the intent to garner publicity in support of their movement. Collazo and Torresola may be aptly described as "convictional" criminals—lawbreakers whose threats of political disruption arise from "altruistic-communal motivation rather than an egoistic drive" (Schafer, 1974: 147).

Additional examples of assassination attempts directed against important American political figures, some successful and some not, are presented by Clarke (1982). Clarke classifies a total of sixteen assassins into four types, Type I of which represents the "good-guy" political criminal as presented here.

Type I assassins view their acts as a probable sacrifice of self for a political ideal. They are fully cognizant and accepting of the meaning, implications, and personal consequences of their acts. Inherently personal motives, such as a neurotic need for recognition, are secondary to their primary political purpose. Type I's may or may not attempt to escape, but the sacrificial theme that characterizes their zeal and commitment suggests that capture, like death, is an acceptable, if not preferred, risk. Emotional distortion is present only to the extent that political ideals supercede survival instincts. If captured, the Type I does not recant on his or her motivating principles or seek clemency or personal publicity (1982:14).

Among Type I assassins Clarke includes, in addition to Collazo and Torresola, the assassins of President Abraham Lincoln, President William McKinley, and Robert Kennedy—respectively, John Wilkes Booth, Leon Czolgosz, and Sirhan Sirhan.

Not all of these five assassins were actually accorded the positive recognition they expected from their perceived supporters. The Puerto Rican Nationalists undoubtedly regarded Collazo and Torresola as heroes, and Sirhan appears to have some support, although not unequivocal, in the Arab world. Czolgosz's image following McKinley's assassination was polarized, even by anarchists. Among those born in Europe he was considered a "courageous martyr in the fight against political oppression" (Clarke, 1982: 59), whereas among American-born and Jewish anarchists (with the important exception of the Jewish anarchist Emma Goldman, who supported him) he was condemned as a lunatic. As for Booth, even though Lincoln was unpopular among many people in the North as well as those in the South, according to Clarke (1982: 25–28, 38–39), there was little support in either region for Booth's plot to prolong the Civil War, and he ended up being a hero to no one.

If political crime encompasses "those behaviors which are defined as criminal because they are regarded as apparent threats and dangers to the political state" (Clinard and Quinney, 1967: 178), then not all political crime would be deemed praiseworthy, because government-threatening activity may be committed for selfish reasons as well as selfless ones. John W. Hinckley, Jr.'s shooting of President Ronald Reagan in 1981 is an example of a political crime in terms of the definition just presented, since any attempt on the life of a president threatens political stability. But there is no evidence of ideological purpose. Rather, Hinckley's act appears to have been motivated solely by a selfish purpose—the desire to make himself known to Jodie Foster, a film actress who was the object of his romantic fantasies. He was therefore considered a bad guy, a judgment attenuated only by a jury verdict that he was legally insane.

Hinckley's case is unusual in that there was not even a pretense of ideological purpose in the act. More often, when political crimes are in fact based on ulterior motives, there will be at least an attempt by their perpetrators to justify them on the basis of some high moral purpose. Schafer (1974) uses the term "pseudoconvictional criminal" to refer to those people who pretend that their criminal acts are based on ideology but who really act out of baser motives—a desire for fame, revenge, and so forth. This distinction corresponds to Clarke's differentiation between the selfless crimes of Type I assassins like Collazo and Torresola, and the motives of his other types. These include Type II assassins, who are driven by a need for recognition, Type III assassins, for whom life is so bereft of meaning that destruction of society and themselves becomes their supreme goal, and Type IV assassins, the most stereotypically insane criminals whose delusions and hallucinations of grandeur or persecution drive them to homicidal behavior against political figures (1982: 14-16).

The process of polarization in interpreting political crime has been exhaustively analyzed by Wagner-Pacifici (1986) in a case study of interpretations of the kidnapping and subsequent murder of the Italian political leader Aldo Moro in 1978. Much of the analysis deals with how the Red Brigades, a prominent left-wing group responsible for the kidnapping, were depicted in the media, by representatives of various political parties, and by government officials. The Red Brigades presented themselves as good guys who represented the majority interests of the Italian people against an oppressive government, who had resorted to violence only as a last resort, and whose members imprisoned for earlier offenses ought properly to be regarded as "political prisoners." They were at the same time referred to by their detractors as "terrorists" and "desperate criminals."

In truth there is often much moral ambiguity in the conduct of groups like the Red Brigades. Wagner-Pacifici presents a telling example of how one experienced politician endeavored to avoid using a term which might support the Red Brigades' image of themselves as representatives of a legitimate political movement.

Prime Minister Andreotti, in his televised speech, spoke of the victims of other kidnappings and, at a critical moment, "caught himself" in a dangerous recognition of the Red Brigades. Alluding, at the end of his speech, to the restoration of Moro and the other kidnapping victims to liberty, Andreotti refers to the kidnappers as "political" and immediately followed and finished the speech with: "I refuse to use this adjective. I would say pseudopolitical or common criminals, whichever. Criminality has no adjectives and criminality is against the soul of our people" (1986: 80–81).

Groups like the Red Brigades, when they articulate a rationale for good guys as perpetrators of violent acts, are presenting an argument based on Marxist assumptions about morality. From the Marxist perspective, the morality of an act depends upon its consistency with "the laws of social development"; praiseworthy criminals are those who facilitate the transformation from capitalism to socialism.

The actions of individuals or groups may be appraised as good or evil according to whether they promote or hinder the interests of a social class as a whole. . . . The objective criterion of social development raises any discussion pertaining to the truthfulness of moral judgments about crime and social justice to a level of analysis that transcends the subjective differences between classes. . . . An objective evaluation of the validity of moral judgments, however, is dependent upon scientific knowledge about the organized methods for establishing desirable social relations. . . . Thus, it is concluded on objective grounds that, to serve the interests of all humanity, it is necessary to advance the interests of the working class at the expense of the ruling class by abolishing capitalism (Schwendinger and Schwendinger, 1977: 10).

As for individual morality, then, a good criminal for the Marxist is one who contributes to the laws of social development by expediting the overthrow of capitalism. However, it would be a distortion to suggest that Marxist morality is primarily concerned with judging individuals. Although concerned with individual welfare, Marxists direct their moral judgments toward larger entities. They minimize the moral responsibility of individuals and attribute moral qualities to social classes, and to entire economic systems.

Engels, for example, considers the forces underlying criminality to be as inevitable as those of the physical laws of nature.

If the influences demoralizing to the working-man act more powerfully, more concentratedly than usual, he becomes an offender as certainly as water abandons the fluid for the vaporous state at 80 degrees Réaumur. Under the brutal and brutalizing treatment of the bourgeoisie, the working-man becomes precisely as much a thing without volition as water, and is subject to the laws of nature with precisely the same necessity; at a certain point all freedom ceases (quoted in Taylor, Walton, and Young, 1974: 210).

And Marxists are not alone in this. Non-Marxist as well as Marxist commentators frequently consider the individual perpetrator to be merely a vessel for the influence of group forces, in effect maintaining that the real good guys or bad guys are the groups themselves. The goals, structures, traditions, socialization practices of collectivities—all of these may negate the moral responsibility of individual members and invite attribution of responsibility to the group. It is to these perceptions—of groups as good guys or bad guys—that we turn in Chapter 4.

4

Bad Groups and Good Groups

Just as theorists like Hobbes see individual nature as the source of bad behavior, so do other theorists identify misconduct with certain qualities of human groups. "Impulsiveness, irritability, incapacity to reason, the absence of judgment and of the critical spirit, the exaggeration of the sentiments"—these are among the major characteristics attributed to collectivities by Gustav Le Bon (1960: 35–36). A contemporary of Freud, Le Bon believed that group situations heighten the tendency for unconscious emotions to control behavior. The person in a crowd "descends several rungs in the ladder of civilization" (1960: 32), exhibiting inclinations "which are almost always observed in beings belonging to inferior forms of evolution—in women, savages, and children, for instance" (1960: 36).

In Le Bon's most famous work, *La Foule* (The Crowd), the author presents the violent and destructive mob of the French Revolution as the prototype for collective action. Made up primarily of "shopkeepers and artisans of every trade: bootmakers, locksmiths, hairdressers, masons, clerks, messengers, etc.," the Revolutionary *foule* is described as a criminal crowd in which normally law-abiding citizens participate in the most heinous actions.

A slaughterer at the Abbaye having complained that the ladies placed at a little distance saw badly, and that only a few of these present had the pleasure of striking the aristocrats, the justice of the observation is admitted, and it is decided that the victims shall be made to pass slowly between two rows of slaughterers, who shall be under the obligation to strike with the back of the sword only so as to prolong the agony. At the prison de la Force the victims are stripped stark naked and literally "carved" for half an hour, after which, when everyone has had a good view, they are finished off by a blow that lays bare their entrails (1960: 162–64).

The group is described as possessing an almost mystical capacity to counteract and overpower a person's normal, rational patterns of thought and action. Although Le Bon recognized that the presence of a crowd might bring forth an excess of lofty sentiments as well as base ones, he clearly viewed all group situations as dangerous, in their propensities to stimulate unreasoned actions.

For most writers it is not collective life in general that causes evil behavior; rather, crime is brought about by exposure to what Tarde refers to as the "putrid environment" (Ferri, 1917: 181). Urban ghettos, for example, are seen as breeding grounds for predatory street gangs whose members graduate to participation in lucrative illegal drug and gambling syndicates, and eventually themselves serve the next generation as role models of success through criminal careers. Frequently it is the whole city as a collectivity that is blamed for conditions giving rise to antisocial conduct, mediated by pathological peer groups or family structures.

The connection between crime and modern life may be traced to the writings of Jean Jacques Rousseau, the eighteenth-century philosopher identified with the view that the history of civilization represents not progress but a decline from an idyllic state of nature. Concomitant with the civilizing process is the development of inequality, which in turn produces spiritual decline, social unrest and conflict.

Rousseau's position is made vivid by his comparison between social relations in the state of nature, and those in groups where governmental sovereignty prevails, which he calls "civil societies." The peaceful character of the state of nature is attributed to a natural feeling of compassion which precedes the development of reason among primitive people. Rousseau contrasts the salutary effects of informal social control with the violence and other outrages that occur in more "civilized" circles whose members are indifferent to wrongs committed by one citizen against another.

It is reason which turns man's mind back upon itself, and divides him from everything that could disturb or affect him. . . . Nothing but such general evils as threaten the whole community can disturb the tranquil sleep of the philosopher, or tear him from his bed. A murder may with impunity be committed under his window; he has only to put his hands to his ears and argue a little with himself, to prevent nature, which is shocked within him, from identifying itself with the unfortunate sufferer. Uncivilized man has not this admirable talent; and for want of reason and wisdom, is always foolishly ready to obey the first promptings of humanity. It is the populace that flocks together at riots and street brawls, while the wise man prudently makes off. It is the mob and the market-women, who part the combatants, and hinder gentlefolks from cutting one another's throats (Rousseau, 1950: 226).

While it was Rousseau who proposed the idea of an equitable social contract as an antidote to the evils of the European civilization he observed during the eighteenth century, the idea that social, and particularly political, development is necessarily evil was formulated by nineteenth-century anarchist writers, such as Bakunin and Kropotkin, who decried the effects of industrialization on human experience. Since evil was for them associated with large-scale economic and political institutions, their solution to the problem was decentralization.   Tolstoy was among the anarchists who preached a return to life on a smaller scale—peasant communes, local churches, and family authority, without the obligation of allegiance to larger, more remote institutions.

Although undoubtedly idealizing the past, what these writers expressed is the view that, whatever may appear to be the worldly benefits of advances in material culture, technology, advanced capitalistic economic systems, or specialized governmental agencies designed to address problems requiring esoteric knowledge—these supposed benefits are more than offset by the dislocations accompanying such "progress." The term "anomie" has become a popular one for denoting a lack of correspondence between the regulations that people require for healthy social relations and the guidelines that their society provides. As noted in Chapter 2, Durkheim originally used the term to refer to a social situation in which institutions like religion, government, and the family had fallen behind in adapting to the needs of the societies they composed—societies whose economies were being transformed from agricultural subsistence to industrial dependence, and whose families were changing from groupings in which extended kin relationships were important and powerful to nuclear households made up of a married couple and their unmarried children.

AMERICAN SOCIETY AS CRIMINOGENIC

The significance of Durkheim's theory as a contribution to sociology is not simply that it attributes deviance to social dislocation rather than human aberration. His concept of anomie (usually translated as "normlessness") explains social problems as stemming from weaknesses that pervade the fabric of certain societies, not just from isolated flaws within a generally strong fabric. As for crime as a social problem, the theory has served as a basis for analysis of American society as a *criminogenic* society. Works with such titles as *Our Criminal Society* (Schur, 1969), and *The Juvenile in Delinquent Society* (Barron, 1954) emphasize crime-inducing forces inherent in the dominant social structure in the United States in moden times (see also Tannenbaum, 1938: chap. 2). Donald Taft and Ralph England (1964: 27–31) have listed characteristics that they see as both pervasive in American society and responsible for high rates of crime. They are:

1. Dynamic quality of American culture.
2. Complexity of American culture.
3. Materialistic values in American culture.
4. Impersonality of American social relations.
5. Restricted group loyalties fostered by American culture.
6. Survival of frontier values.
7. Lack of the viewpoint of social science.
8. Faith in law without expecting or even approving obedience to all laws.

It should be noted that, although Taft and England are nonjudgmental in their presentation, most of the characteristics mentioned in the list have pejorative connotations. The first two, dynamism and complexity, are not inherently bad, but as discussed by these authors they are regarded as problematic because of the difficulties in adjustment and adaptation they entail. Similarly the frontier tradition, though not apparently a total liability, is here identified with violence and an absence of respect for law and order.

A variation on this theme is presented by former Attorney General Ramsey Clark in his book *Crime in America* (1970). The problem of crime, in Clark's view, is rooted in two moral deficiencies in American society: "The apathy of affluence," and "narrow self-interest." These traits are responsible for fundamental social problems that are closely related to crime: poverty, drugs, weapons, ineffective court and prison systems, poor relationships between police and communities.   These problems can be surmounted only through profound changes in basic institutions, including education, health care, housing, and race relations. The obstacle is not a lack of material resources.

If the challenge of change seems staggering, our capacity to meet it is overwhelming. There was never a people that so clearly had the means to solve their problems as Americans today. Movers, builders, doers—we have proven the ability of man to dramatically change his destiny. Now we must show that he can control that destiny. . . . It is only a question of will. What stands in the way are the handicaps of human nature, still manifest in our culture. Old instincts must be altered. Our reflex to violence can be conditioned out of the American character (1970: 339–44).

SUBSOCIETIES AS BAD

In contrast with the far-reaching "criminogenic society" approach are those theories of crime, more in line with the popular view, which assume the fundamental law-abiding tendencies of the society as a whole, while attributing crime to the influence of certain subgroups that adhere to norms and behavior patterns running counter to the legal norms of the larger society. Having said this, we should note that the deviant propensities of any particular subgroup are a matter of degree. One would be hard put to find a subsociety that rejects all the norms of the larger society; subgroups accept and reject selectively. The Old-Order Pennsylvania Amish, for example, reject compulsory school attendance laws but are generally in agreement with the penal code of their state.

Indeed, subgroups in which violation of the criminal code is an explicit norm, inculcated and sanctioned like adherence to law in other groups, are extremely rare. Possibly the only truly well-documented examples are the criminal tribes of India, which engage primarily in crimes against property without violence. Among them, "transmission of criminal patterns and of the sometimes highly specific *modus operandi* follow clear cultural lines, with early training, indoctrination, and ostracism and punishment for non-acceptance of the criminal behavior" (Wolfgang and Ferracuti, 1967: 283).

In the United States the subgroups most frequently held responsible for inducing criminality among their members are made up of recent immigrants, that criminality being accounted for by various aspects of the immigration experience. Crime among immigrants has been variously attributed to (1) culture conflict between the norms of the old and new milieus, (2) change from a rural to an urban environment, or (3) change from a well-integrated and homogeneous society to a disorganized, multicultural one (Sellin, 1938). One salient form of culture conflict consists of instances in which violent norms are imported by carriers of a culture who find themselves at odds with a legal system that is, at least on the surface, intolerant of interpersonal violence.

An inclination toward violent behavior has been observed in many societies, and particularly well documented in the form of vendetta homicide in Macedonia, Sardinia, and Albania. Mexican violence has been connected with a "fatalistic acceptance of death" in that culture, and an extremely high homicide rate in Colombia has prevailed for nearly forty years (beginning well before the current drug wars), where the *violencia columbiana* appears to stem from long standing political conflicts originating in rural areas but more recently expanding into urban areas as well.

One small Italian community known as Albanova, an aggregate of three agricultural villages near Naples with a total population of about 30,000, is reputed to have the highest rate of violent crimes in Europe. It is an isolated area in which relatively minor personal offenses that would be ignored in other communities are interpreted as requiring retaliation and even killing. The adage "if you are slapped, you must wash the slap from your face" is interpreted as obliging offended parties to retaliate by doing more harm than they suffered. In addition to this norm, a number of other explanations for the community's high crime rate have been offered: a genetic propensity to violence intensified by inbreeding in an isolated area, an attraction to weapons such that they have ceremonial significance (it is common practice for a godfather to give his godchild a gun on the occasion of its baptism), and alleged violence-inducing properties of the local wine (Wolfgang and Ferracuti, 1967: 281–82).

Whatever the original source of the violent conduct in this community, it seems clear that its persistence has much to do with norms that are handed down from one generation to another. Should members of a community like this move to a modern American city, it would not be surprising to find them running afoul of the law for carrying out their customary retributive behavior. However necessary the group requirement for retaliation may be, from the standpoint of the larger community's opinion the illegal behavior would be explained as the influence of a bad group.

URBAN COMMUNITIES AS CRIMINOGENIC

"City-bashing" is a tradition in American society going back at least to Thomas Jefferson. There is scarcely a social problem that has not been blamed on city living, and crime is surely one of the most prominent. Anonymity, sheer size and concentration of population, juxtaposition of groups with different customs and values, corrupt municipal government—such phenomena endemic to urban life are depicted as the culprits underlying gang warfare, predatory crime against individuals, and syndicated vice.[1]

This popular view had, as its scholarly counterpart, the research orientation at that fountainhead of sociology in the United States, the University of Chicago. Scholars like Robert Park, Ernest Burgess, and Louis Wirth established a tradition of carrying out, and encouraging their students to carry out, studies of the distribution of mental illness, family disorganization, and crime in that city. This "ecological" approach to the study of crime was based on Burgess's "concentric zone" theory of land use. Supported by observations of Chicago during the early twentieth century but also advanced as applicable to other cities, the theory proposed that cities grow outward from a central business district, so that land use patterns resemble an archery target. The central circle, Zone 1, where the city's major financial and recreational activities are carried on, is occupied by banks, the stock exchange, large hotels, government buildings, department stores and theaters. Zone 2, the first ring outside the circle, is known as the "zone of transition," originally a very respectable residential area, but one abandoned by its original inhabitants and taken over by small-scale commercial operations along with cheap restaurants, flop houses, bars, pawn shops, and other establishments catering to derelicts and other social misfits. Working-class apartment houses and row houses make up much of Zone 3, and zones more remote from the center contain increasingly affluent inhabitants of the city.

For students of deviant behavior it was Zone 2 that commanded attention, and the members of the Chicago school whose attention focused on the ecology of lawbreaking, especially by juveniles, were Clifford Shaw and Henry McKay. Shaw and McKay were white Anglo-Saxon Protestants from nonurban backgrounds. Of the two, Shaw, who had been a Chicago probation officer, was the more ideologically involved. He believed that the only way to counteract problems like delinquency in the urban environment was to implement social control following the model of informal sanctions in the prototypical small town of turn-of-the-century America, an approach that guided the work of the Chicago Area Project for decades (Finestone, 1978: 55).

The connection between a particular urban area and illegal behavior is nowhere more apparent than in Shaw's life history of Stanley, a young "jack roller," that is, a pickpocket who preys on sleeping drunks. Stanley tells how he became enmeshed in the criminal subculture of a particular Chicago neighborhood after having been thrown out of the house by his half sister because he had failed to find a job:

The first place I went was to West Madison Street, the haven of rest for bums, prostitutes, degenerates, and the rest of the scum of the earth who gather there to drift on to some other place. "Floaters" is a good name for them. But this place held lures for me. The lures and the irresistible call drew me on like a magnet, and I was always helpless before them. I was like a canoe on a storm-swept sea, buffeted here and there, helpless and frail. I had about as much chance of controlling my desires to drift with the currents of the underworld as the canoe had of braving the storm (Shaw, 1966: 93).

A pioneering study of delinquency rates within a small, homogeneous immigrant community illustrates the degree to which exposure to an urban environment may account for lawbreaking. In this case it is a question of the bad city environment overcoming the positive forces of subgroup tradition. Pauline Young investigated court records for boys and young men in 108 Molokan families that had begun to settle in a particular area of Los Angeles around 1905. The Molokans are a Russian peasant sect, not unlike the Quakers, who live by a strict moral code. The families were selected for the research because each of them had at least one boy between the ages of nine and nineteen who had delinquency records for the years 1927 and 1929. Court records were further examined to classify the brothers of these boys, ranging in age up to twenty-nine, as delinquent or nondelinquent. The study found that 78 percent of all the boys in these families between the ages of nine and nineteen had court records; 46 percent of those between twenty and twenty-four had such records, but only 5 percent of the young men between twenty-five and twenty-nine were officially classified as delinquent.

The author notes that the oldest group, born in Russia and brought to the United States as young children, was most consistently affected by Molokan values; the middle group was born here but still subject in substantial degree to traditionally strict parental discipline; and the youngest group was least affected by their parents' culture. She rules out economic status, genetic and psychological determinants, broken homes, and other variables as factors accounting for delinquency in some Molokan youth and its absence in others. However, the data show, according to Young, that delinquents and nondelinquents "can . . . be clearly differentiated in terms of their cultural contacts. The evidence points in this study to a direct relationship between the extent of contacts with urban life and the extent of delinquency in this group" (cited in Sellin, 1938: 95).

The community approach in explaining crime was overshadowed by more social-psychological approaches for some forty years, only to be revived in the 1980s as part of a movement to relate planning for economic development in cities to the crime problem. A compendium of essays titled *Communities and Crime* (Reiss and Tonry, 1986) presents the results of recent research efforts to identify the attributes of geographical areas of cities—as distinct from the now typical emphasis on population groups— characterized by high crime rates. Findings from various studies distinguish good communities from bad ones, as indicated by low rather than high rates for certain criminal offenses, on the basis of factors such as gentrification, youth employment opportunities, and aggressive law enforcement.

LOWER CLASS MALE YOUTH SUBCULTURE AS CRIMINOGENIC

Within urban environments, forces conducive to criminal conduct seem to have their most concentrated impact within the subculture of adolescent lower-class males. In his analysis of gang culture, Albert Cohen describes the legal infractions of the gang in pejorative terms: "nonutilitarian, malicious, and negativistic." The "nonutilitarian" characterization refers to the observation that property which has value is frequently simply vandalized, or stolen without any thought for putting it to good use by gang members. "Negativism" refers to the quality of rejecting the dominant culture by doing precisely the opposite of what the larger culture values, and "maliciousness" is expressed in malevolent motivation, "an enjoyment in the discomfiture of others, a delight in the defiance of taboos itself" (Cohen, 1955: 25–27).

A classic among empirical studies is Walter Miller's research on male youth subculture. Trained as an anthropologist, Miller carried out participant observation in a lower-class neighborhood in Boston in order to arrive at an understanding of the issues to which its residents devoted their primary attention. He uses the term"focal concerns" to refer to what most social scientists mean when they talk about group values—those most salient general standards affecting judgment of what is good and what is bad in their own conduct and that of others in their environment. Using his own observation reports, tape recordings of group discussions, and extensive reports by social workers who were attached to his research project, he was able to classify these focal concerns under the rubrics of *trouble, toughness, smartness, excitement, fate,* and *autonomy.* Although these concerns do not lead everyone who is exposed to them inexorably into illegal behavior, they do impinge upon adolescent males in ways that are likely to result in confrontations with legal authority. Excitement, for example, among lower-class boys is sought through a "night on the town," which for them may well lead to a bar-room brawl and subsequent arrest. It is not that the exciting activity is necessarily pursued with an awareness that it will involve criminality, or even harm, and the "harm" is not recognized as such in terms of the subculture's values, but is rather a judgment imposed by the dominant culture.

Neither Cohen nor Miller adopts a simplistic bad-groups approach. Miller, in fact, argues against the "bad-guys" connotation of Cohen's explanation. "No cultural pattern as well established as the practice of illegal acts by members of lower-class corner groups could persist if buttressed primarily by negative, hostile, or rejective motives," states Miller. "Its principal motivational support, as in the case of any persisting cultural tradition, derives from a positive effort to achieve what is valued within that tradition, and to conform to its explicit and implicit norms" (Miller, 1970: 363). And Cohen too, in spite of the pejorative terms he uses to characterize the gang culture, makes clear that he does not wish to condemn the ultimate motivation for lower-class delinquencies. Underlying the malicious, negativistic, and nonutilitarian behavior of gang boys is status frustration.

The working class boy . . . is more likely than his middle class peers to find himself at the bottom of the status hierarchy whenever he moves in a middle class world, whether it be of adults or of children. To the degree to which he values middle class status, either because he values the good opinion of middle-class persons or because he has to some degree internalized middle-class standards himself, he faces a problem of adjustment and is in the market for a "solution."

. . . The delinquent subculture, we suggest, is a way of dealing with the problems of adjustment we have described (Cohen, 1955: 119–21).

Hirschi has suggested that Cohen's explanation of lower-class male delinquency—and it might be said as well of Miller's—can be seen from the perspective of moral judgment as a " 'good-causes-evil' view" (Hirschi, 1969: 5 n). That view may be contrasted with the equally oversimplified "evil-causes-evil" approaches (Cohen, 1970: 125), which seek to demonstrate, for example, that bad neighborhoods or bad families cause bad behavior. The "good-causes-evil" view is based on "functional" assumptions—on the postulate that every element within a culture has arisen in order to facilitate group survival—meet individual sustenance needs, promote harmony among members, encourage reproduction, and so forth. "Good" causes of subcultural delinquency, from this perspective, are good in the sense that they appear to be reasonable adaptations to various disabilities of lower-class existence, while "evil" results are evil as defined by the criminal code.

We may describe the "good-causes-evil" perspective as an "exculpatory" approach, one of a class of theories which deny the personal responsibility of offenders for their actions by attributing the acts to forces beyond the control of the individual. Although these approaches may presume the harm of the actions, and sometimes even the malevolence of the offenders, they absolve not only the individuals but also the groups of blame because they see the groups' norms as adaptive. Just as we spoke of some individual offenders in Chapter 3 as being considered "good" because their material well being is dependent upon their criminal careers, so too can we speak of certain groups as "good" because the criminal conduct they encourage is considered to have survival value. The viewpoint is well expressed by the authors of another classic study of delinquent gangs:

When a society does not make adequate preparation, formal or otherwise, for the induction of its adolescents to the adult status, equivalent forms of behavior arise spontaneously among adolescents themselves, reinforced by their own group structure, which seemingly provide the same psychological content and function as the more formalized rituals found in other societies. This the gang structure appears to do in American society, apparently satisfying deep-seated needs experienced by adolescents in all cultures (Bloch and Niederhoffer, 1958: 17).

Another analysis of the "good-causes-evil" variety is Cloward and Ohlin's "opportunity" theory, which is based on a scheme for classifying deviant behavior originated by Robert Merton (1957). Merton's scheme is based on his thesis that various forms of social deviance can be understood as adaptations to a social system in which there is a lack of integration between socially prescribed goals and institutionalized means for achieving those goals. Taking this thesis as a starting point, Cloward and Ohlin (1960) explain different manifestations of juvenile delinquency in terms of the presence or absence of institutionalized opportunities to achieve culturally prescribed results, those results being the American dream of material success and being your own boss.

One adaptation is the "criminal" subculture, which is present in neighborhoods where legitimate means for achieving success are inadequate, but where there are well-organized illegitimate avenues for attaining prosperity. For delinquent boys these illegitimate opportunities may lead to employment in vice syndicates—business enterprises that purvey morally ambiguous but illegal services and goods like prostitution, gambling, and illegal drugs—or to apprenticeships to professional shoplifters or other skilled adult criminals.

In neighborhoods where there is an absence, not only of legitimate means for attaining culturally valued goals, but also of illegitimate means for attaining them, adaptation takes the form of either a "retreatist" subculture or a "conflict" subculture, according to Cloward and Ohlin. Youths in these categories suffer greater social deprivation than those in the criminal subculture; they are disproportionately members of racial minorities and the underclass. Retreatists respond to the lack of opportunity by becoming detached from the conventional world, most often by seeking gratification and acceptance among like-minded peers through drug use. The conflict subculture, by contrast, instead of detaching itself from the conventional world, relates to it by aggressive acts, although as a matter of convenience the targets of that hostility are at least as likely to be members of the delinquents' own class and race as they are to be members of more privileged groups.

For all of these forms of subcultural delinquency, Cloward and Ohlin's explanation fits the "good-causes-evil" model. Their explanation accepts the premise that young American men, even those of humblest origin, aspire at the outset to success as defined by the dominant majority and only resort to delinquent behavior as barriers arise. Implicitly, it is the social structure's defects which pressure them into delinquent behavior, and so it is also that social structure which bears responsibility for the unfortunate outcome.

THE FAMILY

In opposition to the stereotype of youth gangs as the source of criminal values and behavior patterns, families are regarded, according to the currently prevalent stereotype, as sources of encouragement to follow the straight and narrow path, the path of moral rectitude and obedience to the law. The more youngsters are subject to parental influence—which is what "family" almost invariably means in this context—the less prone they are in this view to succumb to delinquent peer pressure. Families are good groups in the sense that the more parental influence the better. When children go wrong it is usually attributed to the *absence* of parental socialization. Following negative peer group norms implies that (1) parents have been prevented by circumstances from supervising their children properly, because of job pressures, broken homes, and so forth, (2) they have simply neglected their children even though they might have done otherwise, or (3) they have made seemingly appropriate efforts to direct their children properly but have unaccountably failed, perhaps because of unusually strong countervailing forces in the community, or interpersonal conflicts between children and parents. Thus, the problem is one of failure to convey proper values rather than conveying improper values.

This current stereotype may be contrasted with earlier notions of the bad family, which emphasized more direct connections between parental deficiencies and those of their children. One of the earliest institutionalized efforts at crime prevention among children was that of the Philanthropic Society of London, which was organized in 1788 for the purpose of dealing with the offspring of convicted criminals, presumably under the assumption that it was they who were in greatest danger of being themselves involved in criminal activity; only later did the Society turn its attention to youngsters whose own behavior gave evidence of criminal tendencies (Hawes, 1971: 30).

Long-standing beliefs about biological inheritance of criminal tendencies were reinforced as a consequence of the publication of the famous studies of the "Juke" family by Richard Dugdale in 1877 and a follow-up of the same family by A. H. Estabrook in 1916. Together these investigators reported, on the basis of information about some 1200 family members, that the family was to an astonishing degree contaminated by criminality and pauperism. In one branch of the family Dugdale identified 60 percent of the members as criminals. Considering 162 marriageable women in the family, he counted eighty-four "harlots," and concluded that "we find harlotry over twenty-nine times more frequent with the Juke women than in the average of the community." In fact Dugdale also considered an interaction between environment and heredity, but the overwhelming interpretation of his work was to confirm an inevitable connection between "bad breeding" and criminality (Rennie, 1978: 79-82).

Another view of the bad family assigns it a rather passive role in criminogenesis. According to this view the family has no independent role in creating standards of conduct. Rather, the parents mediate between some larger grouping and their children in the socialization process. Thus, if parents have absorbed an attitude of disrespect for legal authority from a peasant culture in which they were brought up, they may be expected to transfer those attitudes to their children. Similarly, if they are members of a social class in which violence is a permissible, or even expected, way of responding to an affront to family honor, they may be considered responsible for their children's adoption of that folkway. On the whole, though, parents are found to condemn their children's criminality, even if they themselves have delinquent backgrounds (Wilson and Herrnstein, 1985: 214, 235).

Against the litany of family shortcomings responsible for starting children on the road to crime may be contrasted the idealized good family as an insulator against the temptation to misbehave. At the first convention of reformatory officials in 1857, the manager of the St. Louis Reform School extolled, as the model for a successful reformatory, "the *time-honored* institution which guided the infancy of nearly all the truly great men and women . . . 'God's University' . . . the well-ordered Christian family" (Rothman, 1971: 235).

Administrators of American institutions for delinquent youth who wanted to move away from the traditional military model found an alternative in an old farm cottage near Hamburg, Germany. There a young man named Johann Henry Wichern, a theology student, established a home in 1833 for twelve boys from the city who were thought to be in danger of becoming criminals. With his mother, Wichern sought to provide these boys with the virtuous family life they had been denied by their own parents. This *Rauhe Haus*, or "rough house," was expanded into a world-famous reformatory as more "families" were established, with staff members trained by Wichern and additional groups of problem children moving into other cottages. The youngsters were indoctrinated with moral values that they could not have assimilated earlier because their own families were thought to lack such values. *Rauhe Haus* values were instilled through a program of agricultural labor, formal education, and participation in religious devotions. The staff members, young students of theology, education, and social work, sought "to recreate the atmosphere in a normal, middle-class family." The youngsters lived and worked as as family units, and the institution developed a reputation as highly successful at reforming "some of the most recalcitrant boys and girls in Hamburg" (Hawes, 1971: 79).

One young American who visited and became strongly influenced by the *Rauhe Haus* philosophy was Charles Loring Brace, the first director of the Children's Aid Society of New York. Brace appears to have had considerable ambivalence about families. He referred to them, on the one hand, as "God's Reformatory" (Hawes, 1971: 88), but he also blamed slum families for their children's misbehavior (Boyer, 1978: 100–2). Above all, he saw merit in the independent spirit of the street urchins, who were condemned by many of his contemporaries as captives of an unalterably wicked nature. To facilitate the proper channeling of those spirits, Brace organized a "placing-out" system, through which groups of New York City youngsters were sent by train to rural communities in the Midwest. There, agents of the society had arranged for the selection of good families for the children to stay with. "When the children arrived, they appeared as a group before the local residents, who then made their choices. After the children had been placed, the western agent of the Children's Aid Society was supposed to visit them and help to adjust any difficulties" (Hawes, 1971: 101).

This was not in fact a program for youngsters with a history of serious delinquencies. Rather, it was seen as a preventive program for homeless and neglected children who, lacking the protective environment of a proper family, needed to be moved in order to avoid corruption by the city's evil forces. The "placing-out" system received a great deal of attention and public support. Between 1854 and 1884 more than 60,000 New York children had been placed in the distant communities. The program had been greatly helped by the *New York Tribune*, and it was a popular beneficiary of contributions from members of the city's upper classes. There was criticism as well, but it came primarily from vested interests—for example, from administrators of reformatories eager to assert the greater efficacy of their approach, and from Catholics who saw "placing-out" as an attempt by the Children's Aid Society to convert children of their faith by placing them in Protestant homes. Some of the support for "placing-out" was stimulated by the Society's *Annual Reports*, which credited the program with significantly reducing the crime rate in New York during its years of operation; it was, on the other hand, also blamed for increasing crime in midwestern communities. Given the ambiguity of the evidence, it seems reasonable to suppose that a significant degree of support for placing out is due to the resonance of public opinion with its underlying philosophy: the ability of a good rural family to help children whose moral careers were threatened by the prospect of city living without the benefit of virtuous parental teaching, example, and discipline.

The "bad family" concept has been reinforced through the findings of a very extensive study of attributes distinguishing delinquent from nondelinquent boys, directed by Sheldon and Eleanor Glueck and carried out at Harvard University during the 1940s and 1950s. The Gluecks found five family-related variables to be among the strongest predictors of delinquency among their research subjects: discipline of boy by father, supervision of boy by mother, affection of father for boy, affection of mother for boy, and family cohesiveness (Glueck and Glueck, 1950: 261). In interpreting their findings, the authors reject explanations of delinquency that rely primarily upon assumptions about the delinquent's lack of "will power." Such theories in their view go "little beyond the discredited explanation that antisocial behavior is the product of the devil operating in the minds and hearts of persons particularly open to satanic enticements" (Glueck and Glueck, 1962: 165).

In attributing a large measure of delinquency to family rather than individual factors, the authors characterize criminogenic families in terms that might be used to explain why yellow fever breaks out in some locations and not others. They appear to adopt the medical model, or, more precisely, a public health model in which the occurrence of disease in a particular person depends on the degree of environmental pollution. Delinquency is attributed to "unwholesome aspects of home life" (1962: 153) and to "inimical" and "malign family influences" (154). As in the public health model, environmental pathology is not all; some people are better able than others to remain healthy in putrid surroundings.

The influences of the home environment, even when they are criminogenic, operate *selectively* to propel toward maladjustment and delinquency certain children who are characterized by specific traits which enhance their vulnerability. . . . In other words, it is differential *contamination*, rather than differential *association*, that is at the core of the etiologic process; and contamination depends not merely on exposure but also on susceptibility as opposed to immunity (1962: 155, italics in original).

As interpreted by the Gluecks, their solid research evidence points toward bad families as those infected by insidious causes of delinquent pathology, in much the same way as the medical model, discussed in Chapter 3, posits biological or psychological pathology in individuals as the cause of their misconduct.

The "diseased family" model of crime causation has become less prevalent among family researchers in the years since the Gluecks' material was published. More common are interpretations treating the family as a mediator between non-family aspects of social structure, such as a shortage of legitimate economic opportunities for the lower class, and tendencies toward lawbreaking (Rodman and Grams, 1967). One recent "meta-analysis," however, has organized a large number of research studies according to their bearing on four general hypotheses focusing on problems of internal family structure: that juvenile misconduct is caused by (1) parental neglect, (2) conflict between parents and children, (3) family disruption due to death, illness, or divorce, or (4) deviant parental attitudes or behavior. Taken together, the studies point to lack of parental supervision, parental rejection, and lack of parental involvement as the strongest predictors of delinquency and juvenile conduct problems. The meta-analysis eschews such terms as "contamination" and "malign influence," as employed by the Gluecks, but it does reflect the diseased-family model insofar as it concludes with a summary of therapeutic interventions aimed at improving parents' socialization of their children as a means of decreasing their children's involvement in delinquency (Loeber and Stouthamer-Loeber, 1986).

There is at least one recent analysis of the connection between criminal behavior and family milieu, however, that departs from the trend away from moral evaluation of families whose children happen to engage in delinquency—and that analysis by an expert practitioner and critic of research methods in delinquency and crime. Hirschi heaps scorn on modern criminologists who "assume that the individual would be noncriminal were it not for the operation of unjust and misguided institutions" (1983: 54)—in particular, a job market that provides too few legitimate opportunities for young people who want to earn money. He advocates renewed attention to the family, and in particular to the importance of punishment as part of parents' responsibility to demonstrate the folly of breaking society's accepted rules.

Hirschi supports his position by citing a report of a demonstration project in which—in order to suppress the misconduct of problem children—it was found necessary not merely to ignore their bad behavior and reward their good deeds, but to punish the transgressions actively. He cites other studies—including the Gluecks'— which have stressed the criminogenic consequences of parental indifference to their offsprings' delicts. But it is the failure to punish that is for Hirschi the major indicator of the bad family. His emphasis on the need for good parents (that is, parents who produce good children) to be ready to use punishment would seem to exceed any prescription the research evidence supports—especially in view of the conclusion in Loeber and Stouthamer-Loeber's survey (1986) that parental discipline is only weakly related to the incidence of delinquency.

SOCIAL CLASSES AND CRIME

Cutting across ethnic, neighborhood, peer and family groups, the social entity on which responsibility for crime in our society is most often placed is that entity known as the "lower class," although what is usually meant by the term is the *lowest* among five or six classes ordered in economic terms. There is a long tradition of attributing crime to the "dangerous and depraved class," with poverty the most reliable indicator of membership in that group. "The criminals in the Roman mines and galleys or nailed to crosses at the Esquiline Gate were not patricians; they were revolted slaves, or the *humiliores*, the pauper rabble who swarmed to the great cities from an impoverished countryside" (Rennie, 1978: 4). The classes perceived as dangerous were made up of people who posed direct threats to the property and safety of respectable citizens in the streets and in their homes. Then as now, people in positions of power who were involved in political corruption, for example, may have in fact done greater harm overall than conventional criminals, but it was not they to whom the term "dangerous class" applied.

The term "dangerous classes" came to be used in the nineteenth century, not only by law-and-order types who advocated harsh punishments, but also by more enlightened people. An Englishwoman named Mary Carpenter published a book in 1851 titled *Reformatory Schools for the Children of the Perishing and Dangerous Classes, and for Juvenile Offenders*, and in 1872 Charles Loring Brace, the first director of the New York Children's Aid Society, published *The Dangerous Classes of New York and Twenty Years Work among Them*. Both authors emphasized the unhealthy elements in a lower-class environment and advocated exposure to the discipline and moral instruction that were characteristic of middle-class and upper-class upbringing in England and America at the time (Hawes, 1971).

A recent derivative of the "dangerous classes" point of view is Banfield's (1974) analysis of the source of the "unheavenly" character of modern American cities. He argues that the cities' problems, and especially crime, are derived from persistent elements in lower-class slum culture. Drawing on Miller's (1970) research on lower-class male youth, Banfield suggests that the adolescent males' preoccupation with excitement and defense of honor apply as well to lower-class adults (1974: 189–90). Above all he emphasizes the "extreme present-orientation of [the lower] class. The lower class person lives from moment to moment, he is either unable or unwilling to take account of the future or to control his impulses" (1974: 54).

Banfield defends his characterization of lower-class culture as "pathological," in contrast to the "normal" cultures of the other classes, "both because of the relatively high incidence of mental illness in the lower class and also because human nature seems loath to accept a style of life that is so radically present-oriented" (1974: 63). He recognizes that there has also been some decay in commitment to the Protestant ethic's traditions among other classes. But since members of other classes do not share in the lower class's special taste for violence as a way of gratifying immediate needs, the forms of excitement they seek, even if illegal, are not experienced as contributing to the "unheavenly" quality of the city. Members of the middle and upper classes, therefore, even when they commit crimes, are good guys to the extent that they choose forms of lawbreaking that do not have specifiable individuals as targets (1974: 188).

Marxist Views on Crime and Social Class

On the surface it might seem that Marx and Engels were not too different from Banfield in their attitude toward the underclass. After all, we have scarcely encountered in our observation of bad-guys images any terms worse than those used by the founding fathers of communism, who refer to the nonworking poor as the "dangerous class," as "social scum, that passively rotting mass thrown off by the lowest layers of old society" (Marx and Engels, 1978: 482).

What this language indicates, however, as a number of writers (e.g., Hirst, 1972; Taylor, Walton, and Young, 1974: 217–20) have observed, is not that Marx and Engels simply adhered to bourgeois stereotypes of the Victorian period. This negative characterization of the *lumpenproletariat* was a necessary derivative of their view that, by failing to contribute to the production of goods, this class serves as an obstacle in the struggle of the good guys of the working class to bring about a socialist revolution. Ordinary crimes of theft, on which the underclass depend for survival, are parasitical in the same way that capitalist exploitation is parasitical: They appropriate goods which rightfully belong to the workers whose labor created their value. Although the possibility of an alliance between workers and the "dangerous class" is mentioned, orthodox Marxism seems to allow little room for the *lumpenproletariat* in the revolutionary process.

There is in fact considerable ambiguity among writers of Marxist persuasion about the moral status of conventional crimes committed by the underclass. Some followers of Marxist principles have discerned a positive revolutionary role for the activities of the criminal classes and therefore come to regard those activities as positively moral, insofar as they promote a solid front against the capitalist oppressor. Especially praiseworthy are infractions committed in the service of explicit political goals, but even ordinary crimes may serve the same purpose.

The urban black community, for example, is hit the hardest by "street" crime, but it is also the locus of tremendous resistance and struggle—as witnessed by the civil rights movement, the ghetto revolts of the 1960s and the antirepression struggles of today. Moreover, of the thousands of blacks who annually go to prison for serious crimes of victimization, many have become transformed by the collective experience of prison life and participate in numerous acts of solidarity, self-sacrifice, and heroism—as witnessed by the conversion of Malcolm X, George Jackson and countless other anonymous militants in the strikes and uprisings at Soledad, San Quentin, Attica, etc. (Platt, 1978: 33).

Whatever ambiguity exists among Marxists concerning the morality of lower-class crime, there is no such ambiguity concerning criminal actions—whether formally incorporated in the criminal code or constructively defined in terms of social harm—carried out by the capitalist class. One criminologist refers to "the unparalleled criminality and terrorism of the ruling class" (Platt, 1978: 33). It is not a question of accidental concentration of bad guys in positions of power. It is rather the economic role of the ruling class as a group to conspire, in pursuit of the profit motive, to deprive the working class of just compensation for the value of its labor. Krisberg (1975: 39) illustrates with the example of an industrial enterprise that pays ninety-five dollars for raw materials, labor, and so forth, to produce a pair of shoes, for which it charges $100. According to the predominant ethic of American society, the five-dollar difference is well-deserved profit. It is seen as a fair return on capital investment, a legitimate component of the selling price without which there would be no incentive for entrepreneurs to build factories, buy machinery and raw materials, hire employees, and market the finished product. According to the Marxist view, however, it is "surplus value," that is, that portion of the market value of the shoes to which the workers are entitled, but which has been improperly withheld from them. Thus, the capitalist is seen as stealing the money for himself.

Compounding tthe inherent criminality of the ordinary productive process, capitalist entrepreneurs, because of their single-minded devotion to maximizing profits, engage in violation of specific criminal laws in the course of conducting everyday business. Consumer fraud, discriminatory employment practices, sale of adulterated food products, working conditions that threaten physical safety and health, pollution of the environment with industrial waste—all of these illegal practices are traced by Marx's followers to an exaggerated zeal for securing the greatest possible return on capital investment.

It is in the nature of the Marxist approach to impute responsibility for these delicts to the social milieu to which the perpetrators belong. The culture of capitalism provides the rationale for the crimes of business. "Our economy, based on competition and on success at that game, promotes a form of life emphasizing the rightness of any activity pursued in the interest of one's business or occupation" (Quinney, 1975: 131). In support of his contention that it is specifically the culture of capitalism which causes middle-class and upper-class people to break laws in the course of their daily work, Quinney cites his own research on prescription law violations by retail pharmacists. Studying drug-store owners licensed to practice pharmacy provides an opportunity to examine the relation between norms and occupational behavior, because there are conflicting expectations for this occupation. Is pharmacy a profession like medicine or dentistry, in which practitioners are expected to be primarily concerned with the health of their patients? Or is it a business like any other, in which the profit motive is dominant? In a comparison of pharmacists with varying degrees of commitment to business and professional values, those pharmacists who subscribe most strongly to the business ethos—who place a high premium on activities like being a good salesman, stocking sundry goods (cosmetics and other items unrelated to the customer's health), and arranging window and counter displays—are the pharmacists most likely to violate the prescription laws. It appears that the expectations of the business world, not criminogenic on the surface, nevertheless provide the basis for professional misconduct (Quinney, 1963).

THE CORPORATION AS BAD GUY

Although it is often said that the general population is unaware of or unconcerned with corporate crime, that view seems to be contradicted by survey results. A clear majority of the public, according to a scientific poll carried out in 1985, does not trust the leaders of American business. More than 50 percent of respondents in all income groups, except the highest, gave a negative answer to the question, "Do you think most American corporate executives are honest, or not?" And even among those with family incomes over $50,000, 43 percent said the business leaders were not honest. Black respondents, as a group, were most distrustful: only 18 percent perceived the majority of executives as honest, and 62 percent disagreed. Eighty-five percent of the total sample were of the opinion that most white-collar criminals are not apprehended, and two-thirds thought the government does not do enough to catch them. When white-collar offenders are convicted, 65 percent of survey respondents felt that the courts treated them too leniently, only 1 percent thought they are treated too harshly, and another 24 percent judged their punishments to be about right (Flanagan and McGarrell 1986: 160-62).

There are no corresponding data indicating what the general public sees as the source of these moral failings, but some academic observers locate it in the corporate structure itself. Quinney (1975: 134–37) maintains that organizational mechanisms—"group involvement and rational planning"—are responsible for establishing and communicating the acceptability and even desirability of illegal business practices. He cites studies of large-scale enterprises in various industries to support his contention that the moral climate of the corporate world provides the foundation and the senior corporate officials provide the role models for illegal behavior. Just as the criminal tribes of India socialize their children into time-honored techniques of theft, so do modern corporations induct new employees into long-standing practices for carrying out white-collar crime. A study of the heavy electrical equipment antitrust cases of 1961 describes the process.

There was considerable agreement concerning the manner in which the men initially became involved in price fixing. "My first actual experience was back in the 1930s," a General Electric official said. "I was taken there by my boss . . . to sit down and price a job." An Ingersoll-Rand executive said, "[My superior] took me to a meeting to introduce me to some of our competitors . . . and at the meeting pricing of condensers was discussed with the competition" (Geis, 1977: 123).

Consider the widely publicized Equity Funding fraud of the 1970s. The Equity Funding Corporation was a conglomerate made up of several insurance companies, savings and loan associations, and other financial-service operations that sold stock to investors and offered services based on outrageously fraudulent misrepresentations. As a result, thousands of people lost a total of hundreds of millions of dollars. Eventually the major corporate officers and managers were indicted, pleaded guilty, and given sentences ranging from a one-year suspended sentence to eight-years imprisonment. One journalist, in his analysis of the case, suggests that corporate crime is a phenomenon *sui generis*, apart from the personal qualities of the participants, many of whom in this case seemed to act more out of loyalty to the corporation than out of personal greed.

What possessed men, some of them professionals in specialties with clearly defined codes of ethics, men whose prior brushes with the law had amounted to traffic violations, to do what they did? . . . In the course of the fraud, these ordinary suburbanites, these guys next door, had engaged in lying, forgery, counterfeiting, bugging, embezzlement, and multiple forms of fraud. . . . But the criminals were victims too, sucked into a vortex they did not have the strength or will to escape. . . . Gradually, the conspiracy of which they were a part seemed to take on a life of its own and grew so enormous, so voracious, that it made vassals of the men who had designed it and thought they were its masters. They could not halt it. By then, some had been so transformed by it that they did not care; they had grown to enjoy their bondage, and thus knew true evil (Blundell, 1978: 155).

THE LEGAL SYSTEM AS GOOD AND BAD

The American legal system, in the abstract, is widely depicted as a glorious achievement of the Founding Fathers. The original Constitution is celebrated as an unprecedented plan for a society in which freedom, equality under the law, and cooperation among citizens with diverse interests would result in greater happiness and fulfillment than had ever before been achieved under any form of government. And the Bill of Rights and subsequent amendments to the Constitution have been similarly praised for giving substance to the founders' grand design.

There are of course other views. One of these is that the architects of the Constitution, having little faith or interest in the common people, designed the system so that their own prerogatives, as wielders of power and owners of wealth, would be preserved at the same time that the rest of the population would be deluded into believing that the system protects the rights of all citizens. Still another view is that the abstract intentions of the Founding Fathers were honorable, but that in implementation the system has somehow failed to live up to its promises, and in fact has been responsible for casting the criminal offender in the role of "aggrieved citizen" (Finestone, 1978: 42).

Beyond the constitutional issues, the overall administration of American criminal law has long been subject to intense criticism. What President William Howard Taft saw of it in 1908 he called a disgrace to civilization (Tannenbaum, 1938: 254). Even earlier, there was a widely perceived connection between the occurrence of crime and imperfections in the criminal justice system. On the rural frontier the machinery for effective operation was simply absent. Given the rough-and-ready lifestyle there seemed to be no way to maintain the kind of police, court, and penal systems necessary to deter bands of free-ranging outlaws.

In urban settings, political corruption is regarded as a primary factor. The rapidly growing cities of the late nineteenth and early twentieth centuries, with their concentrations of foreign born inhabitants, have been depicted as conducive to a tradeoff between "the immigrants [who] were helpless and needed favors, protection, justice" and

the large and powerful interests [who] needed political power. . . . Therefore a partial answer to the question why we have had so much crime in the United States is to be found in the peculiar character of our urban politics, and urban politics are to be explained in part by the use the politicians have been able to make of the immigrant population, Their need for protection, defense, favor, on one hand; their ignorance and indifference to political methods on the other, have made them pliable instruments. On the political side, therefore, large-scale immigration was important in shaping the politics of our large cities, and this in time became an agency for protecting and perhaps even *promoting* certain types of criminal activity (Tannenbaum, 1938: 34–35, italics added).

The immigrants' lack of norms and institutions to help them adapt to a new milieu, discussed previously, underlies the development of corrupt political machines, and those machines in turn become a proximate cause of criminal behavior.

Practically no one has anything good to say about the criminal justice system in its currently operative form, but the wrongs for which it is blamed vary according to the ideology of the critics. There is in fact a polarity of opinion which corresponds to the distinction made by Packer (1968) between the "crime control model" and the "due process model" of justice. The crime control model assumes that the criminal justice system is above all a mechanism for catching criminal offenders and punishing them. The due process model is concerned with protecting the public against wrongful prosecution as well as protecting it against violations by agents of the system of such basic rights as the presumption of innocence, freedom from unlawful arrests and searches, double jeopardy, privilege against self-incrimination, representation by counsel, and trial by jury. When the system is blamed by those who emphasize the crime control model, the charge is inefficiency. "Congress finds that the high incidence of crime in the United States threatens the peace, security, and general welfare of the Nation and its citizens. To prevent crime and to insure the greater safety of the people, law enforcement efforts must be better coordinated, intensified, and made more effective at all levels of government" (Quinney, 1975: 51). Civil libertarians, following the assumptions of the due process model, are fearful that the zeal of crime control advocacy causes the due process guarantees of the formal system to be bypassed by police and prosecutors who presume that an accusation is equivalent to guilt, and by judges seeking to clear the streets of anyone who looks as though he might pose a threat to public safety. Denial of due process is regarded as particularly insidious because it is far more often denied to less-privileged groups than to the more privileged.

The legendary Dean Roscoe Pound of Harvard is often depicted as a defender of entrenched interests, but in the following passages he recognizes the basic overall inequality in application of the criminal law.

In history drastic enforcement of severe penal laws has been employed notoriously to keep a people or a class in subjection. Not only is one class suspicious of attempts by another to force its ideas upon the community under penalty of prosecution, but the power of a majority or even a plurality to visit with punishment practices which a strong minority consider in no way objectionable is liable to abuse. Whether rightly or wrongly used, this power puts a strain upon criminal law and its administration. Also, criminal prosecutions are possible weapons of offense and defense in class and industrial conflicts. Hence suspicion arises that one side or the other may get an advantage through abuse of the prosecuting machinery, giving rise to political struggles to get control of that machinery. Thus considerations of efficient securing of social interests are pushed into the background, and the atmosphere in which prosecutions are conducted becomes political. In practice the result is, when the public conscience is active or public indignation is roused, to be spectacular at the expense of efficiency. When the public conscience is sluggish and public attention is focused elsewhere, the temptation is to be lax for fear of offending dominant or militant political groups (Pound, 1971: 116–17).

A central thesis in Marxist analysis of crime is the tendency for "the more powerful groups [within a society to use] the law and the criminal justice system to advance their own values and interests over those of the less powerful groups" (Greenberg, 1981: 190). This perspective has been applied to penal systems in an extensive scholarly work by Rusche and Kirchheimer (1939). Based on more immediate experience David Du Bois, stepson of the black leader W.E.B. Du Bois and himself a civil rights activist, remarked to an interviewer that a black person "comes into conflict with the police and with the law in demonstrations, and one sees the role that the law enforcement agency plays in protecting the status quo against progressive change. This increases one's understanding of who the real criminal is and where the real crimes lie" (quoted in Carroll, 1974: 27).

The Marxist view actually reverses the establishment perspective, which sees respectable citizens as victims of the dangerous classes. Marxists assert that it is the more powerful groups in society who in a broader sense victimize the less powerful. It is these powerless people whom W.E.B. Du Bois sees as oppressed by the legal system when he says that "thousands of innocent victims are in jail today because they had neither money nor friends to help them" (1968: 390). Bettina Aptheker, another Marxist, writes in a similar vein: "There are many thousands of originally non-political people who are the victims of class, racial and national oppression. Arrested for an assortment of alleged crimes, and lacking adequate legal or political redress, they are imprisoned for long years, in violation of fundamental civil and human rights though they are innocent of any crime" (1971: 47).

During the 1950s and 1960s there was one component of the legal system, the system of juvenile justice, that was targeted for particular blame by critics with varying ideological orientations. Liberal lawyers, social workers, and others involved with the application of criminal law to young people were concerned that an egregious hypocrisy was being perpetrated. In discussing the juvenile court in Chapter 3, we noted its rationale as a protector of young people who have gotten into trouble through no fault of their own and its consequent mandate to serve as the child's protector. From its inception there were some critics who felt that the juvenile courts were too lenient, but the liberals' criticisms of thirty years ago were directed against the very practices that those courts had inaugurated sixty years earlier within the context of liberal ideology. Informal hearings in which restrictive rules of evidence did not apply, exclusion of lawyers from the proceedings, removal of children from their families without proof of wrongdoing—these practices were designed to allow juvenile judges wide latitude in determining how best to promote the child's well-being. But the result of these practices, the liberals contended, was that juveniles were often being treated more harshly than they would have been had they been adults.

In re Gault was a case in point. This was the case of Gerald Gault, a fifteen-year-old boy in Gila County, Arizona, who, while on probation on an earlier charge, was accused of making obscene telephone calls. Neither he nor his family was told what law he was accused of violating. In juvenile court hearings the complaining witness never appeared and thus could not be cross-examined. The youngster was not provided with a lawyer. He was induced to make certain statements with no indication that his words might be held against him, and no transcript was made of the proceedings. Following the proceedings the judge committed Gault to the State Industrial School "for the period of his minority [that is until 21] unless sooner discharged by due process of law." Had he been tried as as adult on the charge of making indecent telephone calls, the maximum penalty under Arizona law would have been a fine of no more than $50 or a jail term of no more than two months.

The case found its way to the U. S. Supreme Court, which handed down a decision in 1967 invalidating Gault's conviction and prescribing minimal due process safeguards that juvenile courts must provide: notice of charges, right to counsel, privilege against self-incrimination, and right to confront and cross-examine opposing witnesses. In this case the Supreme Court's action has led to changes bringing juvenile proceedings closer to the adult justice model. In a case decided the year before *Gault*, the Court itself indicated how the system, as carried out for its first sixty-odd years of operation, violated its own benevolent goals. Under the old system, said the Court, "there is evidence that the child receives the worst of two possible worlds: that he gets neither the protections accorded to adults nor the solicitous care and regenerative treatment postulated for children" (Empey, 1978: 357).

Yet another perspective that holds the justice system responsible for crime is labeling theory. As related to our concern here, the theory asserts that official agencies, by labeling certain people as criminals, set in motion a process that induces them to engage in illegal acts that they might not have done had they not been so labeled. "Being labelled is said to generate negative reactions by others, including attribution of bad character and stereotypical behavioral expectations. These reactions, in turn, limit opportunities for conforming participation and produce changes in the self-image. Limited opportunities for participation and altered self-image lead ultimately to rule-breaking" (Tittle, 1980: 247).

There have been a number of research studies which have sought to test the labeling proposition presented here. Their methodology is based on the contention that, if being labeled by the legal system changes behavior for the worse, then individuals who have been exposed to more severe labeling will be more likely than those less severely labeled to engage in misconduct. Thus, "labelees" may be viewed along a continuum, in which release without formal processing would represent the least degree of labeling, followed by release after minimal processing, release after a trial verdict of "not guilty," release on probation after a plea or finding of guilt, and finally, incarceration.

Overall, research findings have not provided much support for the labeling hypothesis. "The weight of the evidence, then, is contrary to the idea that labelling leads to crime in the general case or that it is the most important variable in the production of criminal careers" (Tittle, 1980:

258).   Nevertheless the legal system continues to be accused of falling short of the most elemental expectation—if it cannot claim to cure the crime problem, it should at least do no harm.

The strongest indication that the legal system continues to be perceived as a doer of harm is the persistence with which the practice of *diversion* is employed, especially as it concerns juveniles. The term "diversion" achieved currency in the 1960s as a response to recommendations in the Task Force Report on Juvenile Delinquency and Youth Crime, as part of the work of the President's Commission on Law Enforcement and the Administration of Justice established by President Lyndon Johnson. Edwin Lemert, a leading labeling theorist, bases his recommendations on concern with the stigmatizing effect of juvenile court processing.

One of the great unwanted consequences of wardship, placement, or commitment to a correctional institution is the imposition of stigma. Such stigma, represented in modern society by a record, gets translated into effective handicaps by heightened police surveillance, neighborhood isolation, lowered receptivity and tolerance by school officials, and rejections of youth by prospective employers. Large numbers of youth appearing in juvenile court have lower class status or that of disadvantaged minorities, whose limited commitments to education already put them in difficulties in a society where education increasingly provides access to economic opportunity. Given this, the net effect of juvenile court wardship too often is to add to their handicaps or to multiply problems confronting them and their families (U. S. President's Commission, 1967b: 92).

Therefore, concludes Lemert, since the juvenile court has such potential to do harm, its guiding principle should be "judicious nonintervention. It is properly an agency of last resort for children, holding to a doctrine analogous to that of appeals courts which require that all other remedies be exhausted before a case will be considered" (U.S. President's Commission, 1967b: 96; for a fuller argument on nonintervention, see Schur, 1973).   Lemert's view was incorporated into the recommendations of the full president's commission. The commission proposed that

the formal sanctioning system and pronouncements of delinquency should be used only as a last resort. In place of the formal system, dispositional alternatives to adjudication must be developed for dealing with juveniles, including agencies to provide and coordinate services and procedures to achieve necessary control without unnecessary stigma. Alternatives already available, such as those related to court intake, should be more fully exploited (U. S. President's Commission, 1967a: 81).

Diversion, therefore, consists of any measures designed to prevent delinquent or criminal suspects from being handled by official agencies of the law. There is some controversy about definitions of diversion. Some writers use the term to apply to any form of processing short of a full adjudicatory hearing; others prefer to use the term only when the matter is referred at initial intake to some entity that is altogether independent of the legal system. Thus, a suspect may be said to be "diverted" if, as an alternative to imprisonment, he is placed on probation, is referred to a community treatment center or drug clinic, or agrees to treatment by a private therapist. The underlying rationale is "minimization of penetration": in recognition of the damage that the juvenile and criminal justice systems are likely to do to the clients they are expected to treat, the contact should be as superficial as possible (Carter and Klein, 1976; Cressey and McDermott, 1974).

BAD GROUPS IN PRISON

Not surprisingly, the components of the criminal justice system that have been charged with doing the greatest harm are those at the end of the line—the custodial institutions to which offenders are remanded after conviction for crime. An unidentified eighteenth-century writer, possibly Henry Fielding, described English jails of the time in these terms:

They are filled with every sort of corruption that poverty and wickedness can generate . . . . In a prison the check of the public eye is removed; and the power of the law is spent. There are few fears, there are no blushes. The lewd inflame the more modest; the audacious harden the timid. Everyone fortifies himself as best he can against his own remaining sensibility, endeavoring to practice on others the arts that are practiced on himself; and to gain the applause of his worst associates by imitating their manners (Erikson, 1966: 14–15).

The preceding quotation expresses the theme, often heard in modern times as well, that the wickedness of prisons rests in the opportunity for the least socialized inmates to control their more civilized companions. At the most elemental level is the freedom for aggressive inmates, known as "gorillas" in modern prison argot (Sykes, 1958: 90), to take whatever they want from others by force. At a more complex level is the tendency for the least moral individuals' standards to become the standards of the convict group, just as Le Bon described the process among crowds. It was therefore their task, in the eyes of the architects of early nineteenth-century American prisons, to establish:

a well-ordered institution [that] could successfully reeducate and rehabilitate [the prisoner]. The penitentiary, free of corruptions and dedicated to the proper training of the inmate, would inculcate the discipline that negligent parents, evil companions, taverns, houses of prostitution, theaters, and gambling halls had destroyed. Just as the criminal's environment had led him into crime, the institutional environment would lead him out of it (Rothman, 1971: 82–83).

The first thing penitentiaries had to do, then, was to devise some way to prevent inmates from exerting their negative influences upon one another. The great debate of the early 1800s was whether to achieve this by physically isolating inmates night and day in individual cells—the Pennsylvania system—or to impose the rule of silence during daytime hours when inmates were together in communal shops and dining halls—the Auburn system (McKelvey, 1977: chap. 1).   But either way the underlying strategy was the same: to stifle the prisoners' natural inclinations to interact as a group.

The isolation system and the silent system are long gone, but the stereotype of inmate groupings as reinforcing deviancy persists in the concept of the inmate social system, which incorporates the notion of an inmate code—a set of informal rules shared and perpetuated by inmates—and an informal hierarchy of prestige and power among inmates, which reflects the code's values and carries out its enforcement (Schrag, 1970). The essence of the code enjoins every inmate to be loyal to other inmates, as individuals and as a group: don't squeal, don't exploit other inmates, don't give in to the wishes of guards or others in authority. And it is widely held to be highly salient for the great majority of prisoners. "Observers of the prison," according to Sykes and Messinger (1970: 403), "are largely agreed that the inmate code is outstanding both for the passion with which it is propounded and the almost universal allegiance verbally accorded it."

It would be folly to suggest that the group norms of prison inmates constitute a code of conduct that we would all do well to live by. Convict groups are not "good" groups in any absolute sense. Indeed, it would be surprising if they were; the criminal justice process as a whole tends to focus on the least upright citizens, and by the time sentencing occurs there is further selection of those with antisocial attitudes. But perceptions of inmate groups may be regarded as coalescing at the negative extreme when they imply that these groups inevitably ensnare the novice and transform him into a hardened criminal. The first panel of a newspaper cartoon shows a judge looking down from his high bench at a young man, saying, "I'm sending you to prison, son. Not only as punishment . . . but, also, to improve yourself." In the second panel the young man is sitting on his bunk in a cell while his cell mate, a tough old con, says, "And another thing. Never pull a heist with a .22. . . . A .38 is better!" (Keefe, 1985). Such stereotypes are contradicted by research indicating that specific criminal techniques are seldom learned in prison, although contacts made there can prove useful to young inmates initially disposed to further their criminal careers (Letkemann, 1973: 122–30).

As for absorbing more antisocial values, some research has shown, in the first place, that there is by no means uniformity among prisoners in adherence to the inmate code and opposition to official rules. One study identifies four major role configurations among inmates, only one of which, the "right guy," consistently follows the inmate code and maintains opposition to the authorities. The "square John," by contrast, accepts the official rules in preference to inmate norms, whereas the "politician" shifts quickly from one to the other, and the "outlaw" subscribes to neither (Schrag, 1961). In another type of study, a comparison among six institutions for juvenile offenders, questionnaires were administered to the boys in each facility asking among other things about the norms against "ratting" to staff in a variety of circumstances: when there is a plan to beat up an adult, to rough up another boy, to escape, or when the informant knew that another boy was stealing from the kitchen. The proportion of boys opposed to ratting about a runaway ranged among institutions from 43 to 71 percent; for the item about a plan to rough up another boy, from 27 to 45 percent. The study's authors conclude that "the findings give little support to the 'solidary opposition' model of the inmate group" (Street, Vinter, and Perrow, 1966: 234).

But what if prisoners as individuals were receptive to being reformed, and receptive to participation in groups that would cooperate with the prison administration toward that end? Even so, according to another set of stereotypes, their purpose would be frustrated because the prison administration, although professing rehabilitation as its ultimate goal, is really more interested in a smoothly running institution which maintains internal order and keeps inmates in custody so that they do not intrude on the free outside community and threaten its safety and property (Irwin, 1980: 123). Such a hypocritical stance, when attributed to the authorities responsible for prison policies and procedures, provides the basis for characterizing prison officialdom as a "bad" group.

There are many variations on this theme. One variation sees prison officials as agents for a society that wants prison to be a painful experience (Newman, 1985). Another sees them as mandated by society to contain the dangerous inmate population at all costs and denied the wherewithal to do anything else (Sykes, 1958: chap. 2). A third variation sees recruitment for prison work as a process selective of bad guys who start out with punitive personalities and gravitate toward prison work as a way of expressing in a socially acceptable way their predispositions to aggression (Shover, 1979: 119). Still another variation sees the task of controlling inmates as inevitably causing good guys to act badly: Given the requirement to exercise control over their uncooperative charges, guards resort to dehumanizing tactics, gradually lose sight of the limitations of necessary control, and eventually impose punishment as an end in itself (Zimbardo, 1972). Another version emphasizes the "corruption of authority": Since there are many more inmates than custodial staff on duty at any given time, it becomes necessary for guards to enlist the aid of certain prisoners to maintain control. But granting special privileges and rewards to induce such cooperation undermines the integrity of the official system and, to the extent that this is known, it is perceived as a corrupt system (Sykes, 1958: 48–58).

Again, we shall not attempt to counter the stereotype that bad groups run prisons by asserting that there is nothing bad about these groups. There is a history of corrupt practices among prison administrators, but it has more to do with political patronage in the appointment and promotion of public officials in general than with correctional agencies in particular. And, as many old-line administrators have retired from top positions in recent years, the long-sought-after professionalization of correctional administration is becoming discernible, as younger graduates of academic criminal justice programs are replacing them as prison superintendents and administrators of municipal, state, and federal correctional agencies.

Even if the allegation seems warranted, that modern prison administrators are simply better at the technocratic aspects of custody and no more oriented toward making the prison a more pleasant or rehabilitative environment than their predecessors, the fact remains that they are operating under the constraints of a public that is almost exclusively concerned with the incapacitative function of the prison (Shover, 1979). In this sense the real bad guy is the public that imposes the constraints.

As for that group which is in most direct contact with inmates, who are variously referred to as guards or correctional officers or "bulls," there is a fairly solid factual basis to counteract the stereotype that these individuals are a sadistic lot (Hawkins, 1976). And yet they are often observed to act violently against prisoners. If not because of personal inclination, why then? Newman (1985: 263–65) explains these acts of aggression as growing out of the stressful position of the guards as "men in the middle": between a public that expects prisoners to be punished and authorizes the guards to use some degree of force on the one hand, and the frustrated, hostile, recalcitrant convicts on the other. In this situation psychologically normal people—and guards seem to be neither more nor less abnormal than average—are likely to regress to the punitive responses of less-civilized ages.

In a similar vein Irwin (1980: 21–24) acknowledges the corruptive contract between guards and prisoners. Instead of condemning it as morally reprehensible he, like Newman, explains it as a consequence of the guard's position in the social structure of the prison. The guard is responsible for seeing that prisoners follow the rules and that they neither abscond nor disturb the internal order of the prison. In fact a number of them have disruptive tendencies, and the guards have "insufficient *immediate* raw power" to maintain order. Therefore they must resort to informal means—sometimes brutality, but more often bestowing favors on certain inmates to secure their help in keeping other inmates in line. Here too, it is not a question of evil intent, and yet the practice is acknowledged as damaging the moral integrity of the system.

ORGANIZED CRIME

Just as the prototypes of the bad individual criminal are the depraved, animal-like throwbacks to savagery depicted by Lombroso, the prototypes of the bad criminal collectivity are the criminal organizations involved in illegal gambling and drugs, labor racketeering, prostitution, loansharking, extortion, cargo hijacking, and pornography. They have been characterized by such terms as "a spreading cancer" (John Barkham, quoted in Maas, 1969: unnumbered preliminary page), an "immoral community" (Tyler, 1962: xii), a "brotherhood of evil" (Sondern, 1959), "corporations of corruption" (Lyndon B. Johnson, quoted in Cressey, 1969: 1). The cancer metaphor is apt. It reflects a number of qualities—incurable, life-threatening, insidious, and metastasizing (spreading from diseased components and eventually destroying a previously healthy organism)—that are frequently used to describe the effects of organized crime on society.

Sometimes underworld organized crime is explained as simply a concatenation of immorally like-minded individuals. But it is also often depicted as an organization with a life of its own, a rationally organized enterprise with all the resources of the best business organizations, but differing from them in the corrupting effect it has on the entire moral structure of society. The task force charged with reporting on organized crime for the president's commission concluded:

Organized crime is not merely a few preying on a few. In a very real sense, it is dedicated to subverting not only American institutions, but the very decency and integrity that are the most cherished attributes of a free society. As the leaders of Cosa Nostra and their racketeering allies pursue their conspiracy unmolested, in open and continuous defiance of the law, they preach a sermon that all too many Americans heed: The government is for sale; lawlessness is the road to wealth; honesty is a pitfall and morality a trap for suckers (U. S. President's Commission, 1967c: 24).

At the opposite pole of the moral spectrum is the view that organized crime is simply a business enterprise like any other, the only difference being that the goods and services purveyed by organized crime happen to be illegal. A frequently cited article by Daniel Bell (1953), titled "Crime as an American Way of Life," illustrates a number of points made by those who go so far as to take a favorable view of organized crime. Bell's approach emphasizes "ethnic succession," the general process by which certain occupations—as well as residential areas, religious and educational institutions, and so forth—are populated at certain times by a particular ethnic group, which subsequently moves up to higher status occupations and is replaced by more recent immigrants. Bell notes that Italian immigrants to the United States, with rural backgrounds and no skills suited for well-paid jobs in the urban communities where they found themselves, had to either accept the dirtiest jobs at the lowest pay, or else become involved in illegal enterprises—first bootlegging and later illegal gambling operations—that were often more lucrative. Thus the Italian group, like the Eastern European Jews and Irish before them, is depicted as choosing criminal occupations for the most American of reasons: because they are the most available means of achieving financial success and a degree of social acceptance.

Although prohibitions against alcohol and gambling have strong roots in America's puritan tradition, this does not mean, according to Bell, that there is a consensus which labels bootleggers and gambling syndicate operators as bad guys. "While Americans made gambling illegal, they did not in their hearts think of it as wicked—even the churches benefited from the bingo and lottery crazes" (Bell, 1953: 140). In fact, he suggests several contributions that urban racketeering makes to the society at large. For one thing, it simply satisfies certain individuals' needs without obviously transgressing the rights of others. For another, it provides a level of material satisfaction for those engaged in such operations that would be unattainable through legitimate jobs. Also, in the process, it reaffirms the value of entrepreneurial endeavor—"such 'normal' goals as independence through a business of one's own, and such 'moral' aspirations as the desire for social advancement and social prestige" (Bell, 1953: 133)—and is not substantially different from the questionable tactics of many "pioneers of American capitalism" (Bell, 1953: 152). And finally, it serves a social control function. "In seeking to 'legitimize itself,' gambling had quite often actually become a force against older and more vicious forms of illegal activity. . . . When the gambling raids started in Chicago, the 'combine' protested that, in upsetting existing stable relations, the police were only opening the way for ambitious young punks and hoodlums to start trouble" (Bell, 1953: 134). In other words, as the leaders of a criminal syndicate, in taking on the organizational sophistication of the world of legitimate corporations, have succeeded in eliminating competing outsiders, they also may protect the larger community from certain unsavory byproducts of those outsiders—for example, lack of "quality control," which can result in such problems as an increase in sexually transmitted diseases from prostitutes whose hygiene is unsupervised, or deaths from accidental overdoses of drugs whose strength varies from batch to batch.

Variations of these polar views of organized crime—as a menace to the very existence of society, or as an enterprise not very different from legitimate business—seem to dominate popular discourse on the subject, resulting in enforcement policies that fluctuate between spasmodic crackdown and benign tolerance. Seldom is organized crime depicted as something in between. And yet an overall view of the phenomenon seems to indicate that if the truth does not lie in the middle, it is at least far from the extreme views that are popularly held.

First, as to the question of real harm inflicted, the answer must be that it depends; in particular, it depends upon what criminal organization one is talking about. One of the most prevalent types of criminal enterprise is the relatively small, relatively independent operation that confines its illegal activities to gambling within a particular area of a large city. Ianni describes one such "family" in the New York City area. The Lupollo family was in fact a group of men, many with kinship ties to one another, who operated a number of successful legitimate businesses along with illegal gambling operations. According to Ianni (who has very likely been accorded as much insider access to the workings of a crime family as any other trained social scientist), the Lupollo family had little contact with other crime groups, and limited its illegal activities to gambling and loan sharking. Lack of contact with other groups suggests that this group, at least, is not part of a conspiracy. There is one senior member of the family whose special function is to keep in touch with the local police and attend testimonial dinners for local politicians. Another, an attorney, entertains businessmen and sports and theatrical celebrities as well as politicians. And when he deals with politicians it is to secure favorable treatment for the family business in pending legislation and the application of federal regulations, much as a corporate executive would do in similar circumstances (1972: 80).

The gambling side of the business is regarded even by the police as innocuous. And even the loansharking operation, though perhaps not harmless from the point of view of some debtors in difficulty, sounds even in this description by one of its clients more like a technical violation of certain provisions of the commercial code than a social threat.

In recent years the family . . . have amassed enough capital now to loan money to different businesses who for one reason or another might need money in a hurry. Some of these businesses might want to expand, others of them might be having financial difficulties of one kind or another, and they need money in a hurry. What happens here is that the men who are in business pick up a marker or give their marker and if they can't pay off their loans in a period of time, the members of the family or whatever else you want to call them, then instead of using force or anything like that, they want to use the money that they have loaned these different business men as a way of buying into different businesses (Ianni, 1972: 98).

We do not suggest that organized crime is an insignificant problem. There are of course organized crime operations that have harmful consequences for the public. Violence is sometimes directed toward respectable citizens who obstruct the goals of the syndicates—by informing, for example—and sometimes bystanders are accidental victims of wars among competing drug dealers. Gus Tyler (1962), a labor union official who is knowledgeable about much of the inner workings of organized crime, has brought together a number of convincing accounts of the impact of organized crime on certain legitimate industries.

And yet there are features of organized crime which suggest that the prophets of doom go too far when they predict that organized crime will end up dominating the major institutions of our society. For one thing, the degree of organization tends to be exaggerated. There is certainly no overarching national, much less international, chain of command. The closest approximation to a national organization is the "Commission" of the Mafia (or Cosa Nostra): a dozen or so Italian-American men, each of whom is regarded as the boss of his own criminal organization in a large city, which meets when necessary to deal with disputes among members, but has never been shown to articulate any overall agenda or goals. Most of its actions are directed toward curbing activities, like violence and drug dealing, that bring too much notoriety to their operations, And increasingly the Mafia's share of the pie is diminishing, as other ethnic groups—Asians, blacks, Hispanics, Israelis—with even less central organization intrude into the market for drugs, illegal gambling, and so forth (Press, 1981).

A second qualification has to do with the stereotype that organized crime ends up becoming the dominant industry in any neighborhood where illicit businesses have a foothold. It would be more accurate to note the extent to which legal and illegal businesses operate side by side. Many successful numbers operators and cocaine distributors ply their trades in the most respectable office buildings, supplying their wares and services to middle-class customers who adhere scrupulously to high ethical standards in their professions and businesses. And even in communities thought to be dominated by organized crime, recruitment is far from automatic. The burden is generally upon the candidate to show that he has the necessary qualities—and recently these qualities have become increasingly the educational attainments of the candidate for an entry-level corporate position—to contribute to the success of the syndicate (Cressey, 1969: 242–47).

Thus, without minimizing the harmful nature of some of the activities in which organized crime is involved, it is inaccurate to hold particular groups ultimately responsible for creating the harms. The desire for illegal alcohol during the days of prohibition, the marijuana craze among young people in the 1960s, the everpresent market for illegal gambling and commercial sex, the current demand for cocaine and its derivatives—none of these was "created" by organized crime. Some of these services or products are widely regarded as innocuous, others as inherently very dangerous, probably most as potentially but not inevitably harmful. Some organized crime groups limit themselves to the more innocuous activities and others seem to have a taste for the most vicious, but the majority might best be characterized as business organizations whose members are somewhat less fastidious about obeying laws than run-of-the-mill legitimate businessmen. As a whole they do not deserve to be regarded as public benefactors, but they are also less than the menace to the whole social fabric that is depicted by those who crusade against them.

NOTE

1. For an extensive treatment of observations about American cities as breeding grounds for moral decay, see Boyer (1978).

5

Victims As Good
and Bad Guys

At first glance it would seem likely that people who have been victims of serious crimes will be perceived sympathetically. Even more common than the assumption that people who commit ordinary crimes are bad is the assumption that victims of those crimes are good. As Schwendinger and Schwendinger (1967: 95) observe, "those who support conventionally governed activity" do so "by maintaining the moral worthiness of possible victims."

The assumption of the victim's goodness is reflected in the etymology of the term *victim*. The Latin word *victima* refers to a creature offered in sacrifice to the gods. It embodies not only the idea that victims suffer, but that they do so unjustly, without having done anything to merit their suffering (Stanciu, 1976). The fictional prototype of the "innocent" victim is Shakespeare's King Lear—innocent, meaning that he has done nothing to deserve the betrayal by his daughters Goneril and Regan, whose wickedness stands in sharp contrast to his own qualities of trust and softheartedness (Lewin, 1976).

And yet not all victims are seen as without responsibility for their suffering. People who engage in direct provocation or temptation, exploitation, greed, carelessness, or ostentatious display, or those who simply fail to share their bountiful resources with others in need are perceived, in some quarters at least, as fit targets for criminal action. Their acts are taken as indicators of some degree of moral blameworthiness; to that degree, blame for the criminal act may be shifted from the perpetrator to the victim.

Although there is a long history of controversy over allocating blame to victims instead of criminals, it is only within the past fifty years that any systematic framework has been developed for considering variations in victim responsibility. Benjamin Mendelsohn (1956) is generally recognized as the first person to have done empirical research in the area. As a lawyer in Rumania prior to World War II, he carried out a questionnaire study of his clients, and subsequently formulated a victim typology, encompassing degrees of victim culpability, from the "completely innocent victim" to "the victim who is guilty alone"—in the latter instance, for example, an attacker who is killed in self-defense by his target. Mendelsohn's continuum for victims corresponds most closely to legal notions of offender responsibility, but it also reflects an underlying moral continuum, according to which innocent victims are good guys, those in the middle are not so good, and the victim who is altogether responsible for his fate is morally equivalent to the bad offender.

Mendelsohn's conception was enlarged by Hans von Hentig (1948), who developed a typology containing some categories that explain victimization in terms of the victim's vulnerability. The very young and the very old, females, those suffering from mental illness or intellectual handicap, members of racial and ethnic minorities, people who are simply lonesome—these victims are regarded as vulnerable because of circumstances beyond their control. The elderly, for example, tend to be physically weak and thus likely targets for robbers because any resistance they might offer is likely to be ineffective. The young are also ideal prey because they are considered "savory" (1948: 404), presumably from the perspective of certain sexual offenders. Von Hentig offers additional examples of the connection between types of crime and victim vulnerability based on psychological states, such as the susceptibility of lonesome widows to matrimonial swindlers. These cases appear to be examples of the "completely innocent victim"—in our terminology, good guys.

But von Hentig also describes victims who suffer because of supposed moral failings: greedy people whose vice makes them prey to confidence games, or alcoholics who torment family members with physical abuse until finally a spouse or one of the children retaliates by killing the tormentor. Such victims are not innocent, and thus, to the degree that they are responsible for their own suffering, bad guys.

In recent years there have been a number of further efforts to classify victims based on the extent and nature of their responsibility (see Karmen, 1990: 113–20). The headings of the following sections represent an effort to explain victim responsibility in connection with particular norms in modern society.

THE MISBEHAVING VICTIM

A common reason for considering victims as bad people is their own antisocial behavior. If they are doing something illegal or otherwise socially harmful at the time they become targets for someone else's crime, the injury they suffer is seen as just retribution for their own misdeeds.

An example encountered almost daily in the urban press is the drug dealer who is robbed, or even killed, in connection with his illegal activities. There is in fact considerable risk of victimization for anyone involved in organized criminal activities—dealing drugs, labor racketeering, procuring, systematic extortion—that involve enriching one's self at the expense of others. Not all participants in vice activities are seen as bad victims; if they are seen as exploited themselves, as in the case of teenage drug dealers or prostitutes, or if the illegal activity is an innocuous one like gambling, they may be regarded with sympathy if they come to harm. But if the victim's activity is considered harmful and his participation is voluntary, the nature of the activity calls forth the public's hope that he will be punished.

Another bad victim is someone who is the target of those confidence games that prey on the victim's willingness to exploit someone else (Maurer, 1940; Sutherland, 1937). In the classic "Spanish prisoner" game, for example, the con operator shows the victim a letter, purportedly from an inmate in a Spanish prison, asking for money to bribe a guard so that the inmate can escape and retrieve a stolen treasure hidden before his capture. The "mark," or victim, is promised a sizable share of the treasure in return for simply putting up bribe money. The "pigeon drop" ruse, another con game, involves a packet containing a large sum of money, supposedly found by chance by the operator, which he offers to share with the mark if the mark will put up some money of his own to show "good faith." When victims of these criminal deceptions lose their "investments," they get little sympathy because their losses result from an unseemly pursuit of the fast buck. Wealth is fine, according to the Protestant ethic, when it accumulates from hard work, but the kind that comes too easily raises questions about greedy motives and exploitation of others, and thus clouds the moral character of the recipient.

Another type of victim is regarded as blameworthy because the misbehavior calls forth retaliation as a natural response—that is, a response that might be expected of a "reasonable person" who finds himself or herself the target of the misbehavior. Such victims are said to have *provoked* another person to hurt them. Provocation may be an unjust claim on one's property, an insult to one's mother, a seduction of one's wife, a threat to one's life. The bad victim's injury is sometimes considered the result of a legally justified act of self-defense, as the jury viewed the paralysis of one of the young men shot by Bernhard Goetz. Or it may fail legal tests for self-defense but still be considered morally deserved because of the behavior that provoked it. The case mentioned in Chapter 3 comes to mind, in which a dozen people pursued and beat to death a thief who had snatched a twenty-dollar bill from a bakery customer. The victim's bad-guy status, it will be remembered, was defined not only by the immediate act, but by evidence of his drug addiction as well, and that definition in turn was responsible for his assailants being perceived as good guys and consequently treated leniently by the court ("Defendant in beating death," 1988; Hays, 1988; McQuiston, 1988).

A more complex situation is one in which the threat is not a one-time confrontation but rather a long-term process. The "tormentor" victim is exemplified in Sinclair Lewis's novel *Babbitt* by Zilla Riesling (the wife of Babbitt's best friend), "who in a moment of excitement and self-humiliation admits her wickedness and threatens to kill herself. But she goes on deviling and [her husband] shoots her" (von Hentig, 1948: 432).

In recent years, as a result of increasing concern with men's physical abuse of women, public attention has been drawn to real-life situations in which a male tormentor has beaten his wife or companion and children over a considerable period of time, until one of the targets of his hostility kills him, often with the applause of the community. One such case, tried in New York City in 1987, was that of a woman who had, following many years of abuse, left her husband and obtained a court order directing him to stay away from her. In violation of that order, he went to her apartment, and after hours of verbal and physical violence, raped her at knife point in front of her children. She then stabbed him to death, but was acquitted by a jury of seven men and five women (Johnson, 1987). Subsequently there appeared a letter in the *New York Times*, signed by four social workers affiliated with a treatment center for rape victims, applauding the jury that acquitted the woman for their courage in rendering a verdict of acquittal on grounds of self defense (Xenarios et al, 1987). Even when there is a possibility that a woman is retaliating after an assault—which is not a legally valid defense—rather than defending herself or others from a present threat, the operative consideration will be a moral evaluation of the man based on his past behavior. If there is clear evidence for a history of severe abuse by the man, the average jury is likely to label him the bad guy and therefore deny him the vindication to which innocent victims are entitled. Thus the legal system reinforces the public's inclination to turn its back on misbehaving victims.

A corresponding distinction between blameless and blameworthy victims is made at the level of research scholarship in criminology, A classic study in criminological research is founded upon a dichotomy between *victim-precipitated* homicides, and homicides that are not victim precipitated. Victim-precipitation, as used for purposes of this study by Wolfgang, corresponds to *provocation* as we have described it previously; victim-precipitated homicides are those for which police reports include certain indications that the victim initiated some misbehavior leading to the fatal act. For example, an incident in which the victim struck the first blow is classified as a victim-precipitated occurrence. Wolfgang and his assistants reviewed records of 588 homicides known to the Philadelphia police between 1948 and 1952, classifying them as victim-precipitated or non-victim-precipitated, and then went on to correlate other factors with the precipitated-nonprecipitated dichotomy—that is, to determine whether the occurrence of victim precipitation in homicide was related to various characteristics of either victims or offenders, such as age, race, or prior criminal conviction (Wolfgang, 1958).

Curtis (1974a; 1974b) expanded Wolfgang's focus on victim precipitation in a study based on police reports in seventeen American cities. He examined typical homicide incidents in which the result, that person A is dead and person B is charged with the crime, is fortuitous—in the sense that it could easily have been the other way around. Most commonly, these incidents involved young, black males in situations accompanied by hard drinking, weapons possession, insulting banter, and displays of physical toughness. Under such circumstances "distinctions between victims and offenders are often blurred and [are] mostly a function of who got whom first, with what weapon, how the event was reported, and what immediate decisions were made by police" (Curtis, 1974b: 597). It is significant that homicides of this nature receive very little public attention. Because both nominal offender and nominal victim are by virtue of their behavior, as well as social status, regarded as bad guys, such incidents do not lend themselves to construction as morality plays, and for that reason are relegated either to the back pages of the newspaper or to total obscurity.

THE ENTICING VICTIM

In interviews with thirty-eight Philadelphia judges, Carol Bohmer discovered a variety of terms applied by her respondents to rapes of women who in their judgment "asked for it" by, for example, accepting a ride home from a stranger they had met in a bar. Various judges described these incidents as "friendly rape," "felonious gallantry," and "assault with failure to please" (1974: 305).

These terms point to a distinctive connotation of rape in the minds of certain segments of the public—that it is not really a crime of the usual sort in which an offender is gratified at the expense of a victim, but is rather an encounter in which the victim frequently also derives, or expects to derive, some kind of satisfaction. This expectation is reflected in questions posed to rape victims in court, asking directly whether they "enjoyed" the intercourse on which the rape complaint was based (Bohmer, 1975: 396). It follows from this view that such victims deserve little sympathy, and when they turn upon the man and accuse him of forcing their participation, they are regarded as bad guys.

This view is derived from a set of assumptions that Brownmiller calls "the male myths of rape"—"all women want to be raped," "no woman can be raped against her will," "she was asking for it," "if you're going to be raped, you might as well relax and enjoy it" (1976: 346). But how is it, given these assumptions, that women end up accusing men of rape?   A corollary set of attitudes seems to apply in different cases.

In some instances it is asserted that the victim did not really want to have intercourse, that she wanted only to lead the man on. The woman's motive may be hostile, deriving perverse gratification from arousing the man and then frustrating him by not delivering what was expected. A variant of this assumption sees the woman as enticing the man in order to secure some nonsexual benefit for herself: a present of jewelry, a job or promotion, a party invitation or dinner at a fine restaurant, or simply the prestige of going out with an attractive or wealthy or powerful man. In any case such women are condemned for their duplicity, and the men who subdue them by force are perceived as entitled to sexual gratification; they are only exacting the reward offered to them in the first place. In these cases there is an element of the provocative victim discussed previously, as well as the enticing victim.

In a second scenario it is believed that the woman intended to go through with the sexual act at the outset of a date but then changed her mind. One study of perceptions of rape in dating situations found that an important variable in victim blaming is whether the victim began to protest at an early, middle, or late stage of the encounter. The longer the woman waited to indicate her objections to the man's sexual advances, the more likely were research subjects to hold her responsible for the rape. In this study, it should be noted, female subjects were more likely than males (all of whom were college students in introductory psychology) to hold women responsible for date rape across the variety of situations they were asked to judge. However, the authors' review of the date rape literature showed variability in findings of sex differences in victim blaming: Some studies find no difference, others find that women exceed men, and still others find that men exceed women in victim blaming (Shotland and Goodstein, 1983).

One indication of the significance attributed to the rape victim's initial disposition toward her assailant is the fact that it was a major focus in one of the classic studies of rape. The study was conducted by Menachem Amir, a student of Wolfgang's, who analyzed police reports in a way similar to Wolfgang's method of studying victim-precipitated homicide, but in this case focused attention on the distinction between victim-precipitated and non-victim-precipitated rape. Amir defines victim-precipitated rape as incidents

in which the victim actually, or so it was deemed, agreed to sexual relations but retracted before the actual act, or did not react strongly enough when the suggestion was made by the offender(s). The term applies also to cases in risky situations marred with sexuality, especially when she uses what could be interpreted as indecency in language and gestures, or constitutes [sic] what could be taken as an invitation to sexual relations (Amir, 1971: 266) .

In Amir's definition of victim-precipitated rape, it is noteworthy that the criteria are quite vague with respect to whether or not there was actual enticement, or consent: "the victim actually, *or so it was deemed*, agreed," "she uses *what could be interpreted as* indecency," "[she offers] *what could be taken as* an invitation" (emphasis supplied). Amir indicates that he did not accept uncritically evaluative statements by witnesses, offenders, or police indicating the presence of provocation, but made his own interpretation. Yet there seems to be incorporated into the classification system itself an assumption that a mere hint of impropriety on the victim's part is sufficient to indicate that she bears responsibility for the ensuing rape. This assumption brings to mind what Clark and Lewis refer to as the "open territory victim" (1977: 123–24): a woman whose demeanor, or past history, or subordinate status stigmatizes her as a bad woman and therefore one who can be victimized with impunity.

A third perception is of a woman who participates willingly in the act of intercourse but subsequently makes a false accusation of rape—to retaliate for some other perceived grievance against the man or to protect her reputation when her involvement in the act becomes known to others. The possibility has recently been mentioned by a state senator from Louisiana as an argument against a rape exception to a strict anti-abortion law, that "women seeking an abortion could falsely claim to have been raped" (Suro, 1990). These stereotypes notwithstanding, a study carried out in Denver in 1973 found that, when rape charges are clearly unfounded, the motive is seldom vindictiveness or an inconvenient pregnancy.

The typical false report these days is not the grieving Lady Windemere who regrets bestowing her favors on a lover who refuses to repay her with his family name, nor is it usually the stereotyped heroine of the 1940s whose indiscretions have placed her in a position which she dare not explain to family or friends. Rather, the typical false rape reporter of this era, we found, is an early teenager, who goes out with her boyfriend, or a small group of other young teenagers, and unexpectedly stays out all night. Sometimes the night's activities include sex, sometimes not. In either case, she returns home as daylight is breaking to find her home ablaze with light and her distraught parents pacing the floor. They may have already called the police and reported her missing. Faced with a hysterical and/or punitive session with her parents—and no good excuse—she may hastily concoct a story about a man, or men, who forced her into a car and raped her at some distant spot (Hursch, 1977: 86).

It is usually easy for an experienced detective to expose the inconsistencies in such a story and elicit a confession that it has been fabricated, so that the allegations go no further. This situation of course is very different from the stereotype of the vindictive accuser, which the author of the Denver study believes has little basis in reality.

Nevertheless, what Karmen calls "the credibility problem" persists: In spite of evidence suggesting that a very small proportion of rape complaints are truly false accusations, "it is part of conventional wisdom to believe that women may lie to get men into serious trouble" (1990: 250). Moreover, as we shall see below when considering victims in the criminal justice system, such beliefs are institutionalized in the formal and informal practices that come into play when rape victims become involved in legal proceedings.

THE CARELESS VICTIM

The following interview is one that the newspaper columnist Art Buchwald claims to have conducted:

Prof. Heinrich Applebaum is a criminologist who feels that unless the police start cracking down on the victims of criminal acts, the crime rate in this country will continue to rise. "The people who are responsible for crime in this country are the victims. If they didn't allow themselves to be robbed, the problem of crime in this country would be solved," Applebaum said.

"That makes sense, Professor. Why do you think the courts are soft on victims of crimes?"

"We're living in a permissive society and anything goes," Applebaum replied. "Victims of crimes don't seem to be concerned about the consequences of their acts. They walk down a street after dark, or they display jewelry in their store window, or they have their cash registers right out where everyone can see them. They seem to think that they can do this in the United States and get away with it" (quoted by Curtis, 1974a: 81).

Is Professor Applebaum's view, that victims are to blame for crime when they display their valuables or go out after dark, shared by anyone else? There is considerable evidence that the general public views victims of typical street crimes as not altogether innocent parties, as people who in some way or another have invited their victimization. J. L. Barkas, whose brother incurred a fatal stab wound in the course of being subject to an otherwise run-of-the-mill mugging, demonstrates this stereotypical attitude as her own preconception prior to her brother's death: "I had believed that one had to do something to become a victim—one had to provoke a burglary by carelessness, an assault by an innuendo that was unconsciously suggestive" (Barkas, 1978: ix). And following the incident, when she realized that her brother's victimization had occurred as a totally random and unprovoked act, she encountered the same stereotype in the behavior of her acquaintances. "If I spoke about my brother's murder, people recoiled. They didn't empathize, they didn't sympathize, they didn't get angry. They said, 'Well, why was he walking down that street?' 'What time of night was it?' They acted as if Seth had done something wrong, as if I were now doing something wrong to mourn him, to be angry, to be devastated" (Barkas, 1978: xi).

However much Buchwald's and Barkas's reports differ in style, their message is the same: seemingly innocent victims are not given the sympathy they deserve, but in a curious reversal of expectations are instead blamed themselves for for their mishaps. The ideas of responsibility noted by these authors are understandable only when it is recognized that in modern urban society certain norms prevail for self protective behavior. It is usual for people to equip their homes and vehicles with expensive locks and alarm systems.[1] Banks, liquor stores, and taxicabs are provided with thick plastic barriers to protect employees from holdups. Many people take pains not to display valuable articles in public; they avoid certain neighborhoods altogether, and venture into others alone only in broad daylight, or in the company of others. Indeed, taking such precautions has become so much a matter of routine that those who shun them are considered foolhardy, even deviant—and so often regarded as having *invited* their victimization as much as if they had performed an affirmative act of provocation.

Curtis in fact incorporates within the rubric of victim-precipitated crime—which we have earlier considered as emanating from overt acts of provocation or enticement—certain robberies arising from " 'temptation-opportunities' where the victim clearly had not acted with reasonable self-protective behavior in handling money, jewelry, or other valuables" (1974a: 92). He gives the example of "a man [who] flashes a great deal of money at a bar and then staggers home alone on a dark street late at night" (1974b: 594). There may be many bars, and many dark streets, where a person might have a very slight chance of encountering someone else who would see the situation as a "temptation opportunity." Many people may indeed engage in such careless behavior without incident, but even so the unfortunate few who do come to grief under these circumstances are themselves targeted for blame.

An unusually forceful example of victim blaming on the basis of carelessness is a crime prevention poster that appeared some years ago in New York subways. "Lock your car and take your keys," said the poster. "Don't make a good boy go bad." If we assume that the poster's creator was in tune with public opinion, the message may be taken to indicate the acceptability of the idea that anyone so negligent as to leave his keys in an unlocked car deserves blame not just for the loss of the car, but for launching a criminal career. The phenomenon of "motorist blaming" has a long history, and Karmen has surveyed the literature in an effort to establish the extent to which car theft is attributable to driver carelessness, or to other factors. Although some studies before 1970 showed a substantial degree of "victim facilitation," as indicated by the proportion of stolen cars in which drivers had left ignitions unlocked or keys available to thieves, these proportions appear to have declined in recent years. Karmen maintains that it is the auto companies themselves who foster the idea that victims of car theft are themselves to blame, as a way of excusing their own failure to build more theft-preventing features into their products (1990: 130–31). But the ability of the companies to get away with blaming individual victims of car theft suggests that public opinion is predisposed to attribute such blame.

VICTIMS WHO ARE UNDESERVEDLY ADVANTAGED

The dominant culture in the United States tends to place high and nearly absolute value on property rights. Even if one's source of income is questionable, the presumption is that possessions bought with it should be protected. Consider by contrast the attitude of a Sardinian shepherd. "The providence of God being merciful to all his creatures, how would he allow it that the shepherds of Gallura possess 500, 800, or 1000 sheep, while we have little flocks of a hundred? Wherefore, if we, through deceit or bravery can steal from them some hundreds, we help, at least in part to effect distributive justice" (Ruffini, quoted by Nader, 1975: 155). Since wealthy sheep owners are perceived simply by virtue of their wealth to be unjustly rich, they are justifiable targets for rustlers and the prevailing view seems to be that they deserve no sympathy for the losses they suffer in order to augment the flocks of their less fortunate neighbors.

Although such views are not the norm in our society, they may be embraced by certain subgroups who assume that those who possess great wealth are morally corrupt and therefore justifiable targets for predatory crime. Radical political groups sometimes prey on wealthy individuals or institutions to finance their activities and rationalize their selection of victims on grounds that their victims have engaged in, or at least acquiesced to, exploitation of the less privileged—as was the case with the Symbionese Liberation Army, the group that allegedly kidnapped the newspaper heiress Patricia Hearst in 1974 and forced her to accompany them in a series of bank robberies.

Some members of the underworld who prey on well-off individuals likewise offer as justification for their crimes the explanation that their victims are bad guys because they have not earned their privileged positions. A victim's negative moral character may be established on the basis that he was not really entitled to the property that was stolen. Robert Allerton, an English thief, justified his stealing from upper-class victims on grounds that they violated the work ethic, while he did not.

But I do work for my living. Most crime—unless it's the senseless, petty-thieving sort—is quite hard work, you know. Planning a job, working out all the details of the best way to do it—and then carrying it out, under a lot of nervous strain and tension—and having to run round afterwards, if it's goods, fencing the stuff, getting a good price for it, delivering it to the fence, and so on—all this needs a lot of thinking and effort and concentration. It certainly is "work," don't kid yourself about that. . . .

A lot of other people don't "work" for their living in the way you mean—but nobody goes on at them like they do at criminals. Quite a large proportion of the "upper classes," for instance. You can see them any day round Piccadilly, Vigo Street, Savile Row—nattily dressed half-wits who've never done a stroke of work in their lives, popping in and out of Fortnum's or Scott's, spending all their time trying to get rid of the money their fathers and grandfathers and great-grandfathers left them. . . . I can steal from people like that without the faintest compunction at all, in fact I'm delighted to do it (Allerton, 1972: 28).

Allerton's view is of course self-serving and extreme, not representative of the mainstream of public opinion. But resentment against members of the privileged classes is shared by many noncriminal members of the lower classes, and many among them share Allerton's disdain to sympathize with those upper-class individuals when they are victims of ordinary property crimes.

Moreover, a lack of sympathy for privileged victims is more extensive when the victims are not individuals but corporations. An undercurrent of resentment against large business enterprises is expressed in acceptance of crimes directed against these enterprises among many people who are not tolerant of the same kinds of crimes directed toward individuals. Part of this may be explained on the basis of "an historic antipathy to the corporate idea" (Smigel and Ross, 1970: 7) in Western culture. Although a University of Michigan study has shown that most Americans believe the benefits of big business outweigh the harms, there is significant unfavorable sentiment as well, based on perceptions that big business earns excessive profits at the same time that it exerts power unfairly over competitors, consumers, and employees (cited in Smigel and Ross, 1970: 8). It is not only political radicals, imbued with the ideology of capitalist exploitation, who justify crime as a vindication of corporate immorality. In interviews with a sample of the adult population of Bloomington, Indiana, it was found that respondents showed less disapproval of theft from large businesses than from small ones. When asked why, the most frequent responses were simply that the larger businesses could better afford the losses and could make them up through increased prices and insurance. But 8 percent of the sample employed negative moral judgments—"they cheat you; they're ruthless"—as a reason for their greater acceptance of crime against larger enterprises (Smigel, 1970: 23).

VICTIMS' MORAL RESPONSIBILITY AND PUBLIC POLICY

The stereotypical victim of crime, as noted at the beginning of this chapter, is thought to be morally worthy because she or he has in no way contributed to being victimized. Such victims seem entitled to expressions of sympathy from their friends and the community at large, and often more. As governments have come to restrict individual retaliation for injuries suffered at the hands of others they have developed substitute mechanisms that are supposed to act formally against the offender on the victim's behalf. These mechanisms—the legal system—are said to serve at least two functions. They relieve individual victims of the uncertainties and costs of carrying out vengeance on their own behalf and they help to assuage the animosities that would persist if the victimized parties felt that their injuries had gone unpunished. The legislative process, the jury system, the authority of judges either elected directly by the people or appointed by elected officials—all of these have a responsibility to safeguard the rights of the criminal defendant, but even more, they should reflect the legal system's intention to do right for any member of the group who might be a victim. This concern was expressed as early as 1776, when Pennsylvania stipulated, in its first constitution, that prisons should be constructed in order that "criminals shall be employed for the benefit of the public, or for reparation of injuries done to private persons" (Sellin, 1973: 12). This protective function of the criminal law, then, is seen as a natural concomitant of a sympathetic view of the victim (Lamborn, 1981).

In practice, however, although criminal justice systems sometimes define innocent victims as good guys and exercise this protective function toward them, at other times these systems treat seemingly good victims as bad guys by ignoring their legitimate claims upon the state to act in their behalf. In the following sections we shall examine variations in the treatment of victims from cross-cultural and historical standpoints, and then consider some explanations for these variations.

Victim Compensation in Premodern Societies

In early times victims' rights were upheld through procedures rooted in custom. The blood feud, or vendetta, is thought to have arisen from a natural instinct for revenge. An injury to a member of one family group led to retaliation against another family whose member was held responsible for the injury. If a family in ancient Athens failed to obtain retribution or vengeance for a crime against one of its own, it was subject to disgrace (Schafer, 1968: 20).

Eventually, in order to reduce the danger that feuding kinship groups would decimate one another, substitutes for the vendetta were sought. Among Germanic tribes in the early Middle Ages there appeared the practice of "composition." Initially a sum of money, the amount determined by agreement of the parties, was paid by wrongdoers to victims or their families;subsequently the practice became a part of the tribal law ("Composition," 1968: 358). "Wergild" was an Anglo-Saxon legal term referring to "money payment made to a family group if a member of that family were killed or in some other way injured" (Jeffery, 1957: 655).

But it was not for long that reparation to victims and their families was the primary emphasis in Western society. When feudal monarchs began to consolidate their power in the later Middle Ages, they formulated the doctrine that they themselves were entitled to compensation from those who had disturbed "the king's peace." And so a dual system developed; wrongdoers might be ordered to pay both compensation to the particular injured party and also a fine to the king. This dual system corresponds to the present distinction between civil law, which regulates the rights and obligations of private parties toward each other, and criminal law, which mediates relations between private parties and the state. Eventually laws were promulgated establishing the primacy of the state to demand reparation from those who threatened it (Hobhouse, 1975; Laster, 1975;

Schafer, 1968), and in practice these payments to royal treasuries soon supplanted payments to individuals or families. Thus the golden age of the victim, to use Schafer's term, was short-lived, lasting from about 500–800 A.D. on the Continent, and from about 600–900 A.D. in England (Diamond, 1971: 57). It could not survive the more potent claims of the feudal kings, that it was their rights which were ultimately violated by the commission of acts that we now call crimes.

In many other "primitive" societies, independent of European influence, there prevailed systems of compensation to private individuals for injuries that are classified as crimes in modern legal codes. And according to outsiders' observations these systems often appeared to do an adequate job of maintaining social order without the necessity for defining and treating such delicts as public offenses. Native American tribes of the Pacific Northwest had well-established schedules for determining compensation to victims or their families. Insults regarded as damaging to the individual or kin group, as well as material injuries, were compensated by payments of shell necklaces and other artifacts whose established value enabled them to be used as money in routine economic transactions. Among the Yurok the penalty for killing a common man was ten strings of shells. For killing a man of high social standing, it was fifteen strings of shells, a woodpecker scalp headband, perhaps a spear head—and a daughter. The offense of uttering the name of a dead man of another family obliged the offender to pay that family two strings of shells. And, if a man seduced a young woman and pregnancy resulted, he was obliged to pay her family twenty woodpecker scalps or five shell necklaces (Redfield, 1967: 9; see also Hoebel, 1972: 52–55).

For another Northwest Coast tribe, the following curious incident has been reported :

In another typical instance, a Tsimshian village was shooting a cannon to honor their dead chief. In their usual enthusiasm for making a big show they overloaded the cannon. It exploded and killed a tribesman. They were much humiliated and "afraid of the slurring remarks of the other tribes," so they decided to kill somebody in a neighboring lineage with whom they were on bad terms because of an inadequate settlement of a previous killing. They managed to wound the first man they met, and then the next day they cheerfully paid damages for the assault, after which the assaulted village joined with the others in the burial of the chief whose resounding mourning rites had touched off the event (Garfield, in Hoebel, 1972: 314).

The Tsimshian incident illustrates the capacity of compensation to alleviate tensions between an injured party and its victimizer. In this case it seems to have resolved, not only the issue of the wound inflicted on a blameless man, but also the perceived inequity carrying over from the earlier homicide. By joining in the burial ceremony, the compensated village expresses its acceptance that it has been adequately repaid and is now prepared to resume normal relations with the aggressor village.

The European Tradition of Social Defense

The positivist, or Italian, school of criminology, although primarily thought of now as an approach to explaining criminal tendencies, was also an important source of ideas on victimization. Some threads of the positivist approach can be discerned in the work of Arnould Bonneville de Marsangy, a French jurist who began writing in the 1830s—about the time when Cesare Lombroso, positivist criminology's founder, was born. Bonneville is probably best known as the father of the *casiers judiciaires*, a record of criminal history compiled by having information about each sentence transmitted to the court clerk in the offender's birthplace, and therefore available upon inquiry to prosecutors in subsequent proceedings. The usefulness of such information was predicated on Bonneville's contention that punishment should be individualized, and that the criminal record is an important factor in the sentencing decision—a view that qualifies him as an important precursor of Lombroso and the Italian School.

Bonneville also foreshadowed the positivists in his concern for victims of crime, and in some ways surpassed them in this respect. He advocated that the criminal courts undertake to assure that offenders answer to the individuals upon whom they have inflicted personal injuries. The criminal courts, he said, ought to decide on the amount an offender should pay his victim, and enforce the payment just as it does a penalty owed to the state. And—far ahead of his time—Bonneville proposed in 1847 a victim-compensation plan to be financed with public funds (Normandeau, 1972).

The Holy Trinity of positivism—Lombroso, Garofalo, and Ferri—were also concerned with victimization, but they differed from Bonneville in their attention to the public as a whole as well as to individual victims. They saw, as the ultimate aim of identifying offenders who were criminal by nature, the need to isolate these unredeemable people for the protection of society. Thus the term "social defense" was adopted by the positivists to refer to their advocacy of long sentences—and for Garofalo and Lombroso, even capital punishment (Allen, 1972: 329; Wolfgang, 1972: 279)—to insure that law-abiding citizens as a group could feel more secure, knowing that the most dangerous criminals would be out of circulation for those years when they posed the greatest threat. Ferri explained that "historically, the principal reason for the rise of the positivistic view of criminal justice was the necessity . . . to put a stop to the exaggerated individualism in favour of the criminal in order to obtain a greater respect for the rights of people who constitute a great majority" (quoted in Taylor, Walton, and Young, 1974: 20). By advocating reparation for crime to both the state and individual victims (Newman, 1985: 219; Wolfgang, 1972: 279), the positivists sought to remedy when possible the imbalance of rights resulting from crime.

Support for the Victim in Modern Europe

To the extent that the proponents of social defense were concerned with the interests of individual victims, they carried on a Continental tradition emphasizing private law, that is, those laws which guard the rights of private persons in relation to one another. This emphasis stands in contrast with the emphasis in Anglo-American countries on public law, which is rooted in a tradition that the courts intercede in private disputes only when there is a threat to the king's peace (David and Brierley, 1968). Partly because of this emphasis in Continental law, countries like France and Sweden have for many years surpassed countries like the United States and England in providing compensation for crime victims through the legal process (Schafer, 1960).

Victim compensation in the Anglo-American system is unwieldy because the state takes priority in bringing criminal charges in situations where there is also infringement of individual rights. "State priority" means, for example, that when one person has intentionally inflicted bodily injury on another, the district attorney as prosecutor for the state tries the case first in criminal court before the injured individual has a chance to sue in civil court for damages he suffered in the same incident. The procedure is different on the Continent, where criminal and civil actions are merged in a single trial. There, each of the three parties—the state, the accused, and victims or their survivors—may be represented by its own lawyer (Hazard, 1977: 901). Formally the lawyer for the "civil plaintiff"—the victim—is concerned with collecting damages arising from the criminal incident. Under this system the victim's interest is strengthened, in contrast with the American system's emphasis on criminal defendants' rights. The Continental system recognizes situations in which the victim's interest, while of course usually opposed to that of the offender, may also be at variance with the public prosecutor. For example, a victim's lawyer might urge the court not to imprison a convicted criminal in order to enable him to continue to work and make restitution, whereas the prosecutor might urge that a prison term be imposed to protect the society as a whole from repetition of the offense.

PRESENT POLICY TOWARD VICTIMS IN THE UNITED STATES

In light of Americans' current concern about protecting themselves from crime, it seems surprising that people who are crime victims are not treated with the measure of sympathy from the general public that would seem to be their due. One would expect that institutions representing the public interest would identify that interest with crime victims, support them, and use what powers they have to restore them to the state they were in before they were victimized.

We have discussed previously those situations in which sympathy is lacking because the sufferer has been defined as a "bad" victim. But for other victims—those who appear innocent of any responsibility for their victimization—the reason for absence of sympathy is not immediately apparent. When it comes to public response, and especially to the response of the criminal justice system, these innocent victims become "forgotten victims."

The courts have ignored the interests of the victim while they have been busy protecting the interests of the defendant. Not only the courts but the entire criminal justice establishment, including legal scholars and criminologists, have largely ignored the victim. There is an enormous literature on the offender: his rights; the role he plays in the criminal process; his perceptions of that process; the influence which that process has and the damage that it can do to his life's prospects by labeling him a criminal; his racial, social, economic, marital, psychological, physical, and behavioral characteristics; and even the effects of his incarceration on his family. Not only is the literature vast but the expenditure of money and concern for the defendant has also been enormous. . . . In comparison, virtually nothing has been done on what happens to that other group of citizens touched by the criminal justice system, namely, the victims (McDonald, 1976: 19).

A similar sentiment was expressed in the platform of the Republican National Convention in 1984, in its accusation that "the Carter–Mondale legal policy had more concern for abstract criminal rights than for the victims of crime" (Committee on Resolutions to the Republican National Convention, 1984: 37).

Inattention to the rights of crime victims cannot, however, be explained simply on the basis of the political party in power. That inattention has a long history, independent of the party affiliation of the Chief Executive. Reiff has emphasized the point by contrasting the treatment of crime victims with the way in which victims of natural disasters have been treated over the years.

The federal government has given aid to victims of fire, flood, earthquakes, tornadoes, and even grasshopper ravages since 1827. . . . In 1975 the Federal Disaster Assistance Administration (FDAA), the government agency responsible for assisting disaster victims, provided $5.5 million through the Department of Labor to persons who were unemployed due to a natural disaster. There is no federal provision for financial assistance to persons unemployed due to a violent crime (Reiff, 1979: 7-9).

There have been a number of efforts to explain why it is that victims are not treated as sympathetically these days as circumstances would seem to warrant. One such effort associates the present lack of support for victims' rights with long-term social change, from collectivities based on personal intimacy to more formalistic social structures.

The golden age of the victim was a part of the *Gemeinschaft*-type social structure, where such relations were familistic, involuntary, primary, sacred, traditional, emotional, personal; but the lessening of the victim's role was a result of the development, to use Tonnies' terminology, of the contractual *Gesellschaft* system, characterized by social interaction that is voluntary, secular, secondary, rationalistic, impersonal (Schafer, 1968: 27).

Victim Invisibility

Rieff's analysis hinges on his contention that victims are "invisible" in the sense that the general public is unaware of their plight. One reason, he suggests, has to do with the fact that most victims are poor and inhabit areas that are not often visited by others, so that there is little opportunity for their suffering to come to the attention of the larger public. This contention is supported in the area of violent crime by studies of victim characteristics. In a comparison among labor force participants—between people who were employed, and those who were unemployed and looking for work—the victimization rates for the unemployed, both white and black, were more than twice as great as the rates for employed individuals (U. S. Bureau of Justice Statistics, 1985: 30).

Moreover, Reiff asserts, victims often consciously seek to make themselves invisible for understandable reasons. The fear of revictimization is exacerbated in many cases by threats from the offenders who were responsible for the original crime to return and do even more harm, so that in general people who have been victimized in the past might reasonably conclude that the best way to avoid further victimization is to make themselves as inconspicuous as possible. Reiff further blames the media, who tend to depict crime scenarios with the major parts played by the criminals as bad guys and the police as good guys, with victims relegated to the role of bit players.

One study has addressed this issue in a limited way, by analyzing newspaper reports of real criminal incidents. Mawby and Brown (1984) analyzed the content of 649 crime stories in British newspapers. Of the ninety-four stories that presented victims judgmentally, thirty-four presented them positively, and sixty in a negative light. But the vast majority presented victims in a nonjudgmental way. Needless to say, the emphasis may be different in the United States, in different media, and in fictional as opposed to real crime stories. But the lack of moral judgment found in Mawby and Brown's study may be taken as a kind of support for Reiff's view that the victim is not so much condemned as consigned to oblivion.

Purposeful Neglect of Victims' Interests

Another view holds that victims are not forgotten fortuitously, nor simply because other parties are more easily visible. This view, more political in tenor, sees the lack of concern for victims as a result of forces that might be threatened if there were more awareness, and consequently pressure, on behalf of victims.

The radical feminist view is one such approach. Its world view is that the subordinate status of women results from a long history of activities carried out by the dominant male group to perpetuate its hegemony. Job discrimination, manipulation of household budgets, the pornography industry, the way in which little girls are dressed and the kind of toys given to them—all of these are offered as examples of efforts by men to gratify their own needs at women's expense.

For many people who hold to this position, the prototypical act by which men express their power over women is the act of rape. Brownmiller (1975) and Clark and Lewis (1977) provide examples of male domination through forced intercourse in situations ranging from war and race dominance to incest and marital rape. These authors contend that the laws of rape were developed, not so much to safeguard the woman's right to refuse to engage in a sexual act, but primarily to protect the property rights of the father of a virgin, and of the husband of a married woman. Yet when it has come to protecting the interests most salient to women themselves, there is considerable evidence that the law has shortchanged them.

One need not be a radical feminist to recognize the extent to which the law of rape, in the Anglo-American tradition, has been primarily concerned with protecting men against unfounded accusations, and in this process has, wittingly or unwittingly, institutionalized certain preconceptions of the typical rape complainant as a bad woman. As we shall note shortly, the more progressive states have modified rape laws in recent years to redress some of the traditional neglect of women's rights, but others have clung to provisions that preserve the long-standing imbalance in favor of men. For the present let us consider some of those legal provisions still in force in many parts of the United States that have served to institutionalize special benefits for (male) rape defendants at the expense of (female) rape victims' interests.

Among legal mechanisms embodying assumptions about the bad character of rape victims, the most notorious has been the provision for inquiring into their sexual histories. This latitude is not allowed for other crimes. In most jurisdictions there are strict limitations on the extent to which evidence of a person's character may be presented to prove whether or not any particular criminal act occurred (Gager and Schurr, 1976: 154–

55). Such evidence may be introduced only in order to "impeach" a witness's credibility, in other words, to raise doubts as to whether the witness has testified truthfully under oath.

But defense lawyers in rape cases have traditionally been permitted to conduct a very broad inquiry into the victim's history of sexual conduct, and if it can be shown that she has had relations with a number of men, that evidence casts doubt upon the requirement that the act occurred without her consent. The so-called "chastity requirement" is expressed in the words of a nineteenth-century case, "And will you not more readily infer assent in the practiced Messalina, in loose attire, than in the reserved and virtuous Lucretia?" (quoted in Gager and Schurr, 1976: 152). A very powerful influence on the admissibility of such evidence was the opinion of John Henry Wigmore, longtime Dean of the Northwestern University Law School and author of the monumental *Treatise on Evidence*, first published in four volumes in 1904 and eventually encompassing ten volumes in the 1940 edition. "In prosecutions for sex offenses . . . Wigmore forcefully argued for the full admissibility of evidence concerning the rape complainant's character and evidence of her prior sexual conduct. . . . Dean Wigmore's attitude reflected a rudimentary fear of baseless criminal prosecution which required careful scrutiny of the credibility of the rape complainant" ("Rape shield paradox," 1987: 649).

And thirty years after Wigmore's death, in a summary of the kind of evidence permissible in rape cases in New York as of 1973, a legal textbook stated,

Thus, where a defendant is charged with forcible rape, the complainant's reputation for chastity is relevant to the issue as to whether the defendant ravished the complainant by force. Since non-consent is an essential element of the crime, the defendant is permitted to show that the complainant was a common prostitute or that her reputation for chastity was bad, upon the theory that it is more probable that an unchaste woman would have consented to intercourse than one of strict virtue (Prince, 1973: 125).

Moreover, when any criminal complainant takes the witness stand—virtually a prerequisite to obtaining a conviction in most rape cases—lawyers in New York have been permitted to inquire about

any immoral, vicious, or criminal act of his life which may affect his character and show him to be unworthy of belief. . . . A female witness may be interrogated as to her chastity, or a male witness questioned concerning his illicit relations with women. . . . As stated by [a New York court in a case decided in 1903], "it has been repeatedly held that men and women whose lives indicate an abandonment or lack of moral principles, and show them to be lewd and debased characters, void of shame or decency, have not usually a great respect for the truth or the sanctity of an oath" (Prince, 1973: 482–83).

Some of these rules of evidence are not peculiar to rape, but widespread suspicion that rape victims may have consented to the act has resulted in greater latitude to present evidence in support of that suspicion.

Moreover, research on decision making in rape cases suggests that typical jurors harbor similarly skeptical views, especially when information about the victim's sexual history is presented to them. In the first place, it has been shown that, although jurors have a marked tendency to prejudge the guilt of defendants charged with most crimes, that bias is far weaker when the defendants are men accused of rape. Of a sample of potential jurors surveyed in New York City, 80 percent believe that criminal defendants are guilty or else the state would not bring them to trial, but only 40 percent apply that belief to rape defendants (Ellison, cited in Randall and Rose, 1984: 62). And in the second place, a number of studies have shown that, when jurors have information about a rape victim's sexual history indicating some blemish on her moral character, they find the defendants less responsible than when no such information is available to them (Borgida and White, 1978; Jones and Aronson, 1973; LaFree, Reskin, and Visher, 1985; L'Armand and Pepitone, 1982).

The effect of sexual history evidence on the outcome of an actual trial for rape may be illustrated in a 1970 case in San Francisco. The complainant, a twenty-three-year-old divorcee, alleged that she was forced into a car at gunpoint by four men, taken to the apartment of one of the men, raped by all of them, and set free in the morning with the threat that she would be killed if she reported the incident. The man in whose apartment the alleged incident occurred was brought to trial. His lawyer, on cross-examining the complainant, tried without success to get her to admit to various sexual indiscretions but succeeded only in establishing that she had worked once or twice as a cocktail waitress, was having a relationship with a man who was separated from his wife, and had two children in foster care. Apparently the jury found sufficient basis in the proceedings to disbelieve her testimony, for the defendant was acquitted of both charges—rape and kidnapping—that had been lodged against him (Griffin, 1984: 118–19).

As a result of the enactment of "rape shield" laws in recent years, most states do not now automatically allow defense attorneys unlimited latitude to question rape victims about their sexual history. It is ordinarily necessary that the lawyer for the accused rapist, in order to be able to ask such questions, show that such evidence is "relevant" to the issue of whether the victim in fact consented to the act of intercourse. However, the difficulty of demonstrating such relevance to the satisfaction of most judges seems not to be very great (Bienen, 1980; "Rape shield paradox," 1987). Probably the new laws have limited the amount of the rape victim's sexual history available to the jury. But in light of what we have observed about jurors' preconceptions, it seems likely that even more limited sexual history evidence would provide them with confirmation for those preconceptions about the bad character of rape victims.

Related to the issue of the complainant's sexual history as evidence of consent is the issue of her resistance. If the circumstances of a rape case make it difficult for the defense to show the victim's bad character through information about her life history, the possibility of her consent may be further suggested by questioning whether she resisted the assault with sufficient determination. "Rape is most assuredly not the only crime in which consent is a defense, but it is the only crime that has required the victim to resist physically in order to establish nonconsent" (Estrich, 1986: 1090). In the past many jurisdictions have been guided by the language of a Wisconsin court, which in 1906 reversed a rape conviction because of what it considered the victim's insufficient efforts to resist: "Not only must there be entire absence of mental consent or assent, but there must be the most vehement exercise of every physical means or faculty within the woman's power to resist the penetration of her person, and this must be shown to persist until the offense is consummated" (quoted in Estrich, 1986: 1123). In this view, anything less than "utmost resistance" casts doubt upon the impeccability of the woman's character that is necessary to make her a credible complainant in a rape prosecution. More recently "earnest" or "reasonable" resistance has come to replace "utmost resistance" as the legal standard, but the problem of how much is enough remains. We might note parenthetically that the resistance requirement not only places a great legal burden on rape complainants but may also be responsible for consequences more damaging than rape itself. One woman was able to forestall the completion of a rape attempt by fighting back, but in the process she sustained injuries requiring 120 stitches on her face. An investigating detective said, "She's scarred for life. And you know what she says now? She says she wishes she hadn't fought, and maybe he wouldn't have cut her up the horrible way he did" (Robin, 1977: 145).

Another legal stumbling block, from the point of view of the rape complainant, has been the presence in the law of special rules for corroboration—requirements that victims' testimony be supported by independent evidence of the facts. In New York State, for example, for many years a man could not be convicted of rape unless there was medical evidence, testimony by an eyewitness to the act, or other proof that there was an act of sexual penetration, that there was force or a lack of consent, and that it was the accused who had committed the act (Gager and Schurr, 1977: 143; Davidson, Ginsburg, and Kay, 1974: 916). New York's corroboration requirements were modified in 1974 as a result of pressure from feminists and other civil rights groups, and other states have made changes in this area as well, but similar requirements still exist in some states (Siegel, 1989: 257). The implication of these unusual requirements for rape prosecution, as of other such requirements, is that women who make rape complaints are especially likely to be of questionable moral character, and so it is especially important not to accept their testimony alone even if it is otherwise convincing. Even in the jurisdictions that have repealed special legal requirements for corroboration of rape, it might be added, prosecutors generally make every effort to present such testimony in order to overcome jurors' bias against rape complainants.

Still another special feature of rape as a crime—the marital exemption—may also be understood to reflect suspicion, if not confirmed belief, of the complainant's lack of virtue. Marital exemption refers to traditional definitions of rape that exclude any sexual intercourse, no matter how forcible, between husband and wife. It is not necessary for our purposes to consider all the rationales for the marital exemption that have been proposed. We should note only that, when women accuse their husbands of forcing sex upon them, they have often been viewed, by men at least, at best of unjustly reneging on a contractual obligation, and at worst of making an unfounded accusation for some nefarious purpose of their own. The male bias is evident in Sir Matthew Hale's famous statement about rape, made more than 300 years ago, that rape is "an accusation easily to be made and hard to be proved, and harder to be defended by the party accused, tho never so innocent" (Estrich, 1986: 1094–95).

Although we have been focusing on "bad" victims of rape, it is not accurate to say that any woman who claims to be a rape victim is looked upon with suspicion, even by the most cynical or prudish observers.

Estrich uses the term "traditional rape" to refer to those cases in which there is no question that the act occurred without the victim's consent. "A stranger puts a gun to the head of his victim, threatens to kill her or beats her, and then engages in intercourse. In that case the law—judges, statutes, prosecutors, and all—agree that a serious crime has been committed." All sympathy is with victims under these circumstances.

But most cases deviate in one or many respects from this clear picture, making interpretation far more complex. Where less force is used or no other physical injury is inflicted, where threats are inarticulate, where the two know each other, where the setting is not an alley but a bedroom, where the initial contact was not a kidnapping but a date, where the woman says no but does not fight, the understanding is different. In such cases the law, as reflected in the opinions of the courts, the interpretation, if not the words, of the statutes, and the decisions of those within the criminal justice system, often tell us that no crime has taken place and that fault, if any is to be recognized, belongs with the woman (Estrich, 1986: 1092).

Estrich's term for the latter scenarios, "non-traditional rape," encompasses "victim-precipitated rape" and "open territory rape," as discussed previously—all designating particular situations in which the victim's moral character becomes the basis for mitigating concern in the criminal justice system.

Similarly, certain cases viewed as "simple rape" have been found to sway juries to acquit defendants in circumstances where there is no real legal defense. In an extensive study of actual jury behavior, researchers differentiated between "aggravated rape"—cases in which there was evidence of extrinsic violence, several assailants were involved, or the defendant and victim were total strangers at the time of the event—and cases of "simple rape"—those in which none of those circumstances applied. Of the sixty-four cases classified as aggravated rape, the juries convicted in forty-six, or 72 percent, whereas the juries found defendants guilty in only twelve, or 29 percent, of the forty-two cases classified as simple rape.

Moreover, among the twelve juries that convicted in the simple rape category, only three actually found the defendants guilty of rape; the others rejected the rape charge and voted to convict the defendants on lesser counts. The authors of the study explain these findings on the basis of what they believe to be jurors' tendencies to believe in "assumption of risk": the idea that defendants should not be liable for the full punishment of the criminal law if their victims did something—like going to a sleazy bar, or accepting a ride from a stranger—to jeopardize their safety. "The jury's stance is not so much that involuntary intercourse under these circumstances in no crime at all, but that it does not have the gravity of rape" (Kalven and Zeisel, 1971: 250).

Underlying the legal process are attitudes of people whose words and actions have a significant influence on that process. In cases of rape, police officers who investigate complaints decide at the outset whether to use all available resources to help the victim, apprehend the perpetrator, and gather evidence that would support a conviction; to follow established procedures but make no special effort; or to discourage the complainant from pursuing the matter. They also write reports and may later testify in court. For doctors and other medical personnel who deal with rape victims shortly after the event, their comments can also affect the victim's decision about taking action and their reports and testimony have a direct effect on the outcome of the legal process. Similarly, the preconceptions of prosecutors, defense lawyers, judges and other court personnel, and jurors— although formally obligated to adhere to objective legal guidelines—also inevitably affect the way in which the matter is ultimately resolved.

Often the preconception is indicated simply by an unsympathetic or derogatory attitude. A judge who presided in one rape case was later censured for having referred to the victim in open court "in an insulting and inexcusable manner" (Griffin, 1979: 79). On another occasion a doctor, about to examine a woman just arrived in a hospital emergency room after being raped, said to her, "Okay, honey, jump up on the table and let's see what this big bad man did to you" (Keefe and O'Reilly, 1976: 394). In still another incident a woman, following a day at the beach, accepted a stranger's offer to take her to a train station. She was wearing shorts and a halter top over her bathing suit. Instead of dropping her off for her train, the stranger drove to an isolated area, forced her to commit oral sodomy and raped her brutally. While being interviewed by one detective following the incident, she was approached by another detective who said, "No wonder you got raped. What do you expect, walking around with your breasts hanging out like that?" (Keefe and O'Reilly, 1976: 393).

To an extent, the attitudes reflected in these examples are simply a counterpart at the level of the informal system of attitudes that were embodied in the traditional formal rules for legal proceedings in rape. But for many participants in the criminal justice system they are also attitudes that persist even when the formal rules have been changed to restrict the admissibility of evidence supporting stereotypes of rape victims as bad women. To the extent that such attitudes persist, the possibility remains that they may subvert the intention of changes in the formal system.

Having devoted considerable attention to rape victims as bad women, we should remind ourselves that this stereotype was introduced as prototypical of a negative victim stereotype whose prevalence might be explained as a result of a conscious effort by a more powerful group—men—to advance their own interests at the expense of a subordinate group—women. Although the laws and informal stereotypes discussed previously are in fact predominantly male products, we have not demonstrated—nor would it be possible to demonstrate—that they resulted from a *conscious* male conspiracy. It seems undeniable that men have occupied positions enabling them to exert such influence, but whether the result has been intentional is more open to question. Indeed, Kalven and Zeisel explained jurors' leniency toward victims of crimes other than rape in terms of "collateral immorality" (1971: 248); they cite defendants who were either acquitted, or found guilty of charges less severe than the evidence apparently supported, in cases of larceny, homicide, and domestic violence because "the victim is . . . stained by some general immorality which has left him vulnerable to the crime" (1971: 247). In some of their cases the victims were male and the leniently treated defendants were female. Such cases serve as exceptions to any possible generalization about preference for male interests in the criminal justice system, but they provide further illustration for our general thesis about the impact of negative victim stereotypes in the criminal justice system.

Psychological Theories

Still another way of explaining the neglect of victims' plight in our legal system is by suggesting that the system is affected by the psychology of those people who are involved in it: lawmakers, law enforcement personnel, and members of the public who have an interest in the system and who act—or fail to act—upon that interest. This explanation emphasizes denial mechanisms as ways of handling the fear of being victimized, particularly denial of the fact that victimization is often unpredictable and therefore unavoidable. As one relative of a murder victim wrote, "[My brother's] murder had proved that crime might touch anyone. If my brother was not somehow to blame for his death, then no one was safe" (Barkas, 1978: xi).

One form of psychological denial consists of maintaining a belief, in the face of evidence to the contrary, that we live in a just world. A considerable body of research in support of the "just world" theory helps to explain public lack of sympathy for victims. According to this theory,

people need to believe that there is justice in the world—not only in a legal sense but in a more basic sense. Good things happen to good people and bad things happen to those who deserve it, including, among the latter, people who are unwilling to avoid suffering or who are in some way blameworthy. This need to believe in a just world influences the perceptions that people have of victims. If an "innocent" victim is suffering, and an observer cannot do anything to alleviate the suffering, then the observer will make himself more comfortable by deciding that the victim is not innocent after all. In this way the observer is able to maintain his view that justice prevails in the world; he simply condemns the victim as undesirable. bad, or deserving his fate (McDonald, 1976: 41).

A fuller treatment of psychological mechanisms will be presented in Chapter 6. There we shall discuss polarization processes that in the most usual cases juxtapose an image of the bad offender with that of the good victim, but in others couple the good offender's image with that of the bad victim.

REHABILITATING THE VICTIM

Notwithstanding the persistence of some attitudes and practices that are unresponsive to the welfare of crime victims, the past twenty years or so have also seen activity directed toward the moral rehabilitation of the victim—a process with social, intellectual, political, economic, and legal components.

A very significant spark for this rehabilitation was fortuitous. In the years before President Lyndon Johnson commissioned an extensive study of American crime in the 1960s, criminologists had been expressing considerable dissatisfaction with what was then the best available source of crime statistics for the United States, the Uniform Crime Reports. These reports, based on data gathered from police agencies by a special division of the Federal Bureau of Investigation, provided information about the frequency and distribution of serious criminal offenses, known as index crimes, which had come to the attention of law-enforcement authorities, as well as information about arrests for these offenses. The offenses included in the reports were murder and non-negligent manslaughter, aggravated assault, robbery, forcible rape, burglary, larceny of fifty dollars or more, and auto theft.

For a number of reasons criminologists suspected that there were substantial distortions in these reports. It was thought that many people simply failed to inform the authorities about offenses that they knew had occurred, and that additional offenses reported to the police were lost in the process between initial report and tabulation by the FBI. Significant strides had been made to standardize reporting procedures for these statistics since their initial publication in the 1930s, but concern about persistent shortcomings stimulated recommendations that police agencies be bypassed and that a nationwide sample survey be carried out on criminal victimization.

Thus, when funds became available in connection with the study by Johnson's Presidential Commission on Law Enforcement and the Administration of Justice, interviews were conducted in 10,000 representative households in the United States to determine whether any members of those households had been victims of crimes during the previous year, and if so, what the circumstances and effects of the offense had been. These data were then extrapolated to the total population so that an estimate of occurrences from the victim survey could be compared with the Uniform Crime Reports. Overall, more than twice the rate of index crimes was uncovered by the interview procedure as compared with that derived from police sources. The discrepancy was interpreted for the most part as indicating shortcomings of official statistics, as compared with the standard established by the victim survey. Those offenses estimated on the basis of the survey, in excess of those documented in the Uniform Crime Reports, were regarded as "hidden crime." According to this measure, the proportion of hidden offenses was about one third for robberies, one half for aggravated assault, two thirds for burglary, and nearly three fourths for forcible rape.

The victim survey technique was considered so great an improvement over previous procedures that it was expanded and has become a routine annual operation of the Department of Justice since that time (U. S. Bureau of Justice Statistics. annual). But beyond its value as a truer indicator of actual offenses throughout the nation, it provided data on the characteristics and behavior of crime victims. The availability of these data, in turn, stimulated interest within the academic community, leading to further research and interpretation of crime from the perspective of the victim.

A climate of opinion favoring concern for crime victims was fostered by several additional forces. At the intellectual level, the issues have been addressed in a series of International Symposia on Victimology, which have been held triennially since 1973 in different countries, with United Nations sponsorship and participation by prominent government officials and university researchers. An academic periodical, titled *Victimology; An International Journal*, has been published in the United States since 1976. And the study of victimology has been increasingly encouraged by research grants from federal agencies and private foundations in the United States and elsewhere.

Another force stimulating attention to crime victims was the Civil Rights movement of the 1960s. As concerns were heightened for the rights of racial and ethnic minorities, of women, of gays and lesbians, of people with mental and physical disabilities, it is not surprising that the notion of crime victims' rights would be advanced.

Within that context, probably the most important force was of a reactive character. The U.S. Supreme Court presided over by Chief Justice Earl Warren handed down a number of decisions during the 1960s reflecting unprecedented concern for the rights of criminal defendants. The *Gideon* decision guaranteed legal representation for indigent defendants in state courts. The *Miranda* and *Escobedo* decisions disallowed the use of coerced confessions in criminal trials, and the *Mapp* case disallowed the use of evidence obtained through an illegal search. The *Witherspoon* decision prevented trial in capital cases by a jury biased in favor of the death penalty. How can this concern for the bad guys be justified, asked the proponents of a law-and-order approach to crime, especially when so little attention has been paid to innocent victims?

As an outgrowth of such sentiments, there developed a number of initiatives on behalf of victims' rights. An early manifestation was the observation by gubernatorial proclamation in California of the week of April 25 through 29, 1977, as "Forgotten Victims Week." Under the sponsorship of that state's District Attorneys Association, symposia were organized to promote awareness that "the victims of violent crime have long been 'forgotten persons' in our society" (Bradley, n.d.: 1). Among many letters of support for the commemorative week was one from the United States Attorney General Griffin Bell, on behalf of President Jimmy Carter. Also, Senators Alan Cranston and S. I. Hayakawa marked the occasion by speaking on the subject to their colleagues in Washington.

Subsequently, "victims' rights weeks" have been observed at the national level (Reid, 1985: 354). In recent years the momentum of the victims' rights movement seems to be increasing; in 1990, there were several hundred meetings held throughout the country during the week from April 22 to April 28, aimed at increasing public concern and mobilizing that concern toward a number of concrete efforts ("Victims' rights are supported," 1990).

One manifestation of this concern has been the establishment of social service centers for victims, providing them with counseling and assistance with the various problems—medical, legal, economic, and so forth—connected with their victimization. As an indication of societal investment in such services, we may note that the Victims Services Agency in New York City in 1989 had 500 employees and an operating budget of 17 million dollars: small in relation to total budget for criminal justice operations, but a substantial commitment nonetheless to services that were nonexistent a decade earlier (Lorch, 1989). In many communities these centers are affiliated with public prosecutors' offices and serve to expedite the availability of victims to identify suspects and testify against them if the suspects are brought to trial (Karmen, 1990; Schneider and Schneider, 1981).

Beyond these facilities for serving victims' short-term needs, the victims' rights movement has provided the impetus for legislation to formalize the process of representing victims' interests. One result is the enactment over the past decade of "right of allocution" statutes in thirty states. These laws require that victims be given the opportunity to be heard at sentencing and parole hearings for cases in which they have been involved, although studies have shown that only a small proportion of victims take advantage of these opportunities (Wiehl, 1989).

Some states have provided a role for victims in ways that may considerably alter traditional adversary relationships in criminal procedure. In Alabama victims are permitted to sit at the prosecution table during trials, suggesting that the prosecutor represents the victim as well as the state as plaintiff in criminal proceedings. Victims may also be involved in plea bargaining in one way or another; when defendants arrange with prosecutors to plead guilty to a lesser charge for some consideration, thirteen states require that the victim be consulted in the process, and three others require that the victims be informed but not consulted (Johnson, 1988).

In other cases victims' interests may be advanced with only minor alteration of the existing legal structure. When a defendant has been convicted or pleaded guilty to a criminal charge, it has been usual practice for a probation officer assigned to the court to conduct a pre-sentence investigation. This investigation involves an assessment of the offender's educational and social background, family situation, work history, psychological strengths and weaknesses, and criminal record. Such information must be excluded from consideration for purposes of determining guilt or innocence, but it is relevant for the probation officer's recommendation to the judge as to the appropriate disposition—whether fine, probation, community service, or prison, and the amount or duration of the penalty. In recent years it has become a widespread practice to include as part of the pre-sentence report a "victim impact statement," in which the victim can indicate the value of the property lost, physical or emotional injury, medical expenses, time and money lost from work, and the like.

Recently there has emerged from victims' supporters a proposal for a Victim's Bill of Rights—more comprehensive than the particular legislative acts just discussed—as a necessary counterforce to present safeguards of criminal defendants' rights in the Fourth, Fifth, Sixth, and Eighth Amendments to the federal Constitution. In fact a legislative package designed for precisely that purpose, known as Proposition 8, was passed in California in 1982. It provides for limitations on plea bargaining, the insanity defense, and the exclusionary rule, and in other ways seeks to promote measures thought to redress the undeserved emphasis on criminal defendants rights that are thought still to prevail in the criminal justice system (Karmen, 1990; Reid, 1985: 357).

Perhaps the most radical innovation, in terms of the philosophy of victims' rights, has been legislation providing monetary compensation by the state to certain crime victims. California initiated such a program in 1965, and New York followed in 1966. Five states altogether had victim compensation programs by 1970, another twenty-three by 1980, and sixteen more by 1988. The New York program, as an example, received 196 claims during its first year of operation. In 1976 more than four thousand claims were submitted, of which 1,510 were approved for reimbursements of more than 42 million dollars. By 1988 more than 25,000 claims were received, and the Crime Victims Board was operating with an annual budget of 421 million, covering support for seventy-two victim services agencies as well as compensation claims (Karmen, 1990; "More help," 1989; Verhouek, 1990).

Generally the programs compensate victims of violent rather than property crimes. Reimbursements are limited to out-of-pocket expenses, like lost wages and medical expenses, but they do not compensate victims for pain and suffering, as might be done through suits against private parties in civil court. Nor do they provide for "double recovery"; payments from insurance policies, other government agencies, or restitution from offenders are deducted from the amount victims are eligible to receive.

Beyond these common features, provisions vary from state to state. Some programs are supported by state taxes, others by penalties imposed on convicted offenders by the state courts, a few by both taxes and penalties, and these revenues have been supplemented since 1984 by the federal government, which at the same time established a victim compensation program of its own for violators of federal criminal statutes. A dozen states provide compensation only for victims who can demonstrate financial hardship resulting from the crime. In New York and Maryland there is no statutory limit to the dollar amount of compensation, while South Carolina has a cap of $3,000, but the range in most states is between 10 and 25 thousand dollars. These differences are to some extent a reflection of differences in ability to pay among states but they also indicate varying ideologies concerning the moral posture and responsibility of victims and the scope of the state's role as a guarantor of public safety, played out within the political arena.[2]

A final feature of victim compensation programs merits our attention, as an indicator of the moral component in their underlying philosophy. When a case comes before a victim compensation board, the board verifies not only the occurrence of the violent act, the applicant's actual injury, the costs incurred, and the absence of reimbursement from other sources. It also considers "evidence of victim facilitation, precipitation, or provocation, or any other signs of contributory misconduct. If it is established that the victim in some manner and in some degree was to blame for the commission of the crime, the grant can be reduced in size or disallowed entirely" (Karmen, 1990: 312). These restrictions embody the distinction similar to that made within the legal system, where good victims can expect vigorous prosecution and bad victims find their interests ignored. The emphasis in victim compensation boards may be different, but they too act sympathetically only toward those who suffer in all innocence.

Further, it has recently been suggested that at least one board has acted to *overextend* the stereotype of the bad victim in just the way that the criminal justice system does. A panel convened to study the New York Crime Victims Board reported that the Board often exceeded the statutory ban on compensating victims who are criminally responsible for the crime. The panel noted numerous cases in which claims were denied because the person was found to be " 'not an innocent victim' or had a 'life style' that may have contributed to the injury" (Verhouek, 1990: B3). Claims by applicants who were described as drug dealers or prostitutes, or who had prior criminal records, were routinely disallowed, notwithstanding lack of evidence of their participation in the particular events on which their claims were based.

The impact of efforts to "rehabilitate" victims of crime over the past two decades has been unmistakable, as shown in support for forgotten victims' ceremonies, in changed rules for criminal prosecution, in the establishment of extensive social services for victims, and in provisions for compensating crime victims with public funds. Nevertheless, the way in which victim compensation has been administered suggests a continuing polarity between good and bad victims that may also be found in other types of programs designed to serve victims' interests. Indeed, there is no assurance that the process of victim rehabilitation itself will not be aborted, or even reversed, whether influenced by results of scientific research, political strategy, or anything else affecting that volatile phenomenon known as public opinion. If that happens—if there is a reversion in the direction of viewing victims as worse guys—we should expect a corresponding tendency to view offenders as better guys. For these stereotypes are not unrelated. To repeat a central theme of this work: there is a connection between perceiving one party in a criminal encounter as good and the other as bad. In the next chapter we shall focus on explaining how this process of moral polarization comes about, and how it serves to distort the reality of crime.

NOTES

1. Advertisements for burglar alarms capitalize on the perception that stinting when it comes to protection against criminal victimization is a moral failing, for example, "Don't look for bargains when it comes to safeguarding your family and your precious possessions."
2. Fuller data on various victim compensation programs and an extensive discussion of the issues are presented in Karman, 1990.

6

Processes of Polarization

For purposes of clarity, we have in previous chapters separated our discussion of bad-guy images of offenders and victims from good-guy images of them. But we have also suggested that people who condemn criminals from a moral standpoint are likely to regard victims as morally worthy, whereas those who sympathize with criminals tend to blame their victims. Most commonly, the offender is perceived as the "bad guy" and the victim as the "good guy": for example, the heartless con man and the naive widow who signs over to him her life savings. Less common but still familiar is the bad victim–good offender duo. When Robin Hood poaches deer from the landlord's estate, no legal justification is put forth. Yet he is considered praiseworthy because he distributes meat from the illegally slaughtered animals to the downtrodden peasants, and the wealthy landowner, resented for his exploitation of the poor, is considered blameworthy.

In other situations offenders and victims are both regarded as bad people, so that when rival drug dealers maim or kill one another, little public sympathy is aroused. And in still other cases both victim and offender are seen as blameless. Parents who work hard but are still unable to provide basic necessities for their children, and who therefore steal from other people no better off than themselves, may be looked upon as sympathetically as are their victims.

Nevertheless, from the point of view of public images, both bad offender–bad victim and good offender–good victim combinations are unsatisfactory. In the case of warring drug dealers there is fear that a pattern of outlaw violence will eventually result in harm to innocent parties, who are then seen as good guys in a larger context. In the case of the needy thief, there is a tendency to look beyond the immediately affected parties and find someone else to hold responsible. When responsibility cannot be imputed to either the victim or the offender, the tendency is to go beyond the immediate actors on the crime scene and blame certain powerful people, or groups, or institutions, for having created the need or for permitting it to persist. Thus, when no bad-guy–good-guy dichotomy is apparent at the outset, public opinion makes an effort to supply the missing agent.

Another thread in our previous discussion has to do with a propensity to magnify reality—to exaggerate the bad qualities of the offender and the good qualities of the victim. Stereotypes of the principals in the fatal shooting of President James Garfield are a case in point. More than 300 editorials, sermons, and speeches that were written or delivered at the time of Garfield's death presented the president as a paragon of virtue, and his assassin as the epitome of evil (Rosenberg, 1968: x–xiii).

We have used the term *polarization* to refer to the tendency to locate participants in criminal events on opposite and extreme sides of a moral continuum. Broadly speaking, the term refers to any phenomenon in which elements are concentrated at the far ends of some dimension with few or none in the middle. Having previously introduced the concept of polarization in a preliminary way and having illustrated its relevance to perceptions of crime, we focus this chapter on the dynamics of polarization processes at two levels, the psychological and the social. At the psychological level our analysis is based on the work of scholars, both clinical observations and controlled research, which has shed light on tendencies in human personality to adopt polarized attitudes toward social objects in general. This leads us to consider the working of psychological polarization in moral judgments of crime. Similarly we consider polarization processes at the social level, starting with explanations of group polarization—in terms of collective action in general—and then show its application to the workings of the criminal justice system.

PSYCHOLOGICAL POLARIZATION

Psychological polarization in fact encompasses a number of related concepts: attitude, prejudice, stereotype, and perception. Attitudes have been defined as "responses that locate 'objects of thought' on 'dimensions of judgment' " (McGuire, 1985: 239). Those dimensions may involve esthetics, morals, or physical satisfactions. Some attitudes are absorbed through exposure to mainstream norms of one's society, others are adopted by selective contact with social groups whose norms are not part of a society-wide consensus, still others are internalized through identification with particularly esteemed individuals with whom one has come in contact.

Essentially, attitude judgments are positive or negative evaluations—that is, favorable or unfavorable sentiments about the "objects of thought," or targets of the attitude. The target may be anything that evokes positive or negative feelings—a racial group, a political candidate, a type of food, a style of music. Attitudes are not observable acts. They are, rather, *dispositions* to accept or reject something. In commonsense language, an attitude is a state of mind. Thus, if some people have a favorable attitude toward a freeze on production of nuclear weapons, it does not necessarily mean that they have taken part in demonstrations against them nor even that they have ever talked about their views on the subject with anyone else. But it does mean that when the occasion arises to vote for a political candidate who espouses such a position, or to contribute to nuclear freeze organizations, such people would be inclined to do so.

Attitudes are important because if properly formulated they direct us toward choices that are beneficial, but if improperly formulated they lead to trouble. Some attitudes are based on extensive experiences with the objects toward which they are directed and crystallized only after reasoned consideration of many factors. Such attitudes are thought to be adaptive by serving as guides for choosing the best toothpaste or laundry detergent, house or car, job or religious affiliation, lover or spouse. Other attitudes are based on no direct experience at all but only on the influence of others who may have just as little basis for judgment. When attitudes are insufficiently founded in experience, we speak of them as prejudgments, or *prejudice*, and they are generally held to result in dissatisfaction for the attitude holder and/or unfair treatment for the object of the attitude.

Fundamental to the distinction between adaptive and prejudiced attitudes is the presence or absence of rational processes.

The norm of rationality is basic for [certain well-known] definitions of prejudice. . . . This norm enjoins a persistent attempt to secure accurate information, to correct misinformation, to make appropriate differentiations and qualifications, to be logical in deduction and cautious in inference.. Prejudice in the sense of deviation from the norm of rationality may occur in the form of hasty judgment or prejudgment, overgeneralization, thinking in stereotypes, refusal to modify an opinion in the face of new evidence, and refusal to admit or take account of individual differences (Harding et al., 1969: 5).

Corresponding to the relationship between attitude and prejudice is the relationship between cognitive structure and stereotype. "Cognitive structures are organizations of conceptually related representations of objects, situations, events, and of sequences of events and actions" (Markus and Zajonc, 1985: 143). "Representation," as used in this definition, is a general term including any sensory, verbal, physical, or other reaction within the organism to some external object. Since reactions to an object may occur on several levels, however, the term "cognitive structure" is used to refer to combinations of reactions and the interrelationship among them.

Like attitudes, cognitive structures serve a useful function.

Cognitive structures simplify when there is too much, and thus they allow the perceiver to reduce an enormously complex environment to a manageable number of meaningful categories. They fill in where there is too little and allow the perceiver to go beyond the information given. These structures help the perceiver achieve some coherence in the environment and in the most general sense provide for the construction of social reality. They are built up in the process of information processing and they function as interpretive frameworks (Markus and Zajonc, 1985: 143).

One type of cognitive structure is the stereotype. But instead of excluding useless information and concentrating on that which helps perceivers to cope rationally with their environment, stereotypes like prejudices are not rationally founded. They are "prepackaged appraisals" (McCall and Simmons, 1978) based on attributes like gender or ethnicity—attributes that indicate little about the qualities that are important in judging a person's suitability for most social positions. Thus, a businessman who does not use a Chinese accountant simply because he feels Asians are untrustworthy may be depriving himself of a valuable service at the same time that he denies the accountant the opportunity to earn a fee for her services.

It is obvious that stereotypes and prejudices are closely related. The concept of stereotype emphasizes cognitive processes. But by calling attention to the effect of the stereotyper's biases, it encompasses evaluation processes, which are basic to the concept of prejudice, as well. Indeed, there is a reciprocal relationship between prejudicial attitudes and stereotyped perceptions. Prior prejudices lead to stereotyped cognitions, and stereotypes shared by group members foster prejudice toward individuals.

Having now identified the principal distinguishing features of prejudices and stereotypes, we now turn to the problem of explaining how they come about. Given the apparent advantages of rational attitudes and cognitive structures, why do people nevertheless allow their views of others to be governed by inadequately tested or irrelevant considerations?

Scholarly attention to these problems has been primarily a product of concern with religious and racial discrimination as manifestations of prejudices and stereotypes, but the resulting insights are applicable to other social policy concerns as well. An outstanding example is the work on the *authoritarian personality* (Adorno et al., 1950), sponsored by the American Jewish Committee around the time of World War II. The culmination of efforts, begun by scholars in the early years of the war in Europe, to try to account for for Hitler's appeal to the German people in terms of Freudian psychology, it undertook an examination of psychodynamic factors prevalent among people who showed anti-semitic attitudes as well as prejudice toward other minorities. Such people were classified by an attitude questionnaire as high on "ethnocentric ideology," as indicated by a scale measuring acceptance or rejection of minority outgroups such as Jews and Negroes.

In intensive clinical interviews comparing subjects who scored high on ethnocentrism with those who did not, it was found that the high scorers were preoccupied with "totalitarian-moralistic" typologizing (Adorno et al., 1950: 443). The high-scoring subjects tended to divide people into those with altogether good qualities and those whose qualities are altogether bad, little recognizing that others (and they themselves as well) are driven by a combination of drives, some of which are selfish and socially condemned, others altruistic and applauded by society. Authoritarians tend to deny that they themselves have any faults. They see themselves as good and rationalize any bad behavior on their part as an aberration. Moreover, they tend to see themselves as victimized: They regard other people in general with distrust and suspicion. In their view the world is a jungle in which other people will destroy you if you do not destroy them first (Adorno et al., 1950: 411). These dynamics, as we shall see, are important for understanding how public attitudes toward crime become polarized.

The authoritarian personality studies were wide-ranging, covering many aspects of the prejudiced personality. An important elaboration, which has explained a perceptual style that transcends outgroup prejudice, has been Rokeach's work on dogmatism. As the term is used by Rokeach, dogmatic thinking refers to "a total cognitive configuration of ideas and beliefs organized into a relatively closed system" (Rokeach, 1960: 183).

Rokeach and his coworkers devoted some attention to institutional factors in dogmatism, for example, how affiliation with the Catholic church or the Communist party is related to closed-mindedness. But their primary focus is on dogmatism as a personality variable. They have shown, for example, that closed-minded subjects—those who score high on their Dogmatism scale—are more likely to give future-oriented responses on the projective Thematic Apperception Test (TAT), while open-minded subjects are more likely to give present-oriented responses. In the qualitative analysis of the content of TAT stories, most subjects in both closed-minded and open-minded groups were found to give rather bland stories, but the stories that did depict threatening situations were all produced by closed-minded subjects. One of these responses reflects a classic good-guys–bad-guys interpretation:

Two men. They look very sinister. The older one is a corrupt city boss, and he's instructing the younger man to go out and take care of an old lady who's got the goods on him. The young man is holding out for some more money. He goes finally to the old lady's house but she's not there. She's left for the State Capitol to tell the authorities about the boss. She'll get there and tell her story, only to discover that the state officials are on the city boss's side (Rokeach, 1960: 372).

Rokeach regards dogmatism as a style of thought that resists information incompatible with one's previous orientation. This concept is an important ingredient in our analysis of polarization. If we wish to understand how it is that polarized attitudes come about, it is reasonable to suppose that people who hold extreme positions will have some kind of psychic mechanism for disregarding or counteracting opposing information that might come their way. At the same time, Rokeach's concept is not identical with polarization. One can conceive of a person whose opinion toward some social issue is only moderately strong but at the same time unshakeable. That person's view would be considered dogmatic, or closed, but not necessarily polarized. As indicated above, the necessary element in polarization is extremism.

Extremist ideology is also linked to personality differences in the work of Sniderman. His research concentrates on self-esteem as a psychological variable. High self-esteem disposes people in our society to learn the traditional norms of our democratic political system, which are expressed as a general orientation toward democratic restraint; people with low self-esteem, by contrast, are suspicious of the democratic idea and inclined toward extremist politics (Sniderman, 1975). At the group level, people who are insecure about their social identities are inclined to compensate by evaluating outgroups negatively in relation to their own ingroups—in other words, by expressing prejudiced attitudes (Stephan, 1985: 625).

The research just mentioned, starting with the authoritarian personality studies, implies that polarization and stereotyping are pathological, in the sense that they are associated with insecurity or other psychological problems. There are other lines of research, however, which see polarization as a *normal* response in certain situations. Linville and Jones (1980), for example, found that their research subjects gave ingroup members less extreme evaluative scores, in both positive and negative directions, than outgroup members with similar credentials. The explanation, they suggest, is that ingroup evaluations are based on extensive prior information, which inhibits the making of extreme judgments. Prior information about groups different from one's own, however, is more limited so that subjects' evaluations of members of those groups is more volatile.

The most extensive treatment of polarization among psychologically normal people is found in the work of Abraham Maslow, who usually refers to the process as *dichotomous thinking* (although he uses "polarities," "polarization," and "dichotomies" interchangeably). He points out "the profound Western tendency, or perhaps general human tendency to dichotomize, to think that between alternatives or differences one must choose *either* one or the other, and that this involves repudiation of the not-chosen, as if one couldn't have both" (Maslow, 1971: 162). Maslow uses, as one example, the masculinity/femininity dichotomy. The usual tendency is to think, simply, that men have certain qualities—independence, strength, and rationality—while women are emotional, dependent, and weak; whereas the truth is that all of these qualities are part of the nature of both men and women. As another example, Maslow points out that most of us see work and play as mutually exclusive categories: Work is what we do to make money, play is what we enjoy doing. What is left out, of course, is the possibility that work is enjoyable.

And more to the point of our interest in moral polarization, Maslow perceives dichotomous styles of thought applied to human nature itself. "The voice of the devil, depravity, the flesh, evil, the selfish, the egocentric, self-seeking, etc., have all been dichotomized from, and opposed to, the divine, the ideal, the good, the eternal verities, our highest aspirations, etc." (Maslow, 1971: 328). The either-or tendency in thinking about categories like masculinity and femininity is also found in thinking about good and evil. Just as our first inclination is to identify people as masculine and therefore not feminine, or the reverse, we are also prone to sort everyone into two pigeonholes in our minds: "bad, not good," and "good, not bad."

But of course even saints have had their moments of greed, hatred of their fellow men, and other sins. And there is often some basis in reality for the perceptions we have noted above of criminals as good guys; many are in fact loyal and generous friends, and even in some of the crimes they commit we find unmistakably laudable motives. Thus dichotomous thinking from Maslow's perspective is essentially *distorted* thinking, a maladaptive way of looking at the world. Although the tendency is widespread, Maslow sees it as pathological, not in the sense that it is limited to people whom clinicians would single out as psychologically impaired—as the authoritarian personality theorists explain it—but in the sense that it falls short of healthy resolution of an issue that is not truly an either/or situation.

POLARIZED ATTITUDES AND CRIME

One of the earliest discussions of the stereotyping process as applied to lawbreakers was written in the 1930s by Frank Tannenbaum, a historian of Latin America, who had become interested in crime when he served as a member of the National Commission on Law Observance and Enforcement. In a book titled *Crime and the Community*, Tannenbaum used the term "dramatization of evil" to describe the process of defining certain youthful acts as social threats, even when from the perspective of the youths themselves they are only "fooling around." "Breaking windows, annoying people, running around porches, climbing over roofs, stealing from pushcarts, playing truant—all are items of play, adventure, excitement. To the community, however, these activities may and often do take on the form of a nuisance, evil, delinquency, with the demand for control, admonition, chastisement, punishment, police court, truant school" (Tannenbaum, 1938: 17).

Tannenbaum pays particular attention to a tendency, which we have called overgeneralization, that is central to the present approach—the tendency to go from the perception of an individual act as bad to a global perception of the perpetrator as a bad person. "There is a gradual shift from the definition of the specific acts as evil to a definition of the individual as evil, so that all his acts come to be looked upon with suspicion" (Tannenbaum, 1938: 17; see also Duster, 1970: 103–29).

He then proceeds to describe how, in the case of a young person, the individual so labeled in turn adopts an antagonistic attitude toward those who impose the negative definition on him, thereby reinforcing their perception of him as incorrigible, and ultimately needing to be dealt with severely by official agencies. Tannenbaum also stresses the role of the peer group as an alternative source of self-definition for the delinquent, who adopts that group's standards, opposed to those of society, as a way of conserving his self-respect.

On one level, it seems so natural for respectable members of the community to have angry and punitive attitudes toward delinquents and criminals when they feel threatened by crime, that the attitude scarcely seems to require explanation. Indeed, the reaction appears so basic to human nature as to raise the possibility that it is a manifestation of a "justice motive" as fundamental as hunger, sex, and achievement drives. "When there is a clear conflict—in goals, values, ways of thinking, being—any relation that exists among . . . contesting parties becomes infused with considerations of *better* or *worse*, *inferior* or *superior*, and not just for the circumscribed here and now but in some enduring, externally objective sense." In a situation of "us" against "them," when "they" are seen lawbreakers who have unjustly gained something at our expense, this perception brings into play the *justice motive*, impelling "the good citizen to use his power directly to neutralize and punish the lawbreakers" (Lerner, 1975: 18; see also Miller and Vidmar, 1981).

The nature of the "justice motive" may be clarified by considering the circumstances giving rise to it and the ways in which it is expressed. One avenue of inquiry that addresses such factors is associated with the "frustration-aggression" hypothesis (Dollard et al., 1939). According to this hypothesis any experience which frustrates individuals' gratification of their needs leads to hostile feelings. In the case of victims of a property crime like auto theft, for example, the crime may prevent the person from going to work or taking a vacation. Inner tension results, and aggression serves to relieve the tension.

At the simplest level, aggression—whether verbal or physical—is directed toward the source of the frustration. Young children instinctively strike out at a person who has taken away a favored toy. But at times something interferes with the direct expression of aggression. Perhaps the frustrated individual has feelings of attachment to, or fear of, whoever has frustrated him. In the former case aggression may lead to loss of love, in the latter to punishment from the frustrator. How then to relieve the tension? By *displacement* of the aggression—directing it against an object that is less likely to cause pain to the aggressor than the original source of frustration.

In earlier times it was convenient to blame evil spirits for whatever frustrations befell individuals and communities and to vent one's fury against them. If unhappiness results from illness, a poor crop yield, warfare, or interpersonal problems, it might begin to occur to sufferers that lazy or neglectful family members, malevolent neighbors, incompetent tribal leaders, or even their own shortcomings are at fault. Yet the consequences of blaming these actors may itself cause further anguish. How much better to lash out against some more remote agency—an alien tribe, animal or ancestral spirits, or the Devil.

In more secular times supernatural spirits are less-acceptable targets for most people so that more tangible agents are blamed. This is the familiar process of scapegoating. Hitler and his followers had the Jews, and Joseph McCarthy and his followers in the 1950s had the international Communist conspiracy to blame for their troubles. So for Americans beset by whatever discontents impinge upon them in the 1990s, how convenient to be able to discharge their daily accumulation of frustration at the criminals responsible for the unspeakable acts described on the evening television newscast or in the daily newspaper. Indeed, it may be said that the killers and rapists presented in the mass media are the modern equivalents of the Devil portrayed by Calvinist preachers of the seventeenth century in terms of the psychic function that these images serve for their respective audiences,

The strength of hostility toward criminals and support for harsh measures against them—"the urge to punish" (Weihofen, 1956)—are so great in some quarters that the simple mechanism of displacement seems insufficient to explain them. The Freudians, in their efforts to account for the apparently irrational degree of this antipathy, rely heavily on the mechanism of *projection*.

Analytic experience has shown that many people attribute to others wishes and experiences of their own which are unacceptable to them and which they unconsciously wish to get rid of, as it were, by the mechanism of projection. It is *as though* such persons said unconsciously, "It's not *I* who have such a bad or dangerous wish, it's *he*" (Brenner, 1974: 92).

As suggested above, the criminal is a very convenient target. The relief that people experience from attributing their own antisocial impulses to others, and then condemning them for harboring those impulses, explains what the psychiatrist Karl Menninger sees as a virtual public "need" for crime.

We condemn crime; we punish offenders for it; but we need it. The crime and punishment ritual is part of our lives. We need crimes to wonder at, to enjoy vicariously, to discuss and speculate about, and to publicly deplore. We need criminals to identify with, to secretly envy, and to stoutly punish. Criminals represent our "bad" selves—rejected and projected. They do for us the forbidden, illegal things we *wish* to do and, like scapegoats of old, they bear the burdens of our displaced guilt and punishment—"the iniquities of us all" (Menninger, 1968: 153).

The figure of repressed modern-day "saints" going out of their way to excoriate sinners is a familiar one. "No one is more bitter in condemning the 'loose' woman than the 'good' women who have on occasion guiltily enjoyed some purple dreams themselves. It is never he who is without sin who casts the first stone" (Weihofen, 1956: 138; see also Alexander and Staub, 1956; Allport, 1954).

The psychic satisfaction of stereotyping criminals as the embodiment of evil has not gone unnoticed by image makers, who have used this insight to further the fortunes of politicians in numerous campaigns. Voters are often attracted to a candidate who promises to be tough on crime, but beyond that, the law-and-order candidate benefits by dramatizing himself as someone with whom voters can identify as the knight in shining armor doing battle with the evil enemy.

George Bush's victory over Michael Dukakis in the 1988 presidential contest was greatly helped, in the opinion of many observers, by the Bush campaign's exploitation of the case of Willie Horton ("George Bush and

Willie Horton," 1988). During the time when Dukakis was governor of Massachusetts, Horton was under a life sentence in that state for murder. He was given a weekend furlough from prison under a plan that Dukakis had not initiated but had apparently supported. While on furlough, Horton raped a Maryland woman and stabbed her companion. The Bush campaign called attention to the incident with frequent showings of a television commercial contrasting Bush's position in favor of capital punishment with Dukakis's position against it. The commercial included a mug shot of Horton, a black man, along with some details of his crimes, at the same time that the words "kidnapping," "stabbing," and "raping" were flashed on the screen. The commercial was widely criticized as appealing to racist tendencies suggested by the selection of a rather ominous looking photograph of Horton, along with the flashing words. But its appeal for many viewers went beyond racism; the commercial was essentially an artfully presented stereotype of the dangerous criminal. Designed to evoke the feeling that Horton was someone who deserved harsh punishment and that Dukakis was too soft, it implicitly invited voters to express their own righteous hostility by supporting a candidate who would treat bad guys like Horton with appropriate severity.

Among psychoanalysts, the theorist whose work suggests most directly the explanation of extreme feelings toward others on both positive and negative sides of the attitudinal spectrum is Melanie Klein. Klein uses the term "splitting" to refer to the tendency for infants, practically from the moment of birth, to respond to painful feelings of frustration and discomfort with "persecutory anxiety," and at the same time, to take comfort from the mother's nurturance, especially the earliest experience of being fed. "The infant directs his feelings of gratification and love toward the 'good breast,' and his destructive impulses and feelings of persecution towards what he feels to be frustrating, *i.e.,* the 'bad' breast. At this stage splitting processes are at their height and love and hatred as well as the good and bad aspects of the breast are largely kept apart from one another" (Klein, 1975: 49). Subsequently the infant's view is extended from the breast, leading to his regard for parents at various times as good or bad, and then at a later period expanded toward other people and objects in the external world.

There is an element of extremism on both sides of the "split." In the case of negative attitudes, the explanation for the exaggeration is similar to that of other psychoanalysts discussed above, as a consequence of the child's *projection* of his own unacceptable impulses—his "bad self"—onto others. Positive object-relations are also magnified, through the process of *idealization*. "The infant's relative security is based on turning the good object into an ideal one as a protection against the dangerous and persecuting object" (Klein, 1975: 49).

In the course of normal psychological development the splitting process becomes attenuated as growing children learn to recognize ambivalence as a combination of positive and negative feelings about a single object. Nevertheless, under certain threatening circumstances splitting reappears in the adult psyche. "Idealization has the effect of a reassurance, and in so far as this process remains operative in the adult, it still serves the purpose of counteracting persecutory anxieties. The fear of enemies and of hostile attacks is mitigated by increasing the power of goodness of other people" (Klein, 1975: 273).

Klein did not mention criminals and victims as objects of split feelings but her observations surely suggest an association between a stereotype of the criminal as bad guy and the victim as good guy. Just as we have noted that displacement and projection are the primary psychological mechanisms underlying strong negative feelings against *offenders*, we should recognize, along with idealization, the role of *identification* as a process tending to evoke a sympathetic public response toward *victims* of crime. Through identification, one person perceives a connection between himself and another, and adopts for himself attitudes, mannerisms, or other attributes of that person. Identification may even be expressed by taking on the afflictions suffered by someone else. Thus, when one person has been victimized by crime, others close to him, whether on a personal basis or simply on the basis that they share a common ethnicity or other group membership, may respond with outrage against the perpetrator just as though they themselves had been directly hurt.

Notwithstanding the natural inclination of the public to identify with crime victims, however, there are frequently circumstances, as noted in Chapter 5, when victims are not looked upon with sympathy but instead regarded as bad people themselves. What are the psychodynamics of this phenomenon? The reader will recall the observations of Barkas, quoted in Chapter 5, who reported on reactions of her friends to her brother's death in a street mugging. They assumed her brother had been doing something wrong, in order to have been victimized. This assumption served to protect her friends from anxiety over the possibility that they themselves might be acting altogether properly, whatever that may mean to them, and still fall prey to a homicidal robber. The function of these perceptions, for those who hold them, may be understood in terms of the mechanism of *denial*, an unconscious process leading the individual to reject some aspect of objective reality that is unpleasant or threatening and to replace it with a fantasy that he or she can live with. In the case of people who insist on the blameworthiness of crime victims, they are thereby denying their own vulnerability to crime. The reality is that many conventional crimes, like murder, rape, and robbery, are to a large extent fortuitous with respect to choice of victim. But that is frightening, because it indicates that you or I, no matter how virtuous or careful, may end up as unlucky targets. How much more reassuring to see victims as wrongdoers themselves, for it suggests that we, by following the straight and narrow path, will be able to escape the pain of victimization.

This process seems to be an essential element of the "just world" delusion (Lerner, 1980). Lerner and his coworkers have hypothesized that human beings are strongly motivated to believe that the world is arranged so that upright people are ultimately rewarded and scoundrels ultimately punished. They have amassed a considerable body of research in support of the hypothesis, from which they conclude: "The 'good guy' may experience temporary adversity and minor defeats at the hands of the 'bad guy,' but ultimately he triumphs. Whenever 'goodness' does not triumph over 'evil' people tend to experience stress and displeasure." The motivation to believe that people end up with their just deserts has often been observed in the realm of religious beliefs and behavior (as well as in rationalizations for oppressive colonial policies and the treatment of disadvantaged people within our own society). It is apparent in the way people respond to any situation—including criminal incidents—when they perceive that an apparently innocent person is victimized. Initially some effort may be made to correct the injustice. But if that is not feasible, "the person who witnesses the injustice . . . can persuade himself that no injustice has occurred after all, . . . that the victim had done something which merited his fate." And if it is not possible to blame the victim for a specific act, then the observers seek a more global way to explain the victimization, by imputing to him a bad character.

The observers . . . try to persuade themselves that the seemingly innocent victim was the kind of person for whom this suffering was not an inappropriate fate. All the observers had to do was decide that the victim was a less than desirable person, at least in some respects—selfish, unintelligent, crude, etc.—and then they could feel more comfortable. Unfortunately, it is relatively easy to see ourselves or anyone else, for that matter, in this negative light. All that is required is selective attention, recall, and emphasis concerning behaviors that we all exhibit from time to time (Lerner, Miller, and Holmes, 1976: 138).

SOCIAL POLARIZATION

At the intersection between psychological and social polarization is a seminal experiment by Moscovici and Zavalloni (1969), which deals with the influence of group dynamics on individual attitudes. Research subjects, in the part of the study to be discussed here, were sixty young men in their last year at a Parisian *lycée* (academic high school). Seated around a table in groups of four, they were initially instructed to fill out individual questionnaires reflecting their attitudes toward one of two subjects salient for them at the time. (The study was conducted in the 1960s.) Some groups were asked to express opinions about Americans, others about General Charles de Gaulle. Next, the groups were told to discuss among themselves the questionnaire items to which they had just responded, reach a consensus on each item, and record it. The groups having done that, each subject responded to the same questionnaire once more.

Comparing results on the initial questionnaire administration with those reflecting group consensus, the experimenters found the groups' position more extreme. Whether the questionnaires dealt with opinions about Americans or de Gaulle, the group discussion process resulted in a more polarized stance, either positive or negative, than the averaged opinions of group members at the outset. Moreover, when individuals were retested they often adopted the group opinion as their own.

This phenomenon might itself be seen as a type of social polarization—the tendency for attitudes to become polarized through group interaction. More commonly, however, social polarization refers to extreme *actions* by parties with conflicting interests. Such actions are considered social, not only because they are determined by actors' social attributes, but also because the acts themselves are collective in nature. There is of course, as we have mentioned in our discussion of attitudes, a connection between extreme attitudes and collective action. One of the early studies of the frustration-aggression hypothesis, in fact, illustrates this connection nicely. Starting with the hypothesis that "the strength of instigation to aggression varies directly with the amount of interference with the goal response" (Hovland and Sears, 1940: 301), the authors selected lynching as an aggressive act that might be explainable on the basis of frustration. They then correlated the annual number of blacks lynched with the per-acre value of cotton in the fourteen Southern states in which cotton was the major cash crop, for each year from 1882 to 1930. Low prices for cotton presumably induce frustration, and the more frustration, the more lynchings might be expected. Indeed, their hypothesis was confirmed. When a trend toward overall improvement in economic conditions had been corrected for, there remained a substantial tendency for the occurrence of more lynchings in bad times, economically speaking, and fewer lynchings in good times.

The example of the lynch mob may remind the reader of our discussion, at the beginning of Chapter 4, of Le Bon's theory of the crowd as an entity whose behavior represents the most barbaric and emotional of mankind's impulses, the least rational and civilized of its capacities. We may best understand such action as an example of collective behavior, the sociological specialty that concerns itself with panics, crazes, fads, mobs, and cults—all those forms of group conduct that are *non-institutionalized*—that is, not guided by long-established and widely accepted rules for behavior such as those that govern conduct in families, schools, churches, business enterprises, and government.

It is just because of this absence of established rules that collective behavior lends itself to extreme, or polarized, forms of expression. Blumer (1969: 74–77) explains collective behavior as resulting from three processes, which develop in order: (1) milling, (2) collective excitement, and (3) social contagion. Milling refers to aimless motion of people among one another, analogous to the movements of animals in a herd, which serves to focus attention away from external stimuli and intensify individuals' preoccupation with the group. Collective excitement is an intense form of milling, under which "people become more emotionally aroused and more likely to be carried away by impulses and feelings, hence rendered more unstable and irresponsible" (Blumer, 1969: 76). And social contagion emerges as the process by which emotions and actions are transmitted, often very rapidly, from a few individuals to many others. As the collectivity passes through these stages, normal processes of rational judgment are superceded, giving rise to emotional expressions of extreme behavior.

Whereas Blumer's view explains extremist tendencies in terms of processes inherent in collective interaction, Brinton sees them as the outcome of a struggle for power between moderates and extremists. Although his

generalizations are limited because they are derived from only four historical cases of successful revolutions, the conclusions are provocative. In
each of his cases—the English Civil War in the seventeenth century, the
American and French Revolutions in the eighteenth, and the Russian
Revolution in the present century—there was a struggle, following the initial overthrow of the established regime, between moderate and extreme
factions of the revolutionary movement. And in each case the extreme
elements won. This fact, according to Brinton, arises from the nature of
the dislocations that are inevitable when attention turns from getting rid of
the old order to deciding among alternatives for the new order. "But the
times were turned topsy-turvy, and as the crisis of the revolution approached, only the man with a touch—or more—of fanatical idealism in
him, or at least with the ability to act the part of such a fanatic, could attain
to leadership" (Brinton, 1965: 146).   In such a struggle the moderates,
with their concern for individual liberties rather than repression of threat,
for civil rights rather than collective security, are destined to lose out.

At the highest level of social organization, polarization is explained by
Marx and Engels as the escalation of conflict in capitalist society between
workers whose struggle is embodied in demands for pay commensurate
with their contribution to the productive process, and investors whose aim
is to meximize the profit on their capital investment. As the line between
classes is drawn, the capitalist becomes greedier and greedier. "This he
shows by reducing the worker's need to the barest and most miserable
level of physical subsistence." (Marx, 1978: 95). Meanwhile the proletar-
ian-workers, drawing strength from groups not directly involved in industrial production, also adopt a more extreme posture.

The law of the falling rate of profit, of competition, overproduction, and periodic
depression, of the pauperization of the masses, will bring about the economic
ruin of intermediate layers of the population such as shopkeepers, artisans, small
masters, and the like. In time, differences in religious belief, regional traditions,
rural and urban life-styles, skills based on craftsmanship and training, even national sentiments, will be erased by the inevitable march of technological and
economic change under capitalism. As these differences disappear, the increasingly homogeneous proletariat will become more organized, disciplined, class-
conscious, and militant. In time, the revolutionary overthrow of the bourgeois-
minority becomes inevitable (Oberschall, 1973: 285).

Other approaches to polarization differ from the Marxist emphasis on
its economic basis. Modern political scientists have sought to explain the

circumstances that give rise to *political polarization*—a special case of social polarization—which is conceptualized as the extreme opposite of *political consensus*. In parliamentary systems with several parties, none of which has a majority of representatives, it is possible to work out differences on issues through compromise and coalition formation when there is a basic consensus that a certain range of problems should be addressed. If on the other hand the electorate, through its representatives, is split into factions representing extreme positions, the possibilities for effective government are stymied.

In discussing European politics in the years following World War II, Lauber (1983) notes a period of consensus through the 1950s and most of the 1960s in which there seemed to be agreement about the need for greater redistribution of wealth. This period was referred to as a period of "The End of Ideology," in which most politicians did not dispute the major premises about the desirability of industrial growth, but only held different opinions about how that might be achieved. And to the extent that there were disagreements, they were not likely to persist since they could presumably be resolved by experimentation and observation of what measures actually did work to achieve the goals upon which there was consensus.

This was considered a political process, not just because substantive issues of governmental action were concerned, but also because the consensus was reflected, in the political structure, by agreement among political parties. In England, for example, the Conservative party accepted the reforms instituted by Labor, and even though Labor had the extension of certain welfare measures as a long-term goal, it set limits on these aspirations for the time being, while the Conservatives made no effort to roll back the governmental activities instituted by Labor. However, starting in the late 1960s, according to Lauber, there was a fragmentation of this consensus, especially around issues like industrial development, the extension of social welfare, and ecology. Some elements continued to advocate further development, others saw it as conflicting with human needs and called for limitations.

Political polarization in the United States has been examined in a study of the ideological orientation of United States senators, as reflected in their roll-call voting for 1979 and 1980 (Poole and Rosenthal, 1984). According to the authors' reasoning. political polarization exists to the extent that senators from a given state differ from each other in voting on the liberal or conservative side of issues. They find substantial heterogeneity between senators in the fifty states, and conclude that the Senate overrepresents the interests of relatively extreme support coalitions and consequently underrepresents the interests of middle-of-the-road constituents.

SOCIAL POLARIZATION AND CRIME

One American institution that has traditionally represented extreme collective action against crime is the vigilante group. Defined as "taking the law into one's own hands" (Brown, 1976: 79), vigilantism has a tradition in American society going back to the Regulators (1767–1769) in the South Carolina back country, who functioned as the only available force for social control in a region where there was no operative legal system.

Although vigilantism now has a pejorative connotation, that was not so for much of our history. Vigilante groups were not by any means made up of marginal members of the community. Very often they were led by its most respected citizens, and supported by many others, including Presidents Andrew Jackson and Theodore Roosevelt (Brown, 1975: 126–27, 162–67). It was taken for granted that, in a society in which sovereignty remained with the people, respected citizens might be expected at any time to have to step in and buttress the existing system of law and order (Burrows, 1976). In most cases they were much more than ad hoc groups; they had a clearcut hierarchy or command, and a formal constitution representing procedures agreed upon by their members.

Vigilante movements are viewed as essentially conservative forces. They advance no new principles but serve rather to carry out existing laws, in circumstances where social stability is threatened. "The potential for vigilantism varies positively with the intensity and scope of belief that a regime is ineffective in dealing with challenges to the prevailing socio-political order" (Rosenbaum and Sederberg, 1976: 7). Thus it is important to realize that, although police powers were not assigned to them through the usual governmental process, they were surrounded by a strong aura of legitimacy.

And yet, for all its support from established authority, vigilantism has a tendency to be expressed in extreme forms of behavior. The vigilante response is often far out of proportion to the initial crime and, in its zeal, is often evoked with little evidence against suspects who may be later proven innocent—as depicted in the popular novel and film, *The Ox-Bow Incident* (Clark, 1972). Originally limited in most cases to whipping and expulsion, around 1850 American vigilante "justice" became almost synonymous with killing (Brown, 1975: 109).

The moral component of vigilantism was clear from the outset. The vigilante mission was envisioned as a confrontation between the respectable classes and those members of the lower class whose idleness or disregard for the law threatened the established values of life, liberty, and property. Leadership of the frontier vigilante movements was supplied by the upper class, their rank-and-file by the middle class. In fact, one way for an ambitious young man from the East to affirm his right to membership in the upper echelon of a frontier community was to take a leadership role in a vigilante movement (Brown, 1975: 104–111). The polarization of values was perfectly expressed by Thomas J. Dimsdale, a public official whose defense of vigilantism was presented in his popular book, *The Vigilantes of Montana*, published in 1866.

Every fibre of our frame vibrates with anger and disgust when we meet a ruffian, a murderer, or a marauder. Mawkish sentimentalism we abhor. The thought of murdered victims, dishonored females, plundered wayfarers, burning houses, and the rest of the sad evidences of villainy, completely excludes mercy from our view. Honor, truth, and the sacrifice of self to considerations of justice and the good of mankind—these claim, we had almost said our adoration; but for the low, brutal, cruel, lazy, ignorant, insolent, sensual and blasphemous miscreants that infest the frontiers, we entertain but one sentiment—aversion—deep, strong, and unchangeable. For such cases, the rope is the only prescription that avails as a remedy (quoted in Brown, 1975: 95).

Thus vigilantism represents polarization as an informal, or at most semi-legitimate, mechanism for doing justice when the community believes itself injured. But extreme degrees of public sentiment may also be expressed in punishment administered by duly constituted authority. Erikson offers the historical example of the Massachusetts Bay Colony toward the end of the seventeenth century. Beset by factional disputes among members of the Colony, a threat that their charter would be revoked by the English ruler, and costly Indian wars, the colonists seemed overcome by a sense of doom. They felt their whole way of life, begun as a great experiment to live without outside interference according to God's law, was gravely jeopardized. It was just at this time, in 1692, that two young girls, residents of Salem Village, began to make strange noises and fall into convulsive fits. The behaviors quickly spread to other adolescent females and were recognized as signs of bewitchment. Pressed by their elders, the girls identified three women in the village as sources of their malady.

But that did not signal an end to the matter. Accusations multiplied and spread beyond Salem Village. Trials were held, but they must have been cursory, for all those accused were found guilty. By the time the hysteria had run its course, "nineteen people had been executed, seven more condemned, and one pressed to death under a pile of rocks for standing mute at his trial. At least two more persons had died in prison, bringing the number of deaths to twenty-two" (Erikson, 1966: 149).

Finally calmer heads prevailed. Reflecting upon the flimsy nature of evidence accepted in the cases already tried, the Colony's leaders revised their procedures, so that of several hundred additional men and women accused or condemned, all were either discharged without trial or pardoned. The community's collective action against individuals alleged to be agents of the Devil had not served to restore the sacred fellowship of earlier years, but it provided a focal point for a transition to more earthly, practical social institutions. It seems to have offered an alternative for the conflicts that might otherwise have destroyed the Colony during the period of crisis. "For a few years, at least, the settlers of Massachusetts were alone in the world, bewildered by the loss of their old destiny but not yet aware of their new one, and during this fateful interval they tried to discover some image of themselves by listening to a chorus of voices which whispered to them from the depths of an invisible wilderness" (Erikson, 1966: 159).

The witchcraft trials differed from lynch mobs insofar as they employed regularized trial procedures to determine guilt and imposed formally prescribed punishments. For this reason the bay colonists' actions may be considered lawful, to distinguish them from the more spontaneous actions of vigilante groups. Nevertheless, both frontier vigilantism and the Salem trials may be seen as manifestations of similar psychological and social dynamics. Legal punishment, according to Alexander and Staub, is nothing more than an institution providing an outlet, essentially irrational, for sadistic impulses which are bottled up in modern society,

Thus our civilization drives the individual more and more into the frame of communal life, his individualism becomes absorbed in the collectivist trends; his hostility and aggressions, which threaten the solidarity of such a complex social organism, are all immobilized and refused an outlet; such a civilization can hardly be willing to sacrifice the last refuge which its sadism finds in a form so well acceptable to the Ego, as in the institutions of criminal justice (1956: 222).

This essentially psychological theory—that violence is a device for allaying anxieties of individual group members—has a sociological counterpart. The sociological approach regards collective punishment as a mechanism for enhancing the solidarity of the punishing group (Dentler and Erikson, 1959). The theory challenges the common notion of deviance as disruptive to the social order. In particular, groups that sense themselves to be living in periods of crisis are seen as unconsciously "creating" deviance—that is, finding some pretext to accuse selected individuals of acts that threaten the community and to carry out punishment in the name of the group—as a way of buttressing their own solidarity and warding off the perceived crisis. This was the conclusion in Erikson's study of the witch persecutions in Massachusetts. On the frontier, vigilantism supported a crude moral order within communities that had yet to develop stabilizing institutions like local government, churches, and families. And in the American South following the Civil War, lynching fulfilled a similar function: The great majority of cases served to reaffirm the myth of white racial superiority, with its correlaries of the purity of white womanhood and the threat of mongrelization resulting from the supposedly strong desire of black men for sexual relations with white women.

In the situations just described, one group takes extreme action against a class of individuals and justifies that action as necessary to preserve its own goodness against some form of corruption. When the circumstances viewed objectively seem not to warrant so forceful a response, we use the term social polarization to describe the choice of the more extreme course of conduct.

Social polarization, in another sense, may be used to describe a situation of group interaction that is structured in advance so as to elicit strongly opposed behaviors from the interacting parties. Marx's view of class relations under capitalism is one example. Team sports are another. Polarizing structures are commonly referred to as *competitive*, in which one actor's achievement entails the failure of another (see Deutsch's discussion of "contriently interdependent goals," 1968: 462).

A vivid instance is the *adversary system*, a term referring to those courtroom procedures in which lawyers for plaintiffs and defendants do battle with each other to seek a verdict favorable to their clients. One of the system's most dramatic forms is the trial of a serious crime. "A big murder trial," wrote Damon Runyon, "possesses some of the elements of a sporting event. I find the same popular interest in a murder trial that I find . . . on the eve of a big football game, or a pugilistic encounter, or a baseball series" (quoted in Frank, 1949: 91; see also Pound, 1930: 163). Members of the public not only speculate on the outcome, but often root for one side or another, and sometimes even bet on their "team" in the legal contest, just as they might on a sports contest.

When one considers the antecedents of the American trial system, it is not surprising that it is a polarized encounter. Medieval European rulers, in their efforts to maintain order among tribes accustomed to settling disputes by violent means, established the judicial combat, or trial by battle, in order to discourage the escalation of conflict. As to behavior and weapons, early judicial combats were indistinguishable from ordinary brawls between two individuals. They differed only in that the ruler or his representative in the judicial combat exercised nominal supervision over the encounter and declared the winner to be after all in the right concerning the disputed matter. The procedures were refined in the later Middle Ages, with elaborate rules concerning the kind of grievances subject to adjudication by combat, the representation of parties by champions, weapons (clubs for commoners, lances for the nobility), armor, permissible tactics, criteria for determining the winner, and consequences for the parties and their champions. Its rationale was reflected in the contemporary conception of everyday life as a struggle between the forces of good and evil in which righteousness prevails. The perspective is depicted in a miniature adorning a fifteenth-century manuscript, which shows "the victor kneeling and returning thanks to God, while the vanquished is lying on his back with Satan grasping at his open mouth as though already seizing the soul of the criminal" (Lea, 1974: 135–36; see also Neilson, 1932).

The modern adversary system is in theory a search for truth. It assumes that "if each of two adversaries is motivated to get in the record all the evidence most favorable to his own case, the chances are maximized of getting all relevant considerations before the court" (Bredemeier, 1969: 56). Nevertheless, in many respects the twentieth-century courtroom trial, especially in criminal cases, seems more akin to the judicial combat than to a procedure appropriate for securing and evaluating all the evidence necessary to enable a jury or judge to reach a just resolution of conflicting testimony. The institution of cross examination, in particular, is often practiced in such a way as to discredit witnesses who are known by their interrogators to be telling the truth by "annihilating" or "demolishing" not only their credibility as to the facts in question, but their moral characters as well (Strick, 1977: 37–57). Such tactics, along with concealing relevant evidence, giving advice that may encourage perjury, and actually presenting witnesses who are expected to lie—although frowned upon in some legal quarters—are part and parcel of the adversary system (Freedman, 1975). As a way of accomplishing its avowed purpose, the search for truth, it has been subject to criticism from within as well as outside the legal profession. According to one professor of law,

Surely no one in his right mind but a lawyer, if he felt it was important for him to find out the truth about anything, would adopt the method of hiring two persons to champion diametrically opposed points of view, set them free to make the most extreme arguments they could on either side, and hope for the truth to emerge by some kind of Hegelian synthesis from these artificial theses and antitheses (Simpson, 1949: 150; see also Frankel, 1980).

How then can one account for the persistence of so inefficient a mechanism for doing justice? The explanation, according to one student of the system, lies in a connection she perceives in American society between the moral polarity, right versus wrong, and the pragmatic polarity, winning versus losing. "Winning was the American dream and ultimate blessedness; losing the nightmare and unforgivable sin" (Strick, 1977: 112). Thus, the winning advocate in a modern courtroom receives the public's acclaim in the same way that the winning boxer, in Runyon's analogy, or the victor in judicial combat, pictured in the medieval manuscript, is celebrated for his superior moral qualities.

In modern society the vast majority of criminal trials are carried on without public attention, but some of them, like those for notorious crimes of violence or those of famous people, serve through the mass media as morality plays for a large audience. A few cases provide the basis for polarized collective action in the form of courthouse demonstrations by supporters of crime victims and supporters of defendants on trial, and there are sometimes actual encounters between the groups of partisans. Such encounters often represent ethnic antagonisms for which the criminal trial represents only the tip of an iceberg. Nevertheless the criminal incident giving rise to the trial, the trial itself, and the actions of the parties' supporters often exacerbate the underlying hostilities.

A recent, widely publicized example is the ethnic group response to the murder of Yussef Hawkins in New York City in 1989. Hawkins, a black teenager, had gone with three friends to an Italian-American section of Brooklyn in response to a newspaper advertisement for a used car. He and his friends were attacked by a gang of young men from the neighborhood and Hawkins was shot to death. Even before the trial, supporters of the black victim paraded through the streets of the Italian neighborhood to affirm their right to safe passage in any part of the city, and they encountered racial slurs along their parade route. Parade leaders, when interviewed on television, indicated that the paraders perceived themselves as protagonists for valued civil liberties and saw the neighborhood residents who taunted them as criminals; a number of neighborhood residents, interviewed at the same time, interpreted the Hawkins supporters as trespassers and defended their menacing response to the paraders as necessary and proper to protect their own turf. This is a classic case of polarization, in which the action of each side increases the extremity of the other's stance.

War on Crime

The adversary structure of the courtroom trial is an important stimulus for moral polarization, but polarization occurs around other components of the criminal justice system as well. On the side of suspected or convicted criminals there are crowds that gather spontaneously to object to police brutality, and prison inmates who riot in protest against overcrowded cells, censorship of mail, bad food, or lack of opportunity to practice their religion. On the other side, as would-be controllers of crime, are some citizens who mobilize to drive prostitutes away from their neighborhoods and others who participate in demonstrations supporting capital punishment. The latter efforts, though lacking any real unifying organization, are often seen as part of a general social effort known as the "war on crime."

The war-against-crime metaphor has been around for well over a century, at least. In 1859 Barwick Baker, an English magistrate, gave an address to the Social Science Association in his country on the topic "How To War with Crime." Baker's speech proposed a "war of extermination" based on a combination of deterrence for nonoffenders and confinement for offenders in facilities graded so that they would begin in solitary confinement and then proceed to progressively less-restricted stages before being finally released. Baker advocated measures that were liberal in his time, or any time; a war against crime for him was not a battle against evil people, but against those inclinations, among others, within the criminal that on occasion tempt him to do wrong (Baker, 1984).

In the early years of Prohibition, the Chicago Crime Commission employed the expression "war on crime" as part of an effort to instill respect for authority in the city's schoolchildren, suggesting some degree of progressive attitude. But for the most part they saw it as a battle against people who were essentially immoral. The commission attributed much of crime to heredity. It took the position that criminals should be sterilized and that future generations be further improved by eugenics laws requiring all applicants for marriage licenses to demonstrate that they were "morally clean."

Though the members of the Chicago Crime Commission often sounded like vigilantes, theirs was not the traditional form of frontier justice. They did not believe in taking the law into their own hands, in resorting to violence themselves, but they supported the exercise of violence by the authorities. Commission members were not a lynch mob as such; they simply applauded official hangings and lobbied bitterly against reprieves (Cipes, 1968: 16).

A concerted effort at the federal level, begun during Lyndon Johnson's presidential administration, has been described in a book titled *The Crime War* (Cipes, 1968). Johnson launched the "active combat against crime" in a special message to Congress on March 8, 1965, with a proposal for an extensive survey of the problem to be undertaken by a blue-ribbon President's Commission. In his message Johnson spoke of the magnitude of the problem and of the need to address it on a national level. But he did not embrace the kind of straightforward "get tough" policy brought to national attention in the Goldwater campaign a year earlier, probably because "getting tough" was often interpreted by nonwhite minorities, a significant segment of Johnson's Democratic constituency, as discriminating against suspects from their groups. Instead, he foresaw a balance. "We are not prepared in our democratic system to pay for improved law enforcement by unreasonable limitations on the individual, protections which ennoble our system. Yet there is the undoubted necessity that society be protected from the criminal and that the rights of society be recognized along with the rights of the individual" ("Text of President's message," 1965). And, when the Commission published its overall report in 1967, it emphasized such Progressive concerns as expanding facilities for rehabilitating offenders and providing more equal educational and occupational opportunities for delinquency-prone youngsters (as discussed in Chapter 1). However, the individual reports by two of the Commission's task forces, the Task Force on Science and Technology and the Task Force on the Police, reflected a conception of the "war on crime" as no mere metaphor. Many of their recommendations took the military model literally, seeking victory through superior intelligence about enemy activity, and troops better trained and equipped with the requisite weapons for battle. And when it came to providing resources for implementation, there was disproportionate emphasis on strategies proposed by these task forces.

Thus, a very substantial portion of the funds appropriated in support of the Omnibus Crime Control and Safe Streets Act of 1968, and later legislation, went for support of communications and surveillance hardware, and such weaponry for police departments as machine guns, gas bombs, tanks and helicopters (Quinney, 1975: 293–301). Some of these resources were designed for combat with organized groups, including political terrorists and criminal syndicates, but most were also justified as tools for apprehending conventional street criminals more efficiently.

Not surprisingly, the Republican candidate who eventually succeeded Johnson in the presidency, being less sensitive to the implications of a "tough" criminal justice system for minority rights, embraced the "war" metaphor with enthusiasm. In accepting his party's nomination in the summer of 1968, Richard Nixon used the language of the military in outlining the focus on crime in his prospective administration. After noting that some courts "have gone too far in weakening the peace forces as against the criminal forces in this country," he announced that his Department of Justice would "launch a war against organized crime in this country," in which the Attorney General would be an "active belligerent against the loan sharks and the numbers racketeers that rob the urban poor" and would "open a new front against the pill peddlers and the narcotics peddlers" ("Transcript of acceptance speeches," 1968).

Following a brief Democratic hiatus under Jimmy Carter, in which there was no notable emphasis on warring against crime, Ronald Reagan took office and surrounded issues that had been conceived by others as problems of strategy and tactics with an unprecedented aura of morality. After eight months in office (and before his famous characterization of the Soviet Union as an "evil empire"), he made a speech to a convention of the International Association of Chiefs of Police in New Orleans containing what were described by a New York Times reporter as "the most detailed statements of his social philosophy since he took office" (Raines, 1981). "The war on crime," Reagan said, "will only be won when an attitude of mind and a change of heart takes place in America, when certain truths take hold and plant their roots deep into our national consciousness. Truths like—right and wrong matter, individuals are responsible for their actions, retribution should be swift and sure for those who prey on the innocent."

At one point Reagan seemed to express a Quaker-like humanism in the assertion that "men are basically good but prone to evil."[1]   But the dominant tenor of the message was Hobbesian. He described the present era as an age of "the human predator," in which, "for all our science and sophistication, for all our justified pride in intellectual accomplishment, we should never forget: the jungle is always there, waiting to take us over." He then indicated his view of the war on crime as a struggle to "restrain the darker impulses of human nature," in which the police are "the thin blue line that holds back a jungle which threatens to claim this clearing we call civilization" ("Excerpts from President's address," 1981; Lescaze, 1981).

The program Reagan presented in the speech was consistent with the view of crime as combat: He indicated that he would introduce federal legislation to strengthen the forces of law and order, such as preventive detention for suspects of violent crimes, and he would also introduce legislation to weaken the armaments of suspects by allowing illegally obtained evidence to be used in criminal prosecutions. He also promised to seek legislation permitting the military to take part in controlling the traffic in illegal drugs.

This last proposal reflected a shift in the war on crime, from the emphasis on domestic criminal syndicates during the Nixon years to the international drug cartels in more recent years. The most reliable government statistics had shown a decrease in the rate of serious crime in the United States between 1976 and 1984, due in large measure to a decline in the proportion of people within the total population who were between fifteen and twenty-four years of age—the group most likely to commit offenses included in the FBI index (Steffensmeier and Harer, 1987). But in the mid-1980s serious crimes of violence began to show a marked increase, especially in the largest cities. Law enforcement officials have been nearly unanimous in attributing this increase to the spread of crack, a powerful and inexpensive cocaine derivative that appeared on city streets during this period. The crack trade greatly intensified competition among street dealers in drugs. They seemed to be shooting one another in unprecedented numbers, and innocent bystanders as well were often injured or killed (James, 1988a; James, 1988b; Morganthau, 1986).

Incidents of serious drug-related crime were widely publicized in all the media, and what had been earlier designated a war on crime now became a war on drugs. The apparent inadequacy of previous antidrug efforts was blamed on a lack of coordination at the federal level, so that in 1988 Congress created the Office of National Drug Control Policy, to be headed by a "drug czar" with responsibility for bringing about that coordination. When George Bush became president in 1989 he appointed William Bennett to the position. Bennett had served in the Reagan cabinet as Secretary of Education, in which capacity he campaigned energetically for emphasizing the teaching of traditional "moral values" in public schools. This emphasis on moral values carried over into Bennett's war on drugs. His appearance at a drug treatment center in a poor, run-down section of Boston was observed by a writer for the *New York Review of Books*. "At one point a black woman in the front row, her voice tinged with challenge, asked: 'Do you believe that people addicted to drugs and alcohol are bad?' Bennett hesitated for a moment, then replied that while some addicts might be unable to control themselves, others do drugs 'because they don't exercise responsibility' and 'care more about themselves than their kids and other people'" (Massing, 1990: 29). As a consequence of this view, Bennett's priorities as drug czar were on rigorous enforcement of drug laws by police, and mandatory imposition of severe punishment by the courts. At the same time, there was less attention given to school-based education for drug prevention, and to treatment programs for drug users—measures that do not lend themselves as readily to the military analogy.

The problem with the concept of addressing the problem of illegal drugs as a war is that it lends itself to what Ralph Brauer has called "rhetorical escalation" (1990: 705). Brauer sees a similarity between depiction of the drug problem by news media and politicians as a war with drug dealers who are called "scum" and "creeps," on the one hand, and the overtones of terms like "japs," "krauts," and "gooks," which were used to refer to the enemy in World War II and the war in Vietnam, on the other hand. Just as the wartime language was instrumental in promoting the image of all members of an enemy nation as evil and subhuman, so the moral rhetoric of drugs comes to taint groups and neighborhoods that in fact have no demonstrable responsibility for the drug problem.

Bennett's approach to the drug problem is in a way reflective of how our society approaches the broader problem of crime. Michael Massing, the *New York Review* writer who observed Bennett's visit to the Boston drug treatment center, observed, "there sometimes seem to be two William Bennetts" (1990: 30). At times he addressed the drug problem as one requiring input from scientific experts and representatives from a broad range of interest groups. But at other times he reverted to a confrontational, moralistic stance. Similarly, social policy toward crime in the United States has wavered between seeing crime as a many-faceted problem, and seeing it as simply a war between the good guys and bad guys. And at a given time, there are some people and groups who embrace a more polarized view of the crime problem, others who take a less polarized view.

POLARIZATION: PERVASIVENESS VERSUS VARIABILITY

The theories of polarization being considered may be roughly divided between explanations emphasizing it as a process intrinsic to human nature and explanations limiting it to certain individuals or social circumstances. At the psychological level, Maslow's theory of dichotomous thinking is representative of approaches pointing to the widespread occurrence of polarization—a perspective emphasizing perceptual and judgmental activities like the formation of stereotypes, which are understandable as derivatives of the need to simplify a world too complex to comprehend in all its objective subtleties. Likewise at the level of collective behavior, Tannenbaum's description of how the public seizes upon a bit of information about a youngster's few delinquent acts, and then goes on to characterize him as an altogether bad person, is understood not as some kind of aberration, but as a reasonable way of responding to an infringement upon the community's well-being.

Moreover, there is an increased potential for law enforcement officials who represent the established community, as Tannenbaum recognized, to distance themselves morally from criminal offenders when those offenders are members of recent immigrant groups whose language, customs, and moral standards differ from those of the better established groups (1938: 42–47). Although New York City's Mayor David Dinkins is fond of referring to his constituents as a "beautiful mosaic" of people whose strength is derived from the contributions of diverse traditions to mainstream American culture, cultural pluralism gives rise to problems as well. Groups that hold on to traditional customs and values tend to keep others at a distance, and as noted above (Linville and Jones, 1980), members of such groups are likely to hold polarized attitudes toward individuals who are members of groups other than their own. One might say that pluralism breeds polarization. And polarization once started feeds upon itself. A group that starts out with a negative stereotype of another group is likely to seize upon an incident showing that group in an unfavorable light as confirmation of the stereotype and as a rationale for placing greater social distance between itself and that other group. At the present time, particularly in central cities, black-white differences constitute the most salient starting point for polarization, with white people tending to identify nonwhites indiscriminately with "the criminal element," and nonwhite people distrusting, if not actually attributing criminal tendencies to, the white population as a whole.

Further exacerbating the tendency toward social polarization is the threat of increased competition between groups. When there is an economic structure of "contriently interdependent goals," to use Deutsch's term (1968: 462), such that one group's achievement entails loss to the other, the threatened group will define the other group as bad and act punitively toward it. There are at least two variations on this theme. One locates the competitive threat between groups within the working class. It explains tension between blacks and whites, for example, as a result of blacks vying with white workers for better-paying jobs that had formerly been reserved for white workers (Blalock, 1967). The alternative explanation, following Marxist principles, considers the threat as class-based: Workers' economic dissatisfaction threatens the political and economic power positions of the elite. In either case, the threatened group responds by "criminalizing" those whom it perceives as challenging its favored position. There is a sizable literature on the relationship between economic stress and punitive reaction toward the threatening groups. Although subject to other interpretations, these studies do tend to show a connection between periods of unemployment and large numbers of people being imprisoned for conventional crimes (Inverarity and McCarthy, 1988; Myers, 1990; Petchesky, 1981).

At another level, the authoritarian personality approach discussed previously addresses the connection between polarization and threat. In this case, however, the threat is conceptualized as a threat to the individual's personality integration. Under the strong influence of Freudian theory, this approach explains dichotomous thinking as a result of traumatizing experiences that have befallen certain individuals, which result in their being "made to feel alone, isolated, and helpless in the world in which they live and thus anxious of what the future holds in store for them. Such a state of affairs should lead to pervasive feelings of self-inadequacy and self-hate" (Rokeach, 1960: 69). These feelings may be compensated for by an overemphasis on the importance of power relationships expressed in unquestioning acceptance of the moral authority of parental figures. Children introduced to the world in such terms are likely to end up with ethical standards that sanction the right of powerful actors to impose punishment on groups and individuals classified as moral and social inferiors. Underlying such views, according to the thinking of authoritarian personality theorists, are the defense mechanisms like those we have mentioned previously—displacement, projection, and denial—which are invoked to defend the individual psyche from generalized anxiety. The work of Rokeach and his associates (1960: 69–70, 347–75) lends support to this theory with evidence that those research subjects who are most prone to dichotomous thinking are also those who evince greatest anxiety on psychological tests.

Just as the authoritarian personality theorists attribute polarized thinking to individuals' perceptions of threats to their self-esteem, so do Durkheim and his followers attribute collective polarization to groups' perceptions of threats to the integrity of their moral and social order. Moreover, the historical example of persecution of witches in seventeenth-century Massachusetts suggests the possibility of a parallel, in the resurgence of support for moral vilification of "the criminal element" in present-day society. Very few Americans take seriously the possibility that our society is likely to sink into oblivion in the near future as a consequence of any kind of governmental decree or assault by savages. And yet it is widely accepted that certain neighborhoods—even entire cities in the United States—are suffering so greatly from various forms of social pathology—family instability, unemployment, crime, mental illness, and deteriorated housing and schools—that the possibilities for their recovery seem practically hopeless. It is perhaps not too far-fetched to say that residents and business people in such neighborhoods who perceive themselves as good guys, and inhabitants of other areas who feel vulnerable to such problems in the near future if not at present, have a sense of evil rampant in their own wildernesses much like that possessed by the seventeenth-century Puritans. For these modern-day moralists extralegal vigilantism, and use of the criminal justice system to impose severe punishment without being too fastidious about the civil rights of accused deviants, may serve the same function as the persecution of witches in the Massachusetts Bay Colony—to reassure themselves that there remains a viable group that observes moral standards they respect, a group that can do something to prevent alien forces from intruding into their community and in effect destroying it.

I am suggesting that the perception of intense and pervasive social threat is a significant factor in explaining the proclivity of public opinion at the present time to accept an image of urban America as a battleground for the white hats of aggressive law enforcers and punishers versus the black hats of street muggers and dope dealers. Nevertheless, recognition of the prevalence of this scenario does not require that one accept its inevitability. We have just suggested some of the factors tending to magnify tendencies to polarization. By implication, then, polarization should be minimized in the absence of such circumstances.

In the following chapter we shall cite some examples of current practice that stress nonpolarization. For psychologists like Maslow, it does not seem likely that most of us, living in the kind of society that we do, will be able to go beyond seeing the world through morally polarized lenses. At the same time, Maslow recognized that there are a few exceptional people, known as "self-actualizing personalities," who are capable of rising above the constraints of polarized thinking. Self-actualization is explained in reference to Maslow's general theory of human motivation, which he sees as comprising a hierarchy of needs. At the bottom are physiological needs, followed in ascending order by the basic needs for safety, belongingness and love, and esteem. The notion of hierarchy suggests that those needs at the bottom must be gratified before people concern themselves with higher ones. Most people in fact do not go beyond these basic needs, but those creative, more fully developed individuals who are called self-actualizers proceed to a higher plane of motivation, the so-called "metamotivations."

Among the fifteen metamotivations attributed to self-actualizers is "dichotomy-transcendence." Dichotomy-transcendence is the capacity to go beyond the limitations of simplistic "black and white, either/or thinking," to recognize gradations, to integrate apparent contradictions. What is significant about this capacity is that such thought is often the basic stuff of creativity. For example, what makes some dramatists great is their capacity to elucidate seeming anomalies within the personalities of their characters in such a way that the character is ultimately understandable as a real person. Similarly, for a few composers, artists, and scientists it is precisely the capacity to bring together disparate elements in their respective products that sets them above the multitudes.

If "dichotomy-transcendence" is now found among a select few, is there not hope for some way to make such metamotivations accessible to larger numbers of people? Maslow speculates on the possibility that more people may be led to transcend dichotomous thinking than the very small group who show from their early years on the rare qualities of the self-actualizer. In his later writings he discusses the possibility, not only of psychotherapy, but of radical changes in education, in the workplace, and in other parts of social structure that may lead to a point where satisfaction of lower-level needs may be taken for granted, and thus provide a basis for creative existence—what he calls the "metalife"—among a larger proportion of the public than was previously believed capable of it.

Can we say that everyone yearns for the higher life, the spiritual . . . ? Here we run full-tilt into inadequacies in our language. Certainly we can say in principle that such a yearning must be considered to be a potential in every newborn baby until proven otherwise. That is to say, our best guess is that this potentiality, if it is lost, is lost after birth. It is also socially realistic today to bet that many newborn babies will never actualize this potentiality, and will never rise to the highest levels of motivation because of circumstances beyond their control that interfere with satisfaction of lower-level motivations, such as unemployment or prejudice in the larger society. There is, in fact, inequality of opportunity in the world today. It is also wise to say of adults that prognosis varies for each of them, depending on how and where they live, their social-economic-political circumstances, degree and amount of psychopathology, etc. And yet it is also unwise (as a matter of social strategy, if nothing else) to give up the possibility of the metalife completely and in principle for any living person. . . . And most certainly, we would be stupid to give up this possibility for future generations (Maslow, 1971: 326).

NOTE

1. In Reagan's prepared text, these words were followed by the statement that "some men are very prone to evil," but that observation was omitted from the speech as delivered. The reader should be cautious, however, about making inferences from this omission; it is possible that technical problems with a teleprompter made the omission unintentional (Lescaze, 1981).

7

Approaches to Nonpolarization

More than sixty years ago an anonymous prisoner wrote, in a popular magazine,

There is a wide gap between the opinions of those who advocate going after the criminal with the cat-o'nine tails and hell-fire, and the blubbers of those who would see him bedded in a hospital, psychoanalyzed, and coaxed back to the paths of rectitude, from which it is assumed he has been drawn by powers beyond his control. There seems to be scant reason to trust either of these extremes of opinion, and it becomes increasingly difficult to find judgments that may not be included with one or the other (Prisoner No. 4000X, 1972: 189).

More recently, an editorial in the liberal journal *Social Policy* speaks to "a need for an alternative to the conservative hard-line approach, but [one that] must also be distinguished from what now seems to many a soft liberal position. That 'liberal' approach to crime emphasizes protecting the rights of the accused, rehabilitating the convicted, and understanding the social causes of criminal behavior. In essence, it sees the accused as society's victim" (Greer and Reissman, 1982).

The present state of affairs has also been described by Morton Hunt as one in which "American attitudes toward the criminal justice system [reflect] a deep and dangerous schism . . . separating two antithetical poles of opinion—a new conservatism on the one side, and a rebellious and often radical dissent on the other" (Hunt, 1973: 426). In spite of differences between them, according to Hunt, adherents of these views share an antagonism toward the ideals of fairness and due process. For that reason he rejects both of these views in favor of a liberal faith in the principles of constitutional democracy, but one which recognizes that the criminal justice system needs to be overhauled, in part through massive infusions of money to create more courts and ancillary personnel to speed up trials. Beyond this, Hunt calls for a commitment to eradicating the inequalities of class and race in education, employment, and housing, which are correlated with crime, and for a similar commitment to improving the correctional system.

Each of the authors just cited calls attention to the deleterious consequences of polarized images of crime, and each points out the possibilities, and advantages, of alternatives to polarization. If one recognizes the problems of polarization, then it seems reasonable to consider remedies—that is, ways of bringing about *nonpolarization*. Such remedies will be the principal subject of the present chapter. Following an examination of the basic barriers that polarization raises against formulating and implementing effective crime policies, we shall identify some general characteristics of nonpolarized approaches and relate them to particular nonpolarized policies and programs.

PROBLEMS WITH POLARIZATION

To begin with, polarized images get in the way of solving the problems of crime because they are usually inaccurate, particularly when it comes to decisions about dealing with criminal offenders. These images suffer, not so much because they are based on untrue observations, but because the observations are not representative of the range of the offender's behavior. In part, to say this means that we acknowledge some validity in the homely wisdom that "there's a little bit of good in the worst of us and a little bit of bad in the best of us." Matza puts it more formally in his analysis of the delinquent as a boy whose illegal acts are simply one part of a life style that is not restricted to, much less dominated by, opposition to the conventions of the larger society.

The delinquent is casually, intermittently, and transiently immersed in a pattern of illegal action. His investment of affect in the delinquent enterprise is sufficient so as to allow an eliciting of prestige and satisfaction but not so large as to become more or less unavailable for other lines of action. In point of fact, the delinquent is available even during the period of optimum involvement for many lines of legal and conventional action. Not only is he available but a moment's reflection tells us that, concomitant with his illegal involvement, he actively participates in a wide variety of conventional activity. . . . He is committed to neither delinquent nor conventional enterprise. Neither, by the canons of his ideology or the makeup of his personality, is precluded (Matza, 1964: 28).

And in fact people who embezzle from banks, or mastermind criminal syndicates, or award government contracts to firms in which they have financial interests, are also often military heroes, tireless hospital volunteers, faithful spouses, or generous contributors to worthwhile charities. This is not to say that a person should be given equal credit for each day that he does not kill someone in balance against the one day on which he does; people who are prone to even occasional misdeeds, if the acts cause serious harm, may deserve society's moral condemnation and punishment. But it is generally true that the more accurate and broader the image we have of lawbreakers the better we are equipped to anticipate how they will respond to various criminal sanctions. Just as an unqualified bad-guy image may underestimate the capacity of some offenders to respond to benign rehabilitation, so may the attribution of good-guy status to other criminals result in dispositions that underestimate their dangerousness.

A telling illustration of the effects of overgeneralization, in contrast to particularization, is a study that contrasted public opinion about juvenile courts in general with survey respondents' views about the proper disposition for particular cases of delinquency (Parker, 1970). The people surveyed, in response to general questions about "strictness," indicated that they thought the courts should be more strict than they perceived them to be. But when they were given relevant information about the circumstances of real cases that had appeared before the juvenile courts in their region, questionnaire respondents recommended dispositions that were in close correspondence with those actually imposed by the judges who handled them.

But it is not only the inaccuracy of these images that poses problems. They are also problematic because they are unfair. When people who have committed typical street crimes are stereotyped as bad guys, there is a failure to balance from a moral perspective the criminal wrong against any meritorious behavior that ought to be counted to the individual's credit. Conversely for other offenders regarded as good guys, and not held to account for infractions because they are subject to deficiencies of intellect, cultural values, or other factors beyond their control, the injustice consists of failure to acknowledge opportunities the individuals may have to choose alternate, noncriminal means of expressing their frustrations.

Injustice becomes a social problem to the extent that it is perceived as such. As we have just noted, the criminal justice system is regarded by a majority of the public as too lenient with bad guys. This kind of perceived injustice, with respect to conventional violent or property crime, is translated into demands for longer prison sentences or capital punishment—demands that are opposed by another segment of the public, which views criminals more sympathetically. In other cases, injustice may be seen by various groups in the form of police harassment of minorities seeking to redress legitimate grievances, inadequate concern for victims' welfare, or unnecessary prison sentences for "petty" offenders.

The results of both of these aspects of polarization—inaccurate overgeneralizations and a public view of injustice associated with accepted practices for dealing (or not dealing) with crime—may be at some times inertia, at other times vacillation, at other times conflict. What do not result, however, are effective approaches—effective not only because they are demonstrably sound according to the criteria of unbiased policy experts but effective also because they are consonant with the sense of justice of the public that must ultimately support them.

The connection between polarization and policy may be summarized by restating the basic themes set forth at the conclusion of Chapter 1.

1. Making moral judgments is a fundamental and often useful process in human thought. A tendency toward extreme—or "polarized"—moral judgment, however, distorts reality and leads to maladaptive action.
2. Conventional criminal events are likely to be the subject of extreme moral judgments, in which perpetrators are seen as very bad people and morally guilty, and victims are seen as very good and morally innocent. Certain criminal events, however, do not fit the conventional stereotype, and in such cases criminals may be seen as good and victims as bad.
3. Current criminal justice policy is affected by moral polarization, which leads to conflict, frustration, and often stalemate.
4. Effective criminal justice policy will take account of moral judgments but try to avoid one-sided or exaggerated elements of polarization.

What follows, then, will consist of identifying general approaches or specific programs directed to the crime problem that appear to avoid the liability of polarization. Although we shall, as a matter of convenience, refer to them as examples of *nonpolarization*, the reader should understand that, strictly speaking, we are interested in approaches that are relatively less polarized in contrast with those that are more polarized. We shall indicate the attributes of these programs that qualify them to be considered as nonpolarized, with the hope that this will encourage attention to other such approaches and programs.

In order to emphasize nonpolarized aspects of the approaches to be discussed here, we shall contrast them with familiar approaches based on polarized assumptions. In a number of cases the proponents of nonpolarized approaches developed them out of an awareness of the shortcomings of polarized approaches; in other cases it is not apparent that a consciousness of the problems of polarization underlay the rationale of the nonpolarized approach.

MORAL BALANCE

Given the pervasive influence of the theories of Sigmund Freud upon the social sciences throughout the twentieth century, it is not surprising that efforts have been made from its earliest years to employ the psychoanalytic perspective in understanding the criminal mind. August Aichhorn, a disciple of Freud's, was a pioneer in applying Freudian therapeutic principles to treatment of juvenile delinquents, and other therapists sought to use those principles to rehabilitate adult offenders. The theory of neurosis, however, although central in psychoanalytic explanation, appears at first glance unsuitable for explaining crime. The neurotic is conceived as a person who has so overpowering a superego that he cannot gratify ordinary impulses without feeling guilty, whereas the criminal is depicted as having so little superego that he transgresses important rules of his society without apparent guilt.

Freud did not himself devote a great deal of attention to criminal psychology, but he did provide a brief description of what he called "the criminal from a sense of guilt" (1963). He used the term to refer to certain individuals whose criminal behavior arises from an unconscious desire for punishment, which serves to alleviate deeply rooted and obscure guilt feelings. This clinical observation was elaborated upon by his disciple Franz Alexander as the "neurotic character" syndrome.

Alexander contrasts the real neurotic's inhibitions from action with the neurotic character's inclination to act out his instinctual drives. And yet the neurotic character may also be distinguished from the real criminal, whose behavior is unconflictedly antisocial. There are in the neurotic character two forces in conflict: one impulsive, the other reacting "in a very moral, even overmoral fashion, for it not only tries to restrict the impulsive activities of the individual, it tries to inflict a self-injury" (Alexander and Staub, 1956: 97).

Alexander and others have treated criminals with a neurotic character by helping them bring to the fore the part of themselves that rejects antisocial, impulsive tendencies, as a way of directing them toward behavior that is more socially acceptable and, in the long run, more gratifying for themselves. Basically, their technique is a modification of the traditional Freudian method, an important element of which is the therapist's acceptance of attitudes and behavior that are rejected by conventional society. In order for patients to bring into consciousness, for purposes of analysis, those painful, long-suppressed memories that are at the root of their neuroses, it is necessary for therapists to eschew moral condemnation. Because it was real or imagined criticism of the unacceptable feelings that made them painful, successful therapy requires the Freudian therapist to adopt a totally accepting attitude, telling patients that it is permissible to bring up even those thoughts that seem most evil and unacceptable, and that the therapist will not reject them for it.

And this moral posture is not simply an expedient fiction; it is integral to the philosophy of orthodox psychoanalysis. The actor is seen as responsible for an act only insofar as his "conscious ego" takes part in it. Conversely, to the extent that the act is an outcome of unconscious processes, the person is thought to be not legally or morally responsible (Alexander and Staub, 1956: 62). And with the emphasis on unconscious determinants of behavior in mainstream psychoanalysis, criminals tend to end up being judged as blameless.

Not all psychoanalysts, however, concur in the view that their approach requires the suspension of moral condemnation. Melitta Schmideberg (1960), one of the few psychoanalytically oriented psychiatrists to have specialized in treating lawbreakers, has criticized modern psychiatry for having idealized a nonjudgmental attitude. In her view, offenders tend to deny their fear of punishment as a response to their anxieties about it. For therapy to be successful, that denial has to be eventually overcome in the course of treatment—a process that is facilitated when the therapist indicates her agreement with society's judgment that crime is wrong and deserves to be punished.

Because of problems encountered in applying nonjudgmental methods to treatment of conventional criminals, some therapists who started working within the psychoanalytic tradition have developed modifications of these methods, in which they accept the validity of conventional moral values. O. H. Mowrer is notable among academic psychologists for his departure from the Freudian explanation of neurosis. Mowrer refers to the Freudian position as the "impulse theory" of neurosis. If a person has been socialized too intensively, the ego becomes alarmed when normal erotic and aggressive impulses are about to emerge into the person's consciousness. In the Freudian view it is the struggle between the fearsome drives and the repressive function of the ego that causes anxiety and depression. Guilt is illusory—that is, it results from incorrectly condemning one's self, which in turn occurs because the individual unrealistically supposes that good people do not harbor sexual and hostile feelings.

Mowrer's view of guilt, by contrast, is that it is not illusory but real, that "in neurosis (and functional psychosis) the individual has committed tangible misdeeds, which have remained unacknowledged and unredeemed and . . . his anxieties thus have a realistic social basis and justification" (1961: 84). For neurotics it does no good to tell them that their guilt feelings are groundless. Therapy for these patients will fail, in Mowrer's view, unless they come to terms with their misdeeds—initially through confession and ultimately through expiation.

Given the dissatisfactions with nonjudgmental Freudian therapy expressed by Schmideberg, Mowrer, and others, it is not surprising that there has been experimentation with alternative techniques. Reality therapy is an approach that has been employed in treating neurotics as well as lawbreakers. We noted earlier, in Chapter 2, the two basic needs recognized by practitioners of reality therapy: the need to love and be loved, and the need to feel worthwhile to one's self and to others. From the second of these there emerges the concept of responsibility. Responsibility, in reality therapy, refers to "the ability to fulfill one's needs, and to do so in a way that does not deprive others of the ability to fulfill their needs" (Glasser 1975: 15). Among half a dozen points of contrast between reality therapy and conventional therapy, notes Glasser, "we emphasize the morality of behavior. We face the issue of right and wrong which we believe solidifies the involvement, in contrast to conventional psychiatrists who do not make the distinction between right and wrong, feeling that it would be detrimental to attaining the transference relationship they seek" (Glasser, 1975: 54).

Parallel to the individual approach of Glasser's reality therapy is a brand of group therapy that has been used with youngsters in a number of educational and correctional institutions, both residential and nonresidential. The approach, known as "Positive Peer Culture," emphasizes responsibility in a way very similar to Glasser's. "Since young people have a well-developed system for displacing responsibility for problems away from themselves, staff must develop an equally effective system for shifting the responsibility back where it belongs. *Reversing* is the process of placing responsibility for action back on those who must do the changing rather than allowing them to project it outside themselves" (Vorrath and Brendtro, 1974: 45).

Staff members in this program appear not to shy away from using confrontational tactics when their clients try to shift the blame for a problem away from themselves. For example, one boy with a drinking problem had made some progress in avoiding alcohol but went on a weekend binge when his brother came home on an army furlough. He insisted to a Positive Peer Culture counselor that he hadn't really fallen off the wagon, that he'd only been drinking over the weekend because his brother wanted to. The staff member retorted, "Do we understand that you are saying you don't have a drinking problem but now you have a new problem of being easily misled by others?" (Vorrath and Brendtro, 1974: 45).

Just as Glasser recognizes a universal need to be loved, the architects of Positive Peer Culture assume that a person must be accepted by others in order to feel positive about himself. But they also stress that the person must feel he *deserves* acceptance. A typical youngster in their program "knows that much of his behavior is irresponsible and damaging to himself or others. . . . If he is to feel deserving of the acceptance he must start making positive contributions to others and stop harmful behavior" (Vorrath and Brendtro, 1974: 10. For an empirical study of the effectiveness of this approach, see McKinney et al., 1978).

Note that, in characterizing these approaches as nonpolarized, we recognize that a nonpolarized view is not necessarily an amoral one. Indeed, moral judgments are explicit in these approaches, but the judgments are balanced, in one way or another taking account of the complexity of human motivations. Malefactors are subjected to neither total acceptance nor total rejection. When they misbehave they are reprimanded on the assumption that they have the capacity to choose to do otherwise, and when they act altruistically they are praised, often with special recognition for handicaps that they have overcome. It is this moral balance that distinguishes approaches like reality therapy and Positive Peer Culture from nonjudgmental therapies.

DEMANDING (AS OPPOSED TO BENEFICENT) REHABILITATION

Proponents of penal reform frequently present innovative proposals in such a way as to imply that, had their ideas occurred to someone else in previous generations, their merits would have been instantly recognized and implemented, and much unneeded suffering would have been avoided. Such a naive assumption, of course, fails to take account of many real obstacles.

Some of these obstacles to correctional reform are obvious. Shortage of funds is a problem not peculiar to correctional systems; there is seldom enough money for hospitals, schools, street cleaning, and other services ordinarily supported by public funds. Therefore, government revenues are likely to be allocated disproportionately to activities that are supported by organized interest groups, which provide money, votes or other valuable commodities to legislators and other decision makers. There are strong organized lobbies for education, agriculture, ethnic minorities, children's rights, labor, business, the medical profession. But probably no segment of society has as little force advocating for it as inmates of correctional institutions. Neither prisoners nor any individuals with a felony conviction record are permitted to vote, so that elected officials have little to gain politically by attending to their interests. And the friends and families of criminals have not been a visible force for correctional reform. With few exceptions, such as Quakers and civil rights groups who feel that the prison system unfairly discriminates against racial or ethnic minorities, there has never been a long-term, effective constituency pressing for the resources needed to make a credible effort to change criminal offenders into useful citizens.

And yet, in view of the costs of criminal recidivism to society, one wonders why efforts at rehabilitation have been so weak and sporadic. Apart from the reasons just mentioned for inattention, there has often been active resistance to rehabilitative measures. The rationale for much of this resistance was discussed in Chapter 2, in terms of the principle of "less eligibility." If the experience designed to rehabilitate criminals seems too pleasant, it is opposed on grounds that it represents an advantage not available to worthier members of the community. Thus, taxpayers will object if asked to support expensive individual psychotherapy for criminal offenders when they themselves might like such treatment but cannot afford it. And, when proposals are advanced to train prison inmates and then place them in satisfying, well-paid jobs upon their release from prison, similar objections will be raised if such opportunities for training and employment are hard to come by for non-lawbreakers.

As a result, those approaches having the widest support are approaches that deemphasize beneficence and emphasize demands that are made upon the participants. The Synanon program for drug addicts is a well-known example. Initiates into this program learn that demands will be made upon them from the outset. "At first, some token roadblocks are thrown in the way of the person who is attempting to enter. He may be given an appointment and made to wait. If he is even a few minutes late for the appointment, he is told to come back another time. . . . Sometimes money is requested as an entrance fee. An effort is made to have the individual *fight his way in*" (Yablonsky, 1967: 194, emphasis supplied).

Throughout the period of residence in a Synanon facility the person is exposed to difficult, often painful encounters. Most dramatic is the "haircut"—a confrontational form of group therapy in which each resident is in turn put on the "hot seat" while others attack him verbally: calling him names, questioning his motives, condemning his values, and so forth. In this program there are no staff members in the usual sense. From the director on down, all "treatment" personnel are or have been addicted to drugs, and there is only a series of steps from the bottom to the top of the hierarchy without a clear line of demarcation between the "treaters" and the "treated." As a result, the confronters in a given encounter can use their own experiences to penetrate the defenses of the confronted resident and emphasize the badness of the lifestyle of addiction. But Synanon residents who have been "clean" for some time also serve as models for initiates to emulate.

A confrontational approach is likewise utilized by Visionquest, a for-profit enterprise designed for serious juvenile offenders, both male and female (Greenwood and Zimring, 1985: 41–53). On the one hand the program provides experiences that would surely be envied by many nondelinquent youngsters. Groups of thirty to forty-five youngsters, led by a similar number of young adult staff members, take part in a wilderness camping experience, travel cross-country on a wagon train, or live on and learn the various skills necessary to operate a sailing vessel. Participation, costing about a hundred dollars a day for each of the youth, is financed by public funds from the juvenile courts—in California, Pennsylvania, and several other states—that commit offenders to the program. Why, one might ask, is the public willing to support so expensive a program? Public support for Visionquest does not appear to depend upon demonstrated effectiveness. In fact, there is evidence that it has not lessened the likelihood of recidivism for one group of participants ("Visionquest," 1988). The answer appears to lie in the fact that, far from coddling the youngsters, the physical demands of the program are very arduous. In this respect, it is similar to "shock incarceration" programs, in which punishment and discipline are the paramount themes (Parent, 1989). Moreover, the opportunity for participation depends upon the youngsters' agreement not to abscond, to abstain from drugs and sex, and to complete at least two components of the program.

Perhaps the most important manifestation of demands made upon participants in the Visionquest program is in the counseling process. Although the junior staff members who do most of the counseling are encouraged to develop affectionate relationships with their charges, there is also considerable emphasis on getting the youths to face up to their past delinquencies and the problems that caused them. Detailed records are kept on all residents, and when they are not living up to expectations of enthusiastic participation or when they violate the rules of the program, they are subject to confrontational interviews with senior staff members who probe for deep-seated conflicts that are thought to give rise to the problem behavior.

What programs like Synanon and Visionquest have in common is that they take account of the dual, good-bad nature of the criminal offender. Instead of denying or minimizing the badness, which has been the downfall of approaches reflecting the Progressive movement, these programs recognize the power of selfish and aggressive motivations and recognize the need to address them vigorously. At the same time, by not settling for mere incapacitation they assert the possibility that, with effort, their clients' better instincts can come to the surface. Especially with their stress on participants' own responsibility for whether they end up following criminal lifestyles or law-abiding ones, these programs take account of the moral dualism in all human nature.

MORAL DEVELOPMENT IN A THERAPEUTIC COMMUNITY

Reality therapy, Positive Peer Culture, Synanon, Visionquest, and other modern correctional approaches emphasize moral responsibility, just as did the sober Quaker gentlemen who prayed with prisoners at the Walnut Street Jail in Philadelphia in the eighteenth century. Among psychologists, however, even though there has been considerable attention to theories of moral development in recent years, very few have directed their attention to penology.

One exception has been the educational psychologist Lawrence Kohlberg. Drawing upon seminal work by the Swiss psychologist Jean Piaget on the moral development of children, Kohlberg developed a theory that accounts for the continuing maturation of ethical judgment into adulthood. According to Kohlberg there are three levels of moral development. The first level, characteristic of children up to about age ten, is termed *preconventional*. At this level the child associates "wrong" with punishment and "right" with the absence of punishment. Most adolescents and adults operate at a second stage, the *conventional* level, which denotes acceptance of right and wrong according to the dictates of one's own society. And some individuals go beyond conventional morality to the *postconventional* level, "at which customs and social rules are critically examined in terms of universal rights and duties and universal moral principles" (Kohlberg et al., 1974: 1). Just as proper intellectual growth is seen as passing through various stages at which increasingly complex modes of logical thought are developed (Piaget, 1957), moral development consists of progression from one moral level to another.

Like intellectual development, moral development is conceived on the one hand as a natural concomitant of increasing age for children but also as a process that may be arrested or slowed down by some experiences and enhanced by others. According to Kohlberg, a majority of adolescent offenders have not gone beyond the preconventional level of moral growth, and the same is true of some adult criminals. It is not necessary for an individual to go beyond the conventional stage in order to be a useful member of society, and indeed someone at the postconventional level might find his conduct at odds with the rules held and enforced by the majority. But crimes like petty theft or vandalism, which represent first steps in lawbreaking, are typically acts of adolescents who have not internalized prevalent community standards. If the connection between delinquents' behavior and arrested moral socialization is understood, that understanding should suggest remedies for the problem.

As a means of fostering moral development, Kohlberg and his associates at the Harvard School of Education established in the 1970s, in cooperation with the Connecticut Department of Correction, a "Just Community," first at the Cheshire Reformatory for Men and subsequently at the Women's Correctional Center in Niantic. By means of group discussion of the moral component of issues encountered in their daily lives, inmates who fell short of accepting conventional moral standards were helped, through exposure to notions of justice at higher levels, to perceive the greater justice of those ways of resolving the issues. Of great importance was the fact that in this program, like others mentioned above, emphasis was placed on group decision-making processes. Conflicts were aired in group meetings, with emphasis on the rights and wrongs for all parties involved. Inmates were given authority to make and enforce certain rules, in line with established principles of justice embodied in a community constitution, which they themselves participated in formulating and periodically revising.

Noteworthy also is the scope of rules that inmates participate in developing. They have a say in rules applying not only to disputes among inmates but also to disputes arising between staff members and inmates. By learning to see justice in rules balancing individual rights with the need for established authority in the microcosm of the therapeutic community, it is expected that inmates will learn to accept and abide by the counterparts of these rules in the larger society. (The Just Community approach appears to have a number of elements in common with exemplars of "peacemaking criminology." See, for example, Rucker, 1991.)

In a systematic evaluation of the Just Community approach at Niantic, Scharf and Hickey (1976) found that among inmates under twenty-four years of age there was a significant change toward higher levels of moral reasoning as a result of participation in the "just community" cottage. Over a five-month period, nearly a third of the seventeen inmates tested shifted more than half a moral stage.

The "Just Community" is based on a model that avoids choosing between treating good guys and punishing bad ones, even within an institution for adjudicated offenders. Its superiority over conventional correctional programs is in part due to an approach in which "within the context of a prison, the seemingly inherent conflicts between rehabilitation and control can be adequately reconciled. Both can be seen as being based on principles of fairness to the inmate and fairness of the inmate to the group or community" (Kohlberg et al., 1974: 11).

RESTITUTION AND COMMUNITY SERVICE

The New Social Defense Movement

Lombroso and his followers, as noted in Chapter 5, justified the punishment of criminal offenders primarily as a means of protecting society, in what came to be known as the theory of social defense. Subsequently, there has developed the New Social Defense movement, which has some roots in utilitarianism as well as in nineteenth-century positivism (Jeffery, 1972: 497; Mannheim, 1972: 35; Newman, 1985: 211–20). Like Beccaria's utilitarianism, Social Defense rejects retribution as a basis for punishment. When punishment is necessary it should take into account the rights of individuals and of society. During the early years of the twentieth century it was invoked as justification for measures designed to remove from society certain categories of offenders thought to be especially dangerous because of mental deficiency or sexual deviance— measures based on the same kind of long-standing fears about the constitutional element in crime that Lombroso had kindled a generation earlier.

More recently, proponents of the Social Defense school have adopted a stance emphasizing the need for prevention and treatment. As explained by one of its leading exponents, Social Defense "proposes above all—and in many respects this is its chief claim——no longer to take expiation or punitive repression as the aim of reaction to crime but rather the prevention of delinquency and the rehabilitation of the offender in a context of social concord" (Ancel, 1987: 3). The idea of "social concord" refers to basic humanistic assumptions embodied in the Social Defense approach. When the normal equilibrium between society and the individual has been disturbed through commission of a criminal act, harmony is restored when the malefactor is somehow enabled to reassume his role as a responsible member of the collectivity. And in the view of modern Social Defense theorists, it is society's responsibility, as well as the offender's, to restore the harmonious relationship. Equilibrium is more likely to be restored by offering treatment than by imposing punishment.

Should punishment be necessary, it ought to avoid the dehumanizing experience of imprisonment whenever possible. Preferable are fines or community service but compensation to individual victims is not mentioned. Since society is clearly the victim when crimes are committed, according to modern Social Defense theorists, it is not surprising that payments to society, in money or in service, are taken to be the proper way of making the victim whole.

Restitution to Individuals

Ancel's concept of "social concord" suggests the function, basic to every legal system, of doing justice—that is, settling disputes in such a way that the outcome seems fair to all parties. But among individual victims that sense of justice is often absent. In Chapter 5, we noted the extent to which Western legal systems have retreated from the "golden age of the victim" (Schafer, 1968), which prevailed during the early Middle Ages. Since that era, especially in the Anglo-American system, criminal proceedings have come to take precedence over civil proceedings.

Thus, for example, although a theft from a private person is both a criminal and civil offense, victimized private parties must wait until the state has carried out its prosecution before they can sue to recover the value of their stolen property. And frequently this means that victims have little chance of recovering anything even if the accused person has been convicted of the crime. Although evidence may have been sufficient to support a conviction by the stringent standard of the criminal courts, where a defendant's guilt must be proven "beyond a reasonable doubt" rather than by the civil court's lesser criterion of proof by "a preponderance of the evidence," by the time the criminal trial has been held and the victim's suit against the perpetrator appears on the civil docket, the offender is often insolvent because the stolen property or the money from its sale has been squandered, hidden, or used to pay the cost of a criminal defense.

In spite of this overall neglect of individual restitution by the criminal justice system, there have been exceptions. Restitution to crime victims is not uncommon in informal pretrial negotiations. In cases of embezzlement, for example, either actual payment to the victim or a promise to repay often accompanies a guilty plea. Even when victims plead not guilty and are convicted at trial, they will not infrequently offer to make restitution. Willingness to make restitution is itself a sign that the offender is a good guy: repentant for the harm done, sympathetic with the plight of the victim, and eager for a chance to undo the damage. As a result, a promise of restitution often works in favor of convicted offenders by persuading the sentencing magistrate to consider probation rather than prison, or a shorter rather than a longer period of confinement.

Although many members of the public find monetary restitution unsat-isfactory as a way of bringing about a sense of justice having been done, there are others who feel that it can go a long way toward restoring confi-dence in the criminal justice system. The problem with relying upon in-formal practices is that the results can be capricious. Among cases involv-ing defendants capable of making restitution, some victims may be lucky enough to encounter a judge or a defense lawyer who raises the issue, and they end up being justly compensated; other less-fortunate victims must absorb the costs themselves.

It is only recently that restitution has been made a formal part of the criminal justice process. The first law specifically authorizing judges to impose restitution as part of the criminal justice process in New York was passed in 1980 and revised in 1983. Originally it limited payments to $5,000 for felonies and $1,000 for misdemeanors; as revised, it allows courts to order convicted offenders to pay their victims the total value of property stolen or destroyed as well as specific expenses incurred, such as medical bills. Although it has been estimated that as many as 20 or 25 per-cent of convicted criminals are financially able to make restitution to their victims, only a few judges make full use of the powers given them under this law (Barbanel, 1983).

Restitution in Kind

When juveniles have damaged property, it is sometimes possible for them to undo the damage through their own efforts. In recent years, when vandals have been found responsible for graffiti on buildings or subway cars, judges have frequently assigned them to a number of hours' work cleaning up the property they themselves have defaced, if practical, or if not, restoring similar defacement caused by others. Often the rationale is that the offenders have no money to pay for the damage at present and no employment to enable them to meet the obligation in the future. And so the work assignment is simply a practical alternative to monetary restitu-tion.

But restitution in kind can be defended as superior to simple payment for damages, even if the offender has financial resources. One college deals with students who steal from its bookstore by requiring them to work in the store for a number of hours, using a pay scale of $2 an hour, equivalent to the value of the item stolen. The hours at work are defended as having a "rehabilitative function" that would not be served by simply writing a check (Winer, 1984).

But how can one determine when the rehabilitative function of restitution is in fact accomplished? In a seminal paper published more than thirty years ago, Eglash proposed the concept of "creative restitution" to refer to a process in which the situation is "left better than before an offense is committed" (1958: 620). He offers the example of an auto thief who not only returns the car to its rightful owner undamaged but also repairs some mechanical problem in the car, or waxes it, or washes it every week for a month. The purpose, Eglash indicates, is to restore the offender's sense of self worth, which benefits when there is a reconciliation between the offender and the victim.

The element of reconciliation has been explicitly addressed in recent programs that have brought together perpetrators and their victims in face-to-face encounters (Karman, 1990: 291–92). With the help of trained mediators, these programs provide opportunities to work out mutually acceptable arrangements for restitution, either in cash or in kind. But they also seek to resolve interpersonal tensions between parties. By allowing victims to confront the perpetrators with their injuries, perpetrators to express regret and make amends, and victims in turn to forgive, these meetings offer the possibility of restoring both parties to a relationship based on something other than the bad offender-aggrieved victim model.

Community Service as Social Restitution

In the situations we have been describing, it is necessary to identify individual victims in order for a reconciliatory process to take place. However, the nature of many criminal offenses—abuse of public office, vandalism, drug trafficking, manipulation in securities markets—is such that the suffering parties are either whole societies or hard-to-identify individuals. Monetary fines—prescribed by statute, imposed by the court and paid to the public treasury—have long been considered an appropriate way of handling these offenses when their severity does not warrant incarceration. The fine is considered not just as equating pain suffered for pain inflicted but as compensation to the state as representative of the private parties who cannot be identified. But the question then arises of how to treat indigent offenders fairly, without imprisoning them simply because they cannot pay the fines that keep more affluent criminals out of prison.

Juvenile offenders on probation, for example, have sometimes in the past been required as a condition of probation to work for money in order to be able to pay fines to the state. This practice was a precursor to a type of legal disposition that has come into very wide use within a short period of time for people who have committed certain types of crimes—the community service order.

The community service order is defined as "a court order that an offender perform a specified number of hours of uncompensated work or service within a given time period for a nonprofit community organization or tax-supported agency" (Carter, Cocks, and Glaser, 1987: 4). Having been used initially by English courts and adopted by a number of jurisdictions in the United States in recent years (Beha, Carlson, and Rosenblum, 1977; Wilson, 1977), community service orders are used as the disposition of choice in situations where incarceration is not warranted and where a financial penalty would be unsuitable, either because the offender has no money or because a monetary fine proportional to the offense is judged to have too little impact on the offender. A number of prominent professional athletes, for example, having been convicted of possessing illegal drugs and thus having set a bad example for youngsters who see them as role models, have been sentenced to work a specified number of hours giving lectures in schools on the detrimental effects of substance abuse. In these instances the fines that might have been imposed would make little dent in the bank accounts of these high-salaried individuals, whereas the time devoted to community service is perceived as requiring some real sacrifice.

Like court orders for restitution to individuals, there is a lack of agreement about the goals that community service sentences should accomplish (Carter, Cocks, and Glaser, 1987; Pease, 1985). In spite of (or perhaps because of) that unclarity, both restitution and community service sentences appeal to both tough-minded and tender-minded critics of the criminal justice system (Perrier and Pink, 1985; Schneider, 1986). Seen as an alternative to simple probation, they appeal to the tough-minded; as an alternative to prison, to the tender-minded. Some conservatives also find them attractive because they see them as punitive, and liberals perceive in them the potential for rehabilitation. Moreover, the idea of providing satisfaction to victims is attractive to members of the public who range across a wide ideological spectrum. At the same time there are critics on both sides: conservatives who find restitution and community service too lenient and liberals who find them too harsh.

One criterion for evaluating these programs is the traditional one for various offender therapies—whether or not the subjects become recidivists (repeat offenders) within a specified time after completion of the treatment. Of the many restitution and community service programs in operation during the past two decades, only a small proportion have been designed so that the group given these dispositions can be compared with a like group handled in other ways.

A comprehensive research study evaluated juvenile offenders in four different juvenile court jurisdictions—one in Oklahoma, one in Idaho, one in Georgia, and one in Washington, D. C. (Schneider, 1986). The design varied somewhat in each area, but for all four programs the experimental groups comprised youngsters who worked to provide money restitution to individual victims or, if the nature of the offense precluded private compensation, performed equivalent work of a community service nature. Each jurisdiction had one or more control groups, usually given probation in its traditional form. For the Georgia and District of Columbia programs it was concluded that, during a two- to three-year follow-up period, boys and girls sentenced to restitution were significantly less likely to recidivate than control youngsters. The Idaho findings showed a trend favorable to restitution, but did not reach statistical significance, and there was no discernible effect in the Oklahoma county.

Another study, this time in New York City, showed no difference in rearrest rates following treatment between adult offenders ordered to perform community service and similar individuals who served jail terms (McDonald, 1986). An Australian study yielded an outcome favoring community service, but methodological problems may be serious enough to invalidate the findings (Rook, as discussed in Pease, 1985). In summarizing the findings of these investigations, researchers who have worked in the area conclude that restitution and community service may inhibit subsequent criminality among juveniles under certain circumstances (McDonald, 1988; Schneider, 1986), but that those dispositions have no demonstrable effect upon recidivism for adult offenders (Pease, 1985; McDonald, 1988).

The ambiguity of results in these studies suggests a need to examine more closely the *processes* as implemented in various settings. Are restitution and community service dispositions so painful that offenders who have endured them resolve to foreswear the kinds of behavior that brought them to the attention of the authorities? Alternatively, is there something about certain of these programs that induces repentance? Is there some connection between offenders' social and psychological characteristics on the one hand, and desistance from repetitive offending on the other? Perhaps variation in the attributes of program directors or other staff is the crucial.difference. Or perhaps some communities respond more positively to restitution than others and it is that positive response, feeding back to offenders, which encourages them to obey the law. Then too, the criterion of recidivism, particularly as indicated by reconviction for any offense within a fairly short period of time, may not be the most significant basis for evaluating the effects of restitution and community service programs.

COMMUNITY SERVICE IN A THERAPEUTIC COMMUNITY

Some insight into the role of restitution in overcoming the problems of polarized approaches to crime may be gained by considering the Delancey Street Foundation, an offshoot of Synanon established in San Francisco in 1971. Its residents, unlike the clients of restitution and community service programs discussed above, are not committed by court order; rather, they are drug addicts and criminals, many recently released from incarceration, who recognize that they need more help readjusting to society than the preparation offered by traditional prison programs. Like Synanon, Delancey Street is a self-help community that does not have a professional staff, as such. All residents have similar backgrounds as social outcasts, and a person who acts as "therapist" for another resident at one moment may, in the next, find herself the subject of others' efforts to force her to deal with her own problems. Delancey Street has its own version of the Synanon "haircut," in which every individual's rationalizations and other defenses for his deviance are subject to forceful and emotional verbal attack by other residents.

These sessions are part of an overall philosophy, as expressed by Delancey's founder and first president, John Maher, based on recognition that problems like drug addiction and crime are indeed connected to social injustices, but that criminals and addicts must nevertheless acknowledge their own responsibility for their situation "if the chain of causation is to be broken" (Hampden-Turner, 1976: 67).

What distinguishes the Delancey approach from Synanon and similar approaches is that, in addition to dealing with moral responsibility at the level of psychological experience, Delancey Street residents must participate in certain activities. They work in a variety of Foundation-owned businesses—a moving company, a restaurant, auto repairs—through which the program not only supports itself financially but also provides its residents with jobs that entail increasing amounts of responsibility. Most important, residents contribute a great deal of time and energy to social action projects for which they receive no financial compensation. Delancey's approach to community service is controversial, for in addition to performing such functions as counseling children on the danger of using illegal drugs and escorting senior citizens in dangerous areas, a number of its activities involve partisanship on behalf of political underdogs. Its residents have, for example, led a successful campaign for the release of an inmate who had served a forty-six-year prison term, supported Cesar Chavez's United Farm Workers, rented their bus to black senior citizens wishing to protest against a local utility, and participated in a voter-registration drive for Spanish-speaking citizens.

Part of the basis for these activities seems to be the idea of making restitution to society for past harms inflicted, but there is also a sense that Delancey workers benefit especially from helping others who are victims of social injustice. However, performing such services is therapeutic even when the recipient is not in need. At a meeting of the Foundation's Board of Directors, Maher said to one of the "square" directors [i.e., a director who was not himself a member of the therapeutic community],

People like you, Dugald, should please not buy your Christmas tree from us. You will get it free—for the same reason we sent your kids to Guatemala. It's important for the family to give things to people who've helped us. Apart from your need to receive it, we need to give it. Okay? We must strive to avoid the dichotomy of dependent insiders and independent outsiders. You help us by depending more, and we become more independent when we help you (Hampden-Turner, 1976: 256).

Our view that the Delancey Street Foundation represents a resolution of the widespread moral dichotomy in approaches to deviance is supported by another of Maher's observations:

See, we're really caught in this bind between right-wing nuts who want to beat everyone on the head and poor, weak-kneed, bleeding heart, vicarious thrill, radical chic creepos who wanna kiss your backside, until you're almost a schizo. A number of our people understand this, and what we want to do is get into a position where our problem, the repressive nature of our relationships with society, is understood, but at the same time *we* are taking personal responsibility for our own change (Hampden-Turner, 1976: 15).

MORAL REDEMPTION AS AN INTEGRATING CONCEPT

The bind that Maher describes is a reflection of the deeply rooted nature of polarization processes. Durkheim (1947: 102) has suggested that social integration is achieved by casting off those individuals who are blamed for some apparent threat to the social order and, as Dentler and Erickson (1959) have shown, it can be beneficial for groups to make the demarcation between certain "bad" individuals and the "goodness" of the group as a whole. But once the mechanisms for this stereotyping and for acting upon such stereotypes have become entrenched within a society, the stereotypes become very difficult to undo. And yet, if one is not going to give up altogether on deviants, one must develop some way of eventually reconciling them with those who cast them out in the first place.

In criminological literature the issue is commonly raised as one of how to reintegrate the offender into the community. In a sense, that is what nonpolarization is all about. The question arises, however, as to the ingredient or ingredients that make for successful reintegration.

In one of the few writings that have addressed this issue within the context of broad theories of criminology, Galaway and Hudson begin by contrasting the classical approach to corrections with the positivist approach. The first of these, in their view, considers crime as the product of "sin"; the second, as the product of "disease." Finding deficiencies in both approaches, they propose an alternative that emphasizes neither the classical model's punitive sanctions nor the positivist model's treatment plan based on differential diagnosis of disease. They propose, rather, the "reconciliative model," with restitution the primary process in implementing it. Galaway and Hudson view crime as "an indication of the estrangement of the individual from the larger society" (1975: 64), and unlike other writers who emphasize restitution in terms of private party payment to restore an imbalance between the offender and the individual victim (Eglash, 1958; Schafer, 1960) they include as well restitution to the community through service, as a way of undoing the "estrangement" resulting from the criminal act. Among benefits of the reconciliatory approach, they mention the opportunities it provides deviants to atone for their misdeeds. Instead of being left with the burden of guilt for harm, the opportunity for restitution leads to expiation of the guilt. Similarly, making restitution enhances the offender's sense of self-worth. Further, it tends to produce a positive social response: As the former malefactor is perceived as less threatening after making restitution, the possibility for participation in communal activities increases.

Galaway and Hudson's reconciliative model, as a response to the crime problem in terms of possibilities of bringing about a rapprochement between criminals and the community, reflects many of the assumptions that led us to emphasize the approaches described earlier in this chapter. But there is an important ingredient that they do not incorporate within their approach—the moral element. Actually, its importance is implicit in the rationale they supply for the reconciliative model. Although they say that restitution "calls forth the strengths and abilities of offenders and does not focus upon 'sins' and 'sicknesses' " (1975: 67), their discussion of expiation of guilt as a function of restitution makes no sense without the assumption that a "sin" was committed in the first place. Similarly, to speak of restitution as an enhancer of self-worth is to acknowledge that something, which if not called "sin" is nevertheless very much like it, caused the individual to doubt his self-worth in the first place.

Because of its moral connotations I shall use the word *redemption* to refer to the process that I believe is fundamental in lessening the good-bad polarities between offenders and society.[1] The term is commonly used in two different though related ways. In one sense of the term we speak of people who have "redeemed" themselves by compensating the victims of their misdeeds, thus reducing if not removing the opprobrium society directs toward them. In this sense, redemption connotes repayment of an obligation. Redemption of pawned jewelry, for example, refers back to a previous arrangement, in which a pawn broker has lent the customer a sum of money, holding the jewelry as security for a period of time. During that period of time there is a contract: The customer is under an obligation to the broker to repay the debt, just as the broker is under an obligation to return the pawned item if the agreed-upon principal and interest on the loan are paid before the deadline. When the item is redeemed the parties are relieved of further obligation to one another. But in a sense there remains a positive relationship on the basis that each party has learned that the other can be trusted.

Similarly, an individual who has committed a criminal act may be said to be in "hock" to society. In theory, the obligation is redeemed by making reparation, that is, compensating the aggrieved party, through paying a fine, serving a prison term, or being executed. But it is only after both parties have agreed on what their obligations are and then gone on to fulfill those obligations, that we can speak of a fully accomplished redemption. In fact, however, there is seldom a real redemption because agreement is lacking on what the offender's obligations should be. When the public feels that criminal sentences are too lenient and when individual victims feel that they have not been compensated for their losses—or when convicted criminals feel they have been treated too harshly, and certain social groups feel that they are harassed as a group by the criminal justice system—then redemption is not possible.

In another sense of the term, redemption refers not simply to repayment of a specific economic debt but to a spiritual transformation—a transformation from a state of sin to a state of grace. Spiritual redemption has to do with the person's relationship to God, but it also has to do with his relationships with other people and his view of himself as well.

Although sometimes used independently, the two meanings of "redemption," the contractual and the spiritual, are related when applied to crime. From the transgressor's point of view a spiritual transformation occurs when he has engaged in expiatory acts; from the viewpoint of the injured party, when that person acknowledges adequate repayment having been made it becomes possible to perceive the offender's transformation from a bad person to a good person.

In reality therapy, Positive Peer Culture, the Just Community, and Synanon-like confrontational approaches, emphasis is upon the offender's moral redemption, whereas restitution and community service place more emphasis on the impact upon individual victims and the community. If one considers these programs from a broader perspective, however, it would seem that all would benefit from dual emphasis on reparation and moral reform. To the extent that members of the public are aware of the pains and deprivations involved in the various techniques aimed at moral rehabilitation and to the extent that they are aware that the clients of these programs have undergone a genuine moral rehabilitation, they should be more likely to feel that the program participants have discharged their obligations. Similarly, the more offenders actually make concrete reparation to their victims, either individual or collective, the more likely they should be to undergo an authentic experience of spiritual redemption.

Insofar as issues of redemption in the offender-public relationship have been addressed, most of the treatment has been speculative. However, there has been some research on the topic. Thorvaldson (1980) interviewed 132 English offenders who had committed a wide range of conventional offenses against property or persons. Of the total, forty-eight had been given community service sentences, forty-two fined, and forty-two placed on probation. The author notes that the community service subsample appeared to have more extensive criminal records than the other two subsamples.

When asked an initial general question about their attitudes toward their sentences, the community service subjects were more likely than the other groups to show that they had internalized the moral principles underlying their sentences, the fined subjects were the most resentful, and the probationers seemed unclear about the functions of the dispositions they had received. Considering redemption in terms of positive moral judgments applied to one's self, one can examine the findings from two of Thorvaldson's scales measuring how his subjects perceived the effects of their sentences. Community-service group members were more likely than those who had been fined to perceive their sentences as increasing their self-esteem and promoting self-understanding, although the probation group scored about the same as the community service group on these measures. Clearly, one cannot infer from these data that community service is superior to more traditional approaches in bringing about a personal redemptive experience for offenders.

With respect to the second question, concerning the effect of reparation on whether offenders are redeemed in the eyes of the public, Thorvaldson offers only indirect evidence. He did not survey the public, but he did ask the offenders in his sample the question, "Do you think your sentence will help you to start with a clean slate so far as society is concerned?" (Thorvaldson, 1980: 88). To this question the responses among the three groups—those sentenced to community-service, fines, or probation—showed no significant differences. As interpreted by the author, this result reflects a pervasive sense among all groups that their criminal convictions will always be held against them no matter what penalty is imposed.

More direct evidence on public perceptions of restitution is based on surveys of American respondents. Gandy (1978) and Gandy and Galaway (1980) found that a substantial majority of people in various samples—police officers, social workers, lawyers, and a representative sample of adult telephone subscribers in Columbia, South Carolina—expressed generally favorable sentiments toward "creative restitution," defined as "a process in which an offender, under appropriate supervision, is

helped to find some way to make amends to those he has hurt by his offense" (Gandy, 1978: 119). As conceptualized in these studies it includes
not only monetary payment to private victims but also personal service to
victims and service to the general community.

Respondents were asked about the appropriateness of various restitu-
tive sanctions for particular classes of offenders. More favorable sentiment was expressed for orders of restitution without additional punishment
for property offenders than for violent ones; similarly, the less punitive
disposition was preferred more often for first offenders than for recidivists.

When asked to give reasons for the appropriateness of restitution, the
most frequent response by far—44 percent of the Columbia sample—mentioned its rehabilitative effect, that "the offender learns something, is re-
educated and returns to society" (Gandy and Galaway, 1980: 97). This is
as close as we can come to empirical evidence that the public is willing to
accept as redeemed those offenders who make reparation, but one should
be cautious in interpreting the findings. Among the three forms of restitution mentioned previously—monetary compensation, personal service, or
community service—monetary payment was most consistently favored;
perhaps this suggests that the victim's welfare rather than the offender's
moral transformation remains uppermost in the public's mind.

CONCLUSION

It would be delightful to conclude this book by asserting that the
criminal justice system is moving steadily toward nonpolarized approaches
to the crime problem. Unfortunately, we have no evidence to support that
assertion. Notwithstanding the examples presented in this chapter, the
overall tendency from the 1970s into the 1990s appears to be toward
greater polarization in public opinion, and that opinion in turn affects the
way in which the criminal justice system operates. Deemphasis on rehabilitation in prisons, along with increasing emphasis on long-term incapacitation and the death penalty, seems to prevail. And concern about dishonesty and profiteering in the halls of government is frequently translated into
the kind of saints-and-sinners dichotomy that we have seen applied to actors in conventional crime encounters.

It is instructive to recall the declaration of principles adopted at the
first meeting of the American Prison Congress, held in Cincinnati in 1870.

Among the principles agreed upon by participants at that meeting were the following: (a) offenders should be provided with rewards for good conduct, (b) discipline should be carried out in such a way as to preserve the inmate's self-respect, (c) the primary goal of prison should be to prepare prisoners for useful occupations after serving their sentences rather than simply to make them manageable captives, and (d) society at large should be made to realize its responsibility for crime conditions. As Sykes (1967) points out, these principles, although widely accepted, are not yet standard practice. In general, many measures that have been advocated by progressive criminologists over the past 200 years are not, for the most part, being implemented at the present time, measures that could well alleviate the crime problem today.

And so it is with nonpolarization. Several ways of dealing with crime that might fairly be characterized as nonpolarized have been developed in recent years. If they have not quickly caught on, we should not be surprised. The polarizing psychological and social processes described in Chapter 6 are not going to melt away overnight. But it is not unreasonable to expect that, to the extent that people become aware of the maladaptive consequences of polarization, there will emerge perceptions and eventually policies free of its constraints. One may hope for a criminal justice system within which, ultimately, nonpolarization will be an important principle.

NOTE

1. Although Eglash prefers the term "creative restitution" (1958), he mentions that he was advised by some people to use the term "redemption" to refer to compensation by offenders to individual victims.

Bibliography

Abbott, Jack Henry. 1981. *In the Belly of the Beast: Letters from Prison*. New York: Random House.

Adorno, T. W., Else Frenkel-Brunswik, Daniel J. Levinson, and R. Nevitt Sanford. 1950. *The Authoritarian Personality*. New York: Harper.

Ain, Stewart, and Don Gentile. 1985. "Court shows mercy." *New York Daily News*, 15 August: 31.

Ajzen, Icek, and Martin Fishbein. 1980. *Understanding Attitudes and Predicting Social Behavior*. Englewood Cliffs, N.J.: Prentice-Hall.

Alexander, Franz, and Hugo Staub. 1956. *The Criminal, the Judge, and the Public*. Rev. ed. Glencoe, Ill.: Free Press.

Alexander, Jack. 1986. "Classification objectives and practices." *Crime & Delinquency* 32 (July): 323–38.

Allen, Francis A. 1972. " Raffaele Garofalo 1852–1934." Pp. 318–40 in Hermann Mannheim (ed.), *Pioneers in Criminology*. 2nd ed. Montclair, N.J.: Patterson Smith.

———. 1981. *The Decline of the Rehabilitative Ideal*. New Haven: Yale University Press.

Allerton, Robert. 1972. "Some comments on being a criminal." Pp. 25–34 in David M. Petersen and Marcello Truzzi (eds.), *Criminal Life: Views from Inside*. Englewood Cliffs, N.J.: Prentice-Hall.

Allport, Gordon. 1954. *The Nature of Prejudice*. Cambridge, Mass.: Addison-Wesley.

American Friends Service Committee Working Party. 1971. *Struggle for Justice: A Report on Crime and Justice in America*. New York: Hill & Wang.

Amir, Menachem. 1971. *Patterns in Forcible Rape.* Chicago: University of Chicago Press.

Ancel, Marc. 1987. *Social Defense: The Future of Penal Reform.* Littleton, Colo.: Fred B. Rothman.

"And the cowardice of hate." 1986. Editorial. *New York Daily News,* 23 December: 24.

Aptheker, Bettina. 1971. "The social functions of the prisons in the United States." Pp. 39–48 in Angela Davis (ed.), *If They Come in the Morning: Voices of Resistance.* New York: The Third Press/Joseph Okpatu.

Asbury, Herbert. 1970. *The Gangs of New York.* New York: Capricorn. (Originally published 1927.)

Attorney General's Survey of Release Procedures. 1973. "State prisons in America." Pp. 23–53 in George C. Killinger and Paul F. Cromwell, Jr. (eds.), *Penology: The Evolution of Corrections in America.* St. Paul: West.

Aubert, Vilhelm. 1952. "White-collar crime and social structure." *American Journal of Sociology* 58 (November): 263–71.

Bachmuth, Rita, S. M. Miller, and Linda Rosen. 1960. "Juvenile delinquency in the daily press." *Alpha Kappa Deltan* 30, 2 (Spring): 47–51.

Baker, J. E. 1977. "Inmate self-government and the right to participate." Pp. 320–32 in Robert M. Carter, Daniel Glaser, and Leslie T. Wilkins (eds.), *Correctional Institutions.* 2nd ed. Philadelphia: Lippincott.

Baker, T. Barwick. 1984. *War with Crime.* New York: Garland. (Originally published 1889.)

Banfield, Edward. 1974. *The Unheavenly City Revisited.* Boston: Little, Brown.

Barbanel, Josh. 1983. "Limits increased for restitutions from criminals." *New York Times,* 20: B3.

Barkas, J. L. 1978. *Victims.* New York: Scribner's.

Barnes, Harry E. 1972. *The Story of Punishment.* 2nd ed. rev. Montclair, N.J.: Patterson Smith.

Barnes, Harry E., and Negley Teeters. 1951. *New Horizons in Criminology.* New York: Prentice-Hall.

Barron, Milton. 1954. *The Juvenile in Delinquent Society.* New York: Knopf.

Beccaria, Cesare. 1963. *On Crimes and Punishments.* Indianapolis: Bobbs-Merrill. (Originally published 1764.)

Becker, Howard. 1966. *Outsiders: Studies in the Sociology of Deviance.* New York: Free Press/Macmillan.

Beha, James, Kenneth Carlson, and Robert H. Rosenblum. 1977. *Sentencing to Community Service.* Washington, D. C.: U. S. Government Printing Office.

Bell, Daniel. 1953. "Crime as an American way of life." *Antioch Review* 13 (June): 131–54.

Bennett, Lawrence A. 1986. "Introduction [to special issue on classification]." *Crime & Delinquency* 32 (July): 251–53.

Bentham, Jeremy. 1970. *An Introduction to the Principles of Morals and Legislation.* Darien, Conn.: Hafner. (Originally published 1789.)

Bienen, Leigh. 1980. "Rape III: National developments in rape reform legislation." *Women's Rights Law Reporter* 6 (Spring): 170–213.

Blackmore, John, and Jane Welsh. 1983. "Selective incapacitation: Sentencing according to risk." *Crime & Delinquency* 29 (October): 504–28.

Blalock. Hubert M. 1967. *Toward a Theory of Minority-Group Relations.* New York: Wiley.

Bloch, Herbert A., and Arthur Niederhoffer. 1958. *The Gang: A Study in Adolescent Behavior.* New York: Philosophical Library.

Bloomberg, Seth A. 1977. "Participatory management." *Criminology* 15 (August): 149–64.

Blumer, Herbert. 1969. "Collective behavior." Pp. 65–121 in Alfred McClung Lee (ed.), *Principles of Sociology.* 3rd ed. New York: Barnes and Noble.

Blundell, William E. 1978. "Equity Funding: 'I did it for the jollies.' " Pp. 153–85 in John M. Johnson and Jack D. Douglas (eds.), *Crime at the Top: Deviance in Business and the Professions.* Philadelphia: Lippincott.

Bohmer, Carol. 1974. "Judicial attitudes toward rape victims." *Judicature* 57 (February): 303–7.

Bohmer, Carol, and Audrey Blumberg. 1975. "Twice traumatized: The rape victim and the court." *Judicature* 58 (March): 390–99.

Borgida, Eugene, and Phyllis White. 1978. "Social perceptions of rape victims: The impact of legal reform." *Law and Human Behavior* 2, 4: 339–51.

Bottoms, Anthony E., and Paul Wiles. 1987. "Housing tenure and residential community crime careers in Britain." Pp. 101–62 in Albert J.

Reiss, Jr., and Michael Tonry (eds.), *Communities and Crime.*
Chicago: University of Chicago Press.

Boyer, Paul. 1978. *Urban Masses and Moral Order in America 1820–1920.* Cambridge: Harvard University Press.

Bradley, Tom. No date. "The forgotten victim." Pp. 1–5 in George Nicholson, Thomas W. Condit, and Stuart Greenbaum (eds.), *Forgotten Victims: An Advocate's Anthology.* Sacramento, Calif.: California District Attorneys Association.

Brauer, Ralph. 1990. "The drug war of words." *Nation,* 21 May: 705–6.

Bredemeier, Harry C. 1969. "Law as an integrative mechanism." Pp. 52–67 in Vilhelm Aubert (ed.), *Sociology of Law.* Hammondsworth, England: Penguin.

Brenner, Charles. 1974. *An Elementary Textbook of Psychoanalysis.* Rev. ed. Garden City, N. Y.: Anchor/Doubleday.

Brinton, Crane. 1965. *The Anatomy of Revolution.* Rev. & expanded ed. New York: Vintage/Random House.

Brockway, Zebulon R. 1969. *Fifty Years of Prison Service.* Montclair, N.J.: Patterson Smith. (Originally published 1912.)

Brown, Edmund G.(Pat). 1970. *Reagan and Reality: The Two Californias.* New York: Praeger.

Brown, Richard Maxwell. 1975. *Strain of Violence: Historical Studies of American Violence and Vigilantism.* New York: Oxford University Press.

———. 1976. "The history of vigilantism in America." Pp. 79–109 in H. Jon Rosenbaum and Peter C. Sederberg (eds.), *Vigilante Politics.* Philadelphia: University of Pennsylvania Press.

Browning, Frank, and John Gerassi. 1980. *The American Way of Crime.* New York: Putnam.

Brownmiller, Susan. 1976. *Against Our Will: Men, Women, and Rape.* New York: Bantam.

Burrows, William E. 1976. *Vigilante!* New York: Harcourt Brace Jovanovich.

Carroll, Daniel. 1974. "Interview with David Du Bois." *Issues in Criminology* 9 (Fall): 21–41.

Carter, Robert M., Richard A McGee, and E. Kim Nelson. 1975. *Corrections in America.* Philadelphia: Lippincott.

Carter, Robert M., and Malcolm W. Klein (eds.). 1976. *Back on the Street: The Diversion of Juvenile Offenders*. Englewood Cliffs, N. J.: Prentice-Hall.

Carter, Robert M., Jack Cocks, and Daniel Glaser. 1987. "Community service: A review of the basic issues." *Federal Probation* 51 (March): 4–10.

Cauthen, Nelson R., Ira E. Robinson, and Herbert H. Krauss. 1971. "Stereotypes: Review of the literature 1926–68." *Journal of Social Psychology* 84 (June): 103–25.

Chaiken, Jan M., and Marcia R. Chaiken. 1982. *Varieties of Criminal Behavior*. Santa Monica, Calif.: RAND Corporation.

Chambliss, William J. 1973. "The Saints and the Roughnecks." *Society* 11(November-December): 24–31.

Chapman, Dennis. 1968. *Sociology and the Stereotype of the Criminal*. London: Tavistock.

Churchill, Mae. 1980. " LEAA: Mission accomplished." *Progressive* 44 (November): 20.

Cipes, Robert M. 1968. *The Crime War*. New York: New American Library.

Clark, Edward P. 1984. "The runner." *Victimology* 9, 1: 12–15.

Clark, Lorenne M. G., and Debra J. Lewis. 1977. *Rape: The Price of Coercive Sexuality*. Toronto: Women's Press.

Clark, Ramsey. 1970. *Crime in America: Observations on Its Nature, Causes, Prevention and Control*. New York: Simon and Schuster.

Clark, Walter V. 1972. *The Ox-Bow Incident*. Gloucester, Mass.: Peter Smith. (Originally published 1940.)

Clarke, James W. 1982. *American Assassins: The Darker Side of Politics*. Princeton: Princeton University Press.

Claster, Daniel S. 1978. "Letting them off when they know what they're doing: Public perceptions of juvenile responsibility." Paper presented at annual meeting of American Society of Criminology, Dallas, Texas, November 9.

Claster, Daniel S., and Deborah S. David. 1977. "The resisting victim." *Victimology* 2 (Spring): 109–17.

Cleckley, Hervey. 1955. *The Mask of Sanity: An Attempt to Clarify Some Issues about the So-Called Psychopathic Personality*. 3rd ed. St. Louis: Mosby.

Clinard, Marshall B., and Richard Quinney. 1967. *Criminal Behavior Systems: A Typology*. New York: Holt, Rinehart, and Winston.

Clinard, Marshall B., and Peter C. Yeager. 1980. *Corporate Crime.* New York: Free Press.

Cloward, Richard A., and Lloyd E. Ohlin. 1960. *Delinquency and Opportunity: A Theory of Delinquent Gangs.* Glencoe, Ill.: Free Press.

Coblentz, Stanton Arthur. 1936. *Villains and Vigilantes.* New York: Wilson-Erickson.

Cohen, Albert K. 1955. *Delinquent Boys: The Culture of the Gang.* Glencoe, Ill.: Free Press.

————. 1970. "Multiple factor approaches." Pp. 123–26 in Marvin Wolfgang, Leonard Savitz, and Norman Johnston (eds.), *The Sociology of Crime and Delinquency.* 2nd ed. New York: Wiley.

Cohen, Jacqueline. 1978. "The incapacitatve effect of imprisonment: A critical review of the literature." Pp. 187–243 in National Research Council, Panel on Research on Deterrent and Incapacitative Effects, *Deterrence and Incapacitation: Estimating the Effects of Criminal Sanctions on Crime Rates.* Washington, D. C.: National Academy of Sciences.

Cohen, Morris. 1961. *Reason and Law.* New York: Collier Books.

Coleman, James. 1957. *Community Conflict.* New York: Free Press.

Committee on Resolutions of the Republican National Convention. 1984. *Republican Platform: America's Future Free and Secure.* Dallas: Republican National Convention.

"Composition." 1968. Pp. 357–58 in *Black's Law Dictionary.* Rev. 4th ed. St. Paul: West.

Conklin, John E. 1972. *Robbery and the Criminal Justice System.* Philadelphia: Lippincott.

————. 1977. *"Illegal but Not Criminal" : Business Crime in America.* Englewood Cliffs, N.J.: Prentice-Hall.

Conrad, John P. 1985. *The Dangerous and the Endangered.* Lexington, Mass.: Lexingtonbooks/Heath.

Cook, Philip J. 1986. "The demand and supply of criminal opportunities." Pp. 1–27 in Michael Tonry and Norval Morris (eds.), *Crime and Justice: An Annual Review of Research.* Vol. 7. Chicago: University of Chicago Press.

Cortés, Juan B., and Florence M. Gatti. 1972. *Delinquency and Crime: A Biopsychosocial Approach.* New York: Seminar.

Covington, Jeanette. 1984. "Insulation from labelling." *Criminology* 22 (November): 619–43.

Craig, Stephen C., and Thomas L. Hurley. 1984. "Political rhetoric and the structure of political opinion." *Western Political Quarterly* 37 (December): 632–40.

Cressey, Donald R. 1969. *Theft of the Nation: The Structure and Operations of Organized Crime in America.* New York: Harper & Row.

———. 1982. "Foreword." Pp. xi–xxiii in Francis T. Cullen and Karen E. Gilbert, *Reaffirming Rehabilitation.* Cincinnati: Anderson.

Cressey, Donald R., and Robert A. McDermott. 1974. *Diversion from the Juvenile Justice System.* Washington, D. C.: U. S. Government Printing Office.

Cullen, Francis T., and Karen E. Gilbert. 1982. *Reaffirming Rehabilitation.* Cincinnati: Anderson.

Curtis, Lynn A. 1974a. *Criminal Violence.* Lexington, Mass.: Lexingtonbooks/Heath.

———. 1974b. "Victim precipitation and violent crime." *Social Problems* 21 (April): 594–605.

Daughen, Joseph R., and Peter Binzen. 1977. *The Cop Who Would Be King: Mayor Frank Rizzo.* Boston: Little, Brown.

David, René, and John E. C. Brierley. 1968. *Major Legal Systems in the World Today: An Introduction to the Comparative Study of Law.* New York: Free Press.

Davidson, Kenneth M., Ruth B. Ginsburg, and Herma H. Kay. 1974. *Sex–Based Discrimination: Text, Cases, and Materials.* St Paul: West.

Davies, John D. 1955. *Phrenology, Fad and Science.* New Haven: Yale University Press.

Dawes, Robyn, and Tom L. Smith. 1985. "Attitude and opinion measurement." Pp. 509–66 in Gardner Lindzey and Elliot Aronson (eds.), *The Handbook of Social Psychology.* 3rd ed. Vol. 1. New York: Random House.

"Defendant in beating death of thief enters plea of guilty." 1988. *New York Times*, 28 September: B3.

Democratic National Committee. 1984. *The 1984 Democratic National Platform.* Washington, D. C.: Democratic National Committee.

Denno, Deborah, and James A. Cramer. 1976. "The effects of victim characteristics on judicial decision making." Pp. 215–26 in William F. McDonald (ed.), *Criminal Justice and the Victim.* Beverly Hills, Calif.: Sage.

Dentler, Robert A., and Kai T. Erikson. 1959. "The functions of deviance in groups." *Social Problems* 7 (Fall): 98–107.

Deutsch, Morton. 1968. "The effects of cooperation and competition upon group process." Pp. 461–82 in Dorwin Cartwright and Alvin Zander (eds.), *Group Dynamics: Research and Theory.* 3rd ed. New York: Harper & Row.

Deutscher, Irwin (ed.). 1973. *What We Say/ What We Do.* Glenview, Ill.: Scott Foresman.

Dewey, Thomas E. 1974. *Twenty against the Underworld.* New York: Doubleday.

Diamond, A. S. 1971. *Primitive Law Past and Present.* London: Methuen.

Dicey, A. V. 1905. *Lectures on the Relation between Law and Public Opinion in England during the Nineteenth Century.* London: Macmillan.

"Does crime pay?" 1981. Letter to the editor. *New York Daily News,* 10 March: 29.

Dollard, John, Leonard W. Doob, Neal E. Miller, O. H. Mowrer, and Robert R. Sears. 1939. *Frustration and Aggression.* New Haven: Yale University Press.

Du Bois, W. E. B. 1968. *Autobiography of W. E. B. Du Bois.* New York: International.

Durkheim, Émile. 1938. *The Rules of Sociological Method.* Glencoe, Ill.: Free Press. (Originally published 1895.)

———. 1947. *The Division of Labor in Society.* Glencoe, Ill.: Free Press. (Originally published 1893.)

———. 1951. *Suicide: A Study in Sociology.* Glencoe, Ill.: Free Press. (Originally published 1897.)

Duster, Troy. 1970. *The Legislation of Morality: Law, Drugs, and Moral Judgment.* New York: Free Press.

Edwards, Allen L. 1940. "Four dimensions of political stereotypes." *Journal of Abnormal and Social Psychology* 35 (October): 566–72.

Eglash, Albert. 1958. " Creative restitution—A broader meaning for an old term." *Journal of Criminal Law, Criminology, and Police Science* 48 (March–April): 619–22.

"Eight youths accused of vigilante acts." 1985. *New York Times,* 29 May: A14.

Elias, Robert. 1986. *The Politics of Victimization: Victims, Victimology, and Human Rights.* New York: Oxford University Press.

"Ellenberger avoids a prison sentence." 1981. *New York Times*, 9 July: B6.

Emerson, Robert M. 1969. *Judging Delinquents*. Chicago: Aldine.

Empey, LaMar T. 1978. *American Delinquency: Its Meaning and Construction*. Homewood, Ill.: Dorsey.

Erikson, Kai T. 1966. *Wayward Puritans: A Study in the Sociology of Deviance*. New York: Wiley.

Estrich, Susan. 1986. "Rape." *Yale Law Journal* 95 (May): 1087–1184.

"Excerpts from President's address on programs for fighting crime in U. S." 1981. *New York Times*, 29 September: A18.

Farrington, David P. 1987. "Implications of biological findings for criminological research." Pp. 42–64 in Sarnoff A. Mednick, Terrie E. Moffitt, and Susan A. Stack, *The Causes of Crime: New Biological Approaches*. Cambridge: Cambridge University Press.

Federal Bureau of Investigation. Published annually. *Uniform Crime Reports*. Washington, D. C.: U. S. Government Printing Office.

Feinberg, Joel. 1970. *Doing and Deserving: Essays on the Theory of Responsibility*. Princeton, N.J.: Princeton University Press.

———. 1984. *The Moral Limits of the Criminal Law*. New York: Oxford University Press.

Ferri, Enrico. 1917. *Criminal Sociology*. Boston: Little, Brown.

Finestone, Harold. 1976. "The delinquent and society: The Shaw and McKay tradition." Pp. 23–49 in James F. Short, Jr. (ed.), *Delinquency, Crime, and Society*. Chicago: University of Chicago Press.

Fink, Arthur E. 1938. *Causes of Crime: Biological Theories in the United States 1800–1915*. Philadelphia: University of Pennsylvania Press.

Firth, R. W. 1964. "Taboo." Pp. 714–15 in Julius Gould and William L. Kolb (eds.), *A Dictionary of the Social Sciences*. New York: Free Press.

Fishman, Mark. 1978. "Crime waves as ideology." *Social Problems* 29 (June): 531–43.

Flanagan, Timothy J., and Edmund F. McGarrell (eds.). 1986. *Sourcebook of Criminal Justice Statistics*. 1985. Washington, D. C.: U. S. Government Printing Office.

Fogel, David. 1979. *"We Are the Living Proof": The Justice Model for Corrections*. 2nd ed. Cincinnati: Anderson.

Foucault, Michel. 1977. *Discipline and Punish: The Birth of the Prison.* New York: Pantheon.

Frank, Jerome. 1949. *Courts on Trial: Myth and Reality in American Justice.* Princeton: Princeton University Press.

Frankel, Marvin E. 1980. *Partisan Justice.* New York: Hill & Wang.

Freedman, Monroe H. 1975. *Lawyers' Ethics in an Adversary System.* Indianapolis: Bobbs-Merrill.

Freud, Sigmund. 1961. *Civilization and Its Discontents.* New York: Norton. (Originally published 1929.)

———. 1963. "Some character-types met with in psychoanalytic work." Pp. 157–81 in Sigmund Freud, *Character and Culture* (ed. Philip Rieff). New York: Collier Books. (Originally published 1916.)

Gager, Nancy, and Cathleen Schurr. 1976. *Sexual Assault: Confronting Rape in America.* New York: Grossett & Dunlap.

Galaway, Burt, and Joe Hudson. 1975. "Sin, sickness, restitution: Toward a reconciliative correctional model." Pp. 59–70 in Burt Galaway and Joe Hudson (eds.), *Considering the Victim: Readings in Restitution and Victim Compensation.* Springfield, Ill.: C. C. Thomas.

Gandy, John T. 1978. "Attitudes toward the use of restitution." Pp. 119–29 in Burt Galaway and Joe Hudson (eds.), *Offender Restitution in Theory and Action.* Lexington, Mass.: Lexingtonbooks/Heath.

Gandy, John T., and Burt Galaway. 1980. "Restitution as a sanction for offenders: A public's view." Pp. 89–100 in Joe Hudson and Burt Galaway (eds.), *Victims, Offenders, and Alternative Sanctions.* Lexington, Mass.: Lexingtonbooks/Heath.

Garfield, Brian. 1972. *Death Wish.* New York: David McKay.

Gearty, Robert, and Don Gentile. 1986. "White gang chases black to his death." *New York Daily News,* 21 December: 3–4.

Geberth, Vernon J. 1980. "Crime and violence: Are the courts the catalyst?" *Law and Order* 28, 9 (September): 44–52.

Geis, Gilbert. 1977. "The heavy electrical equipment antitrust cases of 1961." Pp. 117–32 in Gilbert Geis and Robert F. Meier (eds.), *White Collar Crime: Offenses in Business, Politics, and the Professions.* Rev ed. New York: Free Press.

Gelb, Leslie H. 1985. "The mind of the President." *New York Times Magazine,* 6 October: 20.

Genet, Jean. 1964. *The Thief's Journal.* New York: Grove. (Originally published 1949.)

"George Bush and Willie Horton." 1988. Editorial. *New York Times*, 4 November: A34.

Gerard, Roy. 1973. "Institutional innovations in juvenile corrections." Pp. 149–62 in George C. Killinger and Paul F. Cromwell, Jr. (eds.), *Penology: The Evolution of Corrections in America*. St. Paul: West.

Gest, Ted. 1987. "The public fights back." *U. S. News and World Report*, 29 June: 16–17.

Givens, Ron. 1985. "Mercy—or murder?" *Newsweek*, 9 September: 25.

Glaser, Daniel. 1978. *Crime in Our Changing Society*. New York: Holt, Rinehart, and Winston.

Glasser, William. 1975. *Reality Therapy: A New Approach to Psychiatry*. New York: Perennial/ Harper & Row.

Glover, Edward. 1960. *The Roots of Crime*. London: Imago.

Glueck, Bernard. 1959. "Analytic psychiatry and criminology." Pp. 90–112 in Sheldon Glueck (ed.) , *The Problem of Delinquency*. Boston: Houghton Mifflin. (Originally published 1933.)

Glueck, Sheldon. 1962. *Law and Psychiatry: Cold War or Entente Cordiale?* Baltimore: Johns Hopkins.

Glueck, Sheldon, and Eleanor Glueck. 1950. *Unraveling Juvenile Delinquency*. Cambridge: Harvard University Press.

———. 1956. *Physique and Delinquency*. New York: Harper.

———. 1962. *Family Environment and Delinquency*. London: Routledge & Kegan Paul.

Goodman, Walter. 1983. "Literary criminals." *New York Times Book Review*, 24 July: 27.

Gorelick, Steven M. 1989. " 'Join our war': The construction of ideology in a newspaper crimefighting campaign." *Crime & Delinquency* 35 (July): 421–36.

Graber, Doris A. 1980. *Crime News and the Public*. New York: Praeger.

Greenberg, David F. (ed.). 1981. *Crime and Capitalism*. Palo Alto, Calif.: Mayfield.

Greenberg, David F., and Drew Humphries. 1981. "The cooptation of fixed sentencing reform." Pp. 367–86 in David F. Greenberg (ed.), *Crime and Capitalism*. Palo Alto, Calif.: Mayfield.

Greenwood, Peter. 1982. *Selective Incapacitation*. Santa Monica, Calif.: RAND Corporation.

Greenwood, Peter, and Franklin E. Zimring. 1985. *One More Chance: The Pursuit of Promising Intervention Strategies for Chronic Juvenile Offenders*. Santa Monica, Calif.: RAND Corporation.

Greer, Colin, and Frank Reissman. 1982. "Crime prevention: An alternative perspective." *Social Policy* 12 (Spring): 2.

Griffin, Susan. 1979. *Rape: The Power of Consciousness*. New York: Harper and Row.

———. 1984. "Rape: The all-American crime." Pp. 114–25 in William J. Chambliss (ed.), *Criminal Law in Action*. 2nd ed. New York: Wiley.

Grimsted, David. 1968. *Melodrama Unveiled: American Theater and Culture 1800–1850*. Chicago: University of Chicago Press.

Guze, Samuel B. 1976. *Criminality and Psychiatric Disorders*. New York: Oxford University Press.

Hamilton, Fred. 1973. *Rizzo*. New York: Viking.

Hamparian, Donna, Richard Schuster, Simon Dinitz, and John D. Conrad. 1978. *The Violent Few: A Study of Dangerous Juvenile Offenders*. Lexington, Mass.: Lexingtonbooks/Heath.

Hampden-Turner, Charles. 1976. *Sane Asylum*. San Francisco: San Franciso Book.

Harding, John, Harold Proshansky, Bernard Kutner, and Isidor Chein. 1969. "Prejudice and ethnic relations." Pp. 1–76 in Gardner Lindzey and Elliot Aronson (eds.), *The Handbook of Social Psychology*. 2nd ed. Vol. 5. Reading, Mass.: Addison-Wesley.

Hare, Robert D. 1970. *Psychopathy: Theory and Research*. New York: Wiley.

Hart, H. L. A. 1961. *The Concept of Law*. London: Oxford University Press.

Haskins, George Lee. 1960. *Law and Authority in Early Massachusetts*. New York: Macmillan.

Hawes, Joseph M. 1971. *Children in Urban Society: Juvenile Delinquency in Nineteenth-Century America*. New York: Oxford University Press.

Hawkins, Gordon. 1976. *The Prison: Policy and Practice*. Chicago: University of Chicago Press.

Hays, Constance L. 1988. "Charges dropped against 7 in fatal beating." *New York Times*, 28 June: B1.

Hazard, John. 1977. "Furniture arrangement as a symbol of judicial roles." Pp. 897–903 in Lawrence M. Friedman and Steward

Macaulay (eds.), *Law and the Behavioral Sciences*. 2nd ed. Indianapolis: Bobbs-Merrill.

Healy, William A. 1915. *The Individual Delinquent: A Textbook of Diagnosis and Prognosis for All Concerned in Understanding Offenders*. Boston: Little, Brown.

————. 1917. *Mental Conflicts and Misconduct*. Boston: Little, Brown.

Heidensohn, Frances. 1985. *Women and Crime*. New York: New York University Press.

Heinz, Anne M., Herbert Jacob, and Robert L. Lineberry (eds.). 1983. *Crime in City Politics*. New York: Longman.

Hibbert, Christopher. 1963. *The Roots of Evil: A Social History of Crime and Punishment*. Boston: Little, Brown.

Hippchen, Leonard J. 1978. " Trends in classification philosophy and practice." Pp. 1–11 in Leonard J. Hippchen (ed.), *Handbook on Correctional Classification: Treatment and Reintegration*. Cincinnati: Anderson.

Hirschi, Travis. 1969. *Causes of Delinquency*. Berkeley: University of California Press.

————. 1983. "Crime and the family." Pp. 53–68 in James Q. Wilson (ed.), *Crime and Public Policy*. San Francisco: ICS Press.

Hirst, Paul Q. 1972. "Marx and Engels on law, crime, and morality." *Economy and Society* 1 (February): 28–56.

Hobbes, Thomas. 1968. *Leviathan*. Baltimore: Penguin. (Originally published 1651.)

Hobhouse, L. T. 1975. "Law and justice." Pp. 5–18 in Burt Galaway and Joe Hudson (eds.), *Considering the Victim: Readings in Restitution and Victim Compensation*. Springfield, Ill.: C. C. Thomas. (Originally published 1906.)

Hobsbawm, Eric. 1969. *Bandits*. New York: Delacorte.

Hoebel, E. Adamson. 1972. *The Law of Primitive Man*. New York: Atheneum.

Holl, Jack M. 1971. *Juvenile Reform in the Progressive Era: William R. George and the Junior Republic Movement*. Ithaca, N. Y.: Cornell University Press.

Honderich, Ted. 1969. *Punishment: The Supposed Justifications*. New York: Harcourt, Brace & World.

"Honor students form Texas vigilante group." 1985. *New York Times*, 29 March: A16.

Hooton, Earnest A. 1939. *Crime and the Man.* Cambridge: Harvard University Press.

Hovland, Carl I., and Robert R. Sears. 1940. "Minor studies of aggression: VI. Correlation of lynchings with economic indices." *Journal of Psychology* 9 (April): 301–10.

Howe, Irving. 1976. *World of Our Fathers.* New York: Harcourt Brace Jovanovich.

Hubbard, Geoffrey. 1974. *Quaker by Convincement.* Hammondsworth, England: Penguin.

Hudson, Joe, and Burt Galaway (eds.). 1980. *Victims, Offenders, and Alternative Sanctions.* Lexington, Mass.: Lexingtonbooks/Heath.

Hunt, Morton. 1973. *The Mugging.* New York: Signet/New American Library.

Hurley, Patricia A. 1977. "Assessing the potential for significant legislative output in the House of Representatives." *Western Political Quarterly* 32 (March): 45–58.

Hursch, Carolyn J.. 1977. *The Trouble with Rape.* Chicago: Nelson-Hall.

Ianni, Francis A. J. 1972. *A Family Business: Kinship and Social Control in Organized Crime.* New York: Russell Sage.

Inciardi, James. 1975. *Careers in Crime.* Chicago: Rand McNally.

"Inside Prisons" (videotape). No date. Crime File series. Washington, D.C.: National Institute of Justice.

Inverarity, James, and Daniel McCarthy. 1988. "Punishment and social structure revisited: Unemployment and imprisonment in the United States, 1948–1984." *Sociological Quarterly* 29 (June): 263–79.

Irwin, John. 1980. *Prisons in Turmoil.* Boston: Little, Brown.

Jacoby, William G. 1986. "Levels of conceptualization and reliance on the liberal-conservative continuum." *Journal of Politics* 48 (May): 423–32.

James, George. 1988a. "Serious crime rises again in New York." *New York Times*, 23 March: B1, B6.

———. 1988b. "Crime totals confirm fears in Queens." *New York Times*, 21 April: B1, B6.

Jeffery, C. Ray. 1957. "The development of crime in early English society." *Journal of Criminal Law, Criminology, and Police Science* 47 (March–April): 647-66.

————. 1972. "The historical development of criminology." Pp. 458–98 in Hermann Mannheim (ed.), *Pioneers in Criminology*. 2nd ed. Montclair, N.J.: Patterson Smith.

————. 1979. "Biology and crime: The new neo-Lombrosians." Pp. 7–18 in C. R. Jeffery (ed.), *Biology and Crime*. Beverly Hills, Calif.: Sage.

————. 1980. "Sociobiology and criminology: The long lean years of the unthinkable and the unmentionable." Pp. 115–24 in Edward Sagarin (ed.), *Taboos in Criminology*. Beverly Hills, Calif.: Sage.

Johnson, Elmer. 1974. *Crime, Correction, and Society*. 3rd ed. Homewood, Ill.: Dorsey.

————. 1977. "Commentary: Potential of inmate self-government." *Criminology* 15 (August): 165–78.

Johnson, Julie. 1987. "Queens woman acquitted in killing of husband." *New York Times*, 1 October: A1, B4.

Johnson, Kirk. 1988. "Crime victims getting a day, and a say, in court." *New York Times*, 1 April: B7.

Johnston, R. J. 1981. "Testing the Butler Stokes model of a polarization effect around the national survey in partisan preferences: England, 1979." *British Journal of Political Science* 11(January): 113–17.

Jones, Cathaleene, and Elliot Aronson. 1973. "Attribution of fault to a rape victim as a function of respectability of the victim." *Journal of Personality and Social Psychology* 26 (June): 415–19.

Jones, Russell A. 1982. "Perceiving other people: Stereotyping as a process of cognition." Pp. 41–91 in Arthur G. Miller (ed.), *In the Eye of the Beholder: Contemporary Issues in Stereotyping*. New York: Praeger.

Kalven, Harry, Jr., and Hans Zeisel. 1971. *The American Jury*. Chicago: Phoenix/University of Chicago Press.

Kant, Immanuel. 1974. *The Philosophy of Law*. Clifton, N.J.: Kelley. (Originally published 1796.)

Karmen, Andrew. 1980. "Auto theft: Beyond victim blaming." *Victimology* 5, 2–4: 161–74.

————. 1990. *Crime Victims: An Introduction to Victimology*. 2nd ed. Pacific Grove, Calif.: Brooks/Cole.

Katz, Jack. 1988. *Seductions of Crime: Moral and Sensual Attractions in Doing Evil*. New York: Basic Books.

Keefe, Mary L., and Henry T. O'Reilly. 1976. "The plight of the rape victim in New York City." Pp. 391–402 in Emilio C. Viano (ed.), *Victims & Society*. Washington, D. C.: Visage.

Keefe, Michael. 1985. Cartoon. P. 55 in Bonnie Szumski (ed.), *American Prisons: Opposing Viewpoints*. 4th ed. St. Paul, Minn.: Greenhaven.

Keeton, Robert E. 1973. *Trial Tactics and Methods*. 2nd ed. Boston: Little, Brown.

Kellogg, Frederick R. 1977. "From rehabilitation to desert: The evolution of criminal punishment." *Criminology* 15 (August): 179–92.

Kelly, Orr. 1982. "Corporate crime: The untold story." *U. S. News & World Report*, 6 September: 25–29.

Klansky, Nadine. 1988. "Bernard Goetz, a 'reasonable man': A look at New York's justification defense." *Brooklyn Law Review* 53 (Winter): 1149-69.

Klein, Herbert T. 1968. *The Police: Damned If They Do—Damned If They Don't*. New York: Crown.

Klein, Melanie. 1975. *Envy and Gratitude and Other Works 1946–1963*. New York: Free Press.

Knapp, Kay A. 1982. "Impact of the Minnesota Sentencing Guidelines on sentencing practice." *Hamline Law Review* 5 (June): 237–56.

Kohlberg, Lawrence., Kelsey Kauffman, Peter Scharf, and Joseph Hickey. 1974. *The Just Community Approach to Corrections*. Niantick, Conn.: Connecticut Department of Corrections.

Kooistra, Paul G. 1989. *Criminals As Heroes: Structure, Power, and Identity*. Bowling Green, Ohio: Popular Press.

Kornhauser, Ruth Rosner. 1984. *Social Sources of Delinquency*. Chicago: University of Chicago Press.

Krase, Jerome. 1979. "Stigmatized places–stigmatized people: Crown Heights and Prospect-Lefferts Gardens." Pp. 251–62 in Rita Seiden Miller (ed.), *Brooklyn USA: The Fourth Largest City in America*. New York: Brooklyn College Press and Columbia University Press.

Kreml, William P. 1977. *The Anti-Authoritarian Personality*. Oxford, England: Pergamon.

Krisberg, Barry. 1982. "Gang youth and hustling: The psychology of survival." *Issues in Criminology* 9 (Spring): 115–31.

———. 1975. *Crime and Privilege: Toward a New Criminology*. Englewood Cliffs, N. J.: Prentice-Hall.

LaFree, Gary D., Barbara F. Reskin, and Christy A. Visher. 1985. "Jurors' responses to victims' behavior and legal issues in sexual assault trials." *Social Problems* 32 (April): 389–407.

Lamborn, LeRoy. 1981. "The culpability of the victim." Pp. 160–64 in Burt Galaway and Joe Hudson (eds.), *Perspectives on Crime Victims*. St. Louis: Mosby.

L'Armand, K., and A. Pepitone. 1982. "Judgments of rape: A study of victim-rapist relationship and victim sexual history." *Personality and Social Psychology Bulletin* 8 (March): 134–39.

Laster, Richard E. 1975. "Criminal restitution: A survey of its past history." Pp. 19–28 in Burt Galaway and Joe Hudson (eds.), *Considering the Victim: Readings in Restitution and Victim Compensation*. Springfield, Ill.: C. C. Thomas.

Lauber, Volkmar. 1983. "From growth consensus to fragmentation in Western Europe: Political polarization over redistribution and ecology." *Comparative Politics* 15 (April): 329–49.

Laufer, William S., and James M. Day. 1983. *Personality Theory, Moral Development, and Criminal Behavior*. Lexington, Mass.: Lexingtonbooks/Heath.

Lea, Henry C. 1974. *The Duel and the Oath*. Philadelphia: University of Pennsylvania Press. (Originally published 1866.)

Le Bon, Gustave. 1960. *The Crowd*. New York: Viking. (Originally published 1895.)

Lemert, Edwin. 1951. *Social Pathology*. New York: McGraw Hill.

Lerman, Paul. 1975. *Community Treatment and Social Control*. Chicago: University of Chicago Press.

Lerner, Melvin J. 1975. "The justice motive in social behavior: Introduction." *Journal of Social Issues* 31 (Summer): 1–19.

———. 1980. *The Belief in a Just World: A Fundamental Delusion*. New York: Plenum.

Lerner, Melvin J., Dale T. Miller, and John G. Holmes. 1976. "Deserving and the emergence of forms of justice." Pp. 133–62 in Leonard Berkowitz and Elaine Walster (eds.), *Advances in Experimental Social Psychology*. Vol. 9. New York: Academic Press.

Lescaze, Lee. 1981. "Reagan blames crime on 'human predator'." *Washington Post*, 29 September: A2.

Letkemann, Peter. 1973. *Crime As Work*. Englewood Cliffs, N. J.: Prentice-Hall.

Levine, James P., Michael C. Musheno, and Dennis J. Palumbo. 1980. *Criminal Justice: A Public Policy Approach.* New York: Harcourt Brace Jovanovich.

Levy, Howard, and David Miller. 1970. *Going to Jail: The Political Prisoner.* New York: Grove Press.

Lewin, John R. 1976. "The victim in Shakespeare." Pp. 451–64 in Emilio C. Viano (ed.), *Victims & Society.* Washington, D.C.: Visage.

Lewis, Michael. 1970. "Structural deviance and normative conformity: The 'hustle' and the gang." Pp. 176–99 in Daniel Glaser (ed.), *Crime in the City.* New York: Harper & Row.

Linville, Patricia W., and Edward E. Jones. 1980. "Polarized appraisals of out-group members." *Journal of Personality and Social Psychology* 38 (May): 689–703.

Lippman, Walter. 1922. *Public Opinion.* New York: Macmillan.

Lipton, Douglas, Robert Martinson, and Judith Wilks. 1975. *The Effectiveness of Correctional Treatment: A Survey of Treatment Evaluation Studies.* New York: Praeger.

Loeber, Rolf, and Magda Stouthamer-Loeber. 1986. "Family factors as correlates and predictors of juvenile conduct problems and delinquency." Pp. 29–149 in Michael Tonry and Norval Morris (eds.), *Crime and Justice: An Annual Review of Research.* Vol. 7. Chicago: University of Chicago Press.

Lombroso, Cesare. 1972. "Introduction." Pp. xxi–xxx in Gina Lombroso-Ferrero, *Lombroso's Criminal Man.* Montclair, N.J.: Patterson Smith. (Originally published 1911.)

Lombroso, Cesare, and Guglielmo Ferrero. 1903. *The Female Offender.* New York: D. Appleton.

Lombroso-Ferrero, Gina. 1972. *Lombroso's Criminal Man.* Montclair, N. J.: Patterson Smith. (Originally published 1911.)

Lorch, Donatella. 1989. "Hospital counselors relieve emotional scars of violence." *New York Times,* 13 August: 32.

Lukas, J. Anthony. 1985. *On Common Ground: A Turbulent Decade in the Lives of Three American Families.* New York: Knopf.

Maas, Peter. 1969. *The Valachi Papers.* New York: Bantam.

MacNamara, Donal E. J. 1977. "The medical model in corrections." *Criminology* 14 (February): 439–48.

Mack, Mary Peter. 1969. *A Bentham Reader.* New York: Pegasus.

Madlin, Nancy. 1983. "ABC's 'eyewitness anonymous'." *Columbia Journalism Review* 22, 2 (July–August): 32–33.

Mannheim, Hermann. 1972. "Introduction." Pp. 1–35 in Hermann Mannheim (ed.), *Pioneers in Criminology*. 2nd ed. Montclair, N.J.: Patterson Smith.

March, William. 1954. *The Bad Seed*. New York: Rinehart.

Markus, Hazel, and R. B. Zajonc. 1985. "The cognitive perspective in social psychology." Pp. 137–230 in Gardner Lindzey and Elliot Aronson (eds.), *The Handbook of Social Psychology*. 3rd ed. Vol. 1. New York: Random House.

Mars, Gerald. 1983. *Cheats at Work: An Anthropology of Workplace Crime*. London: Unwin Paperbacks.

Martinson, Robert. 1974. "What works?—Questions and answers about prison reform." *Public Interest* 35 (Spring): 22–54.

———. 1979. "New findings, new views: A note of caution regarding sentencing reform." *Hofstra Law Review* 7 (Winter): 243–58.

Martinson, Robert, Ted Palmer, and Stuart Adams. 1976. *Rehabilitation, Recidivism, and Research*. Hackensack, N.J.: National Council on Crime and Delinquency.

Marx, Karl. 1978. "Economic and philosophic manuscripts of 1844." Pp. 66–125 in Robert C. Tucker (ed.), *The Marx-Engels Reader*. 2nd ed. New York: Norton.

———. 1981. "The labeling of crime." P. 54 in David Greenberg (ed.), *Crime & Capitalism*. Palo Alto, Calif.: Mayfield. (Originally published 1859.)

Marx, Karl, and Friedrich Engels. 1978. "Manifesto of the communist party." Pp. 469–500 in Robert C. Tucker (ed.), *The Marx-Engels Reader*. 2nd ed. New York: Norton. (Originally published 1848.)

Maslow, Abraham. 1954. *Motivation and Personality*. New York: Harper.

———. 1971. *The Farther Reaches of Human Nature*. New York: Viking.

Massing, Michael. 1990. "The two William Bennetts." *New York Review of Books*, 1 March: 29–33.

Matza, David. 1964. *Delinquency and Drift*. New York: Wiley.

———. 1969. *Becoming Deviant*. Englewood Cliffs, N. J.: Prentice-Hall.

Maurer, David W. 1940. *The Big Con*. Indianapolis: Bobbs-Merrill.

Mawby, Rob I., and Judith Brown. 1984. "Newspaper images of the victim: A British study." *Victimology* 9,1: 82–94.

McCall, George J., and J. L. Simmons. 1978. *Identities and Interactions*. Rev. ed. New York: Free Press.

McCleary, Richard. 1978. *Dangerous Men: The Sociology of Parole*. Beverly Hills, Calif.: Sage.

McDonald, Douglas C. 1986. *Punishment without Walls: Community Service Sentences in New York City*. New Brunswick, N.J.: Rutgers University Press.

———. 1988. "Restitution and community service." *Crime File Study Guide* series. Washington, D. C.: National Institute of Justice.

McDonald, William F. 1976. "Criminal justice and the victim: An introduction." Pp. 17–55 in William F. McDonald (ed.), *Criminal Justice and the Victim*. Beverly Hills, Calif.: Sage.

McGuire, William J. 1985. "Attitudes and attitude change." Pp. 233–346 in Gardner Lindzey and Elliot Aronson (eds.), *The Handbook of Social Psychology*. 3rd ed. Vol. 2. New York: Random House.

McKelvey, Blake. 1977. *American Prisons: A History of Good Intentions*. Montclair, N. J.: Patterson Smith.

McKinney, Fred, David J. Miller, Leo Beier, and Stephen R. Bohannon. 1978. "Self-concept, delinquency, and Positive Peer Culture." *Criminology* 15 (February): 529–38.

McQuiston, John T. 1988. "Man fatally beaten by East Harlem mob angry at $20 theft." *New York Times*, 21 March: A1, B3.

Mednick, Sarnoff A. 1987. "Introduction—Biological factors in crime causation: The reactions of social scientists." Pp. 1–6 in Sarnoff A. Mednick, Terrie E. Moffitt, and Susan A. Stack (eds.), *The Causes of Crime: New Biological Approaches*. Cambridge: Cambridge University Press.

Mednick, Sarnoff A., Terrie E. Moffitt, and Susan A. Stack. 1987. *The Causes of Crime: New Biological Approaches*. Cambridge: Cambridge University Press.

Mendelsohn, Benjamin. 1956. "The Victimology." *Études Internationales de Psycho-Sociologie Criminelle* 1(July–September): 25–36.

Menninger, Karl. 1968. *The Crime of Punishment*. New York: Viking.

"Merciless jury." 1985. *Time*, 27 May: 66–67.

Merton, Robert K. 1957. *Social Theory and Social Structure*. Rev. & enl. ed. Glencoe, Ill.: Free Press.

Miller, Arthur G. (ed.).   1982. *In the Eye of the Beholder: Contemporary Issues in Stereotyping.* New York: Praeger.

Miller, Dale, and Neil Vidmar. 1981. "The social psychology of punishment reactions." Pp. 145–72 in Melvin J. Lerner and Sally C. Lerner (eds.), *The Justice Motive in Social Behavior: Adapting to Times of Scarcity and Change.* New York: Plenum.

Miller, Jerome G. 1988. "Address given in acceptance of the August Vollmer award." *The Criminologist* 13, 1 (January–February): 7, 13–14, 18.

Miller, Walter B. 1970. "Lower class culture as a generating milieu of gang delinquency." Pp. 351–63 in Marvin Wolfgang, Leonard Savitz, and Norman Johnston (eds.), *The Sociology of Crime and Delinquency.* 2nd ed. New York: Wiley.

Monahan, John. 1981. *Predicting Violent Behavior: An Assessment of Clinical Techniques.* Beverly Hills, Calif.: Sage.

Montagu, Ashley. 1976. *The Nature of Human Aggression.* New York: Oxford University Press.

———. 1978. "Introduction." Pp. 3–11 in Ashley Montagu (ed.), *Learning Non-Aggression.* New York: Oxford University Press.

Moquin, Wayne, and Charles Van Doren (eds.). 1976. *The American Way of Crime: A Documentary History.* New York: Praeger.

"More help for more victims." 1989. Editorial. *New York Times*, 19 June: A14.

Morganthau, Tom. 1986. "Crack and crime." *Newsweek*, 16 June: 16–22.

Morris, Norval. 1966. "Impediments to penal reform." *University of Chicago Law Review* 33 (Summer): 627–56.

———. 1974. *The Future of Imprisonment.* Chicago: University of Chicago Press.

Morris, Norval, and Michael Tonry. 1980. "Introduction." Pp.vii–ix in Norval Morris and Michael Tonry (eds.), *Crime and Justice: An Annual Review of Research.* Vol. 2. Chicago: University of Chicago Press.

Moscovici, Serge , and Marisa Zavalloni. 1969. "The group as a polarizer of attitudes." *Journal of Personality and Social Psychology* 12 (June): 125–35.

Mowrer, O. Hobart. 1961. *The Crisis in Psychiatry and Religion.* Princeton, N.J.: Van Nostrand.

Myers, Martha A. 1990. "Economic threat and racial disparities in incarceration: The case of postbellum Georgia." *Criminology* 28 (November): 627–56.

Nader, Laura. 1975. "Forums for justice: A cross-cultural perspective." *Journal of Social Issues* 31 (Summer): 151–70.

National Research Council. Panel on Research on Deterrent and Incapacitative Effects. 1978. *Deterrence and Incapacitation: Estimating the Effects of Criminal Sanctions on Crime Rates.* Washington, D. C.: National Academy of Sciences.

Navasky, Victor, with Darrell Paster. 1976. "Background paper." Pp. 25–145 in Twentieth Century Fund Task Force on the Law Enforcement Assistance Administration, *Law Enforcement: The Federal Role.* New York: McGraw-Hill.

Neilson, G. 1932. "Trial by combat." Pp. 304–343 in William S. Carpenter and Paul T. Stafford (eds.), *Readings in Early Legal Institutions.* New York: F. S. Crofts.

Nettler, Gwynn. 1978. *Explaining Crime.* 2nd ed. New York: McGraw-Hill.

New York Radical Feminists. 1974. *Rape: The First Sourcebook for Women.* New York: Plume/New American Library.

Newman, Daisy. 1972. *A Procession of Friends.* Garden City, N.Y.: Doubleday.

Newman, Graeme. 1985. *The Punishment Response.* 2nd ed. Albany, N.Y.: Harrow and Heston.

Normandeau, André. 1972. "Arnaud Bonneville de Marsangy 1802–1894." Pp. 129–37 in Hermann Mannheim (ed.), *Pioneers in Criminology.* 2nd ed. Montclair, N.J.: Patterson Smith.

Norris, Frank. 1981. *McTeague.* New York: Signet/New American Library. (Originally published 1899.)

"Notes on people." 1977. *New York Times,* 3 November: C2.

Oberschall, Anthony. 1973. *Social Conflict and Social Movements.* Englewood Cliffs, N. J.: Prentice-Hall.

Packer, Herbert L. 1968. *The Limits of the Criminal Sanction.* Stanford: Stanford University Press.

Paolucci, Henry. 1963. "Translator's introduction." Pp. ix–xxiii in Cesare Beccaria, *On Crimes and Punishments.* Indianapolis: Bobbs-Merrill.

Parent, Dale G. 1989. *Shock Incarceration: An Overview of Existing Programs.* Washington, D.C.: U. S. Department of Justice.

Parker, Howard A. 1970. "Juvenile court actions and public response." Pp. 252–65 in Peter G. Garabedian and Don C Gibbons (eds.), *Becoming Delinquent: Young Offenders and the Correctional System.* Chicago: Aldine.

Pease, Ken. 1985. "Community service orders." Pp. 51–94 in Michael Tonry and Norval Morris (eds.), *Crime and Justice: An Annual Review of Research.* Vol. 6. Chicago: University of Chicago Press.

"N. Y. Penal Law." 1987. *McKinney's Consolidated Laws of New York Annotated.* Book 39. St. Paul: West.

Perrier, David C., and F. Steven Pink. 1985. "Community service: All things to all people." *Federal Probation* 49 (June): 32–38.

Petchesky, Rosalind P. 1981. "At hard labor: Penal confinement and production in nineteenth-century America." Pp. 341–57 in David F. Greenberg (ed.), *Crime and Capitalism.* Palo Alto, Calif.: Mayfield.

Petersilia, Joan, Peter W. Greenwood, and Marvin Lavin. 1978. *Criminal Careers of Habitual Felons.* Washington, D.C.: U. S. Government Printing Office.

Piaget, Jean. 1957. *Logic and Psychology.* New York: Basic Books.

Platt, Anthony M. 1969. *The Child Savers: The Invention of Delinquency.* Chicago: University of Chicago Press.

———. 1978. " 'Street' crime—a view from the left." *Crime and Social Justice* 8 (Spring–Summer): 26–34.

Pollak, Otto. 1950. *The Criminality of Women.* Philadelphia: University of Pennsylvania Press.

Pontell, Henry N. 1984. *A Capacity to Punish.* Bloomington, Ind.: Indiana University Press.

Poole, Keith T., and Howard Rosenthal. 1984. "The polarization of American politics." *Journal of Politics* 46 (November): 1061–79.

Porter, William Sydney [O. Henry]. 1953. "The cop and the anthem." Pp. 37–42 in *The Complete Works of O. Henry.* Vol. I. Garden City, N.Y.: Doubleday. (Originally published 1906.)

Potholm, Christian P. 1976. "Comparative vigilantism: The United States and South Africa." Pp. 175–93 in H. Jon Rosenbaum and Peter C. Sederberg (eds.), *Vigilante Politics.* Philadelphia: University of Pennsylvania Press.

Pound, Roscoe. 1930. *Criminal Justice in America.* New York: Holt.

———. 1971. "Criminal justice in the American city." Pp. 101–20 in Abraham S. Goldstein and Joseph Goldstein (eds.), *Crime, Law, and Society.* New York: Free Press. (Originally published 1922.)

Press, Aric. 1981. "How the mob really works." *Newsweek*, 5 January: 34–43.

Prince, Jerome. 1973. *Richardson on Evidence*. 10th ed. Brooklyn, N.Y.: Brooklyn Law School.

Prisoner No. 4000X. 1972. "A criminal looks at crime and punishment." Pp. 189–93 in David M. Petersen and Marcello Truzzi (eds.), *Criminal Life: Views from Inside*. Englewood Cliffs, N. J.: Prentice-Hall. (Originally published 1927.)

Putnam, Robert D. 1971. "Studying elite culture: The case for ideology." *American Political Science Review* 65 (September): 651–81.

Quinney, Richard. 1963. "Occupational structure and criminal behavior: Prescription violation by retail pharmacists." *Social Problems* 11 (Fall): 179–85.

———. 1972. "Who is the victim?" *Criminology* 10 (November): 314–23.

———. 1975. *Criminology: Analysis and Critique of Crime in America*. Boston: Little, Brown.

Radzinowicz, Leon. 1966. *Ideology and Crime*. New York: Columbia University Press.

Rafter, Nicole H. 1985. *Partial Justice: Women in State Prisons, 1800–1935*. Boston: Northeastern University Press.

Raines, Howell. 1981. "Reagan proposes revision of laws to combat crime." *New York Times*, 29 September: A1, A19.

Randall, Susan, and Vicki McN. Rose. 1984. "Forcible rape." Pp. 47–72 in Robert F. Meier (ed.), *Major Forms of Crime*. Beverly Hills, Calif.: Sage.

"The rape shield paradox: Complainant protection amidst oscillating trends of state judicial interpretation." 1987. *Journal of Criminal Law and Criminology* 78 (Fall): 644–98.

Redfield, Robert. 1967. "Primitive law." Pp. 3–24 in Paul Bohannon (ed.), *Law and Warfare: Studies in the Anthropology of Conflict*. Garden City, N.Y.: Natural History Press.

Reiff, Robert. 1979. *The Invisible Victim*. New York: Basic Books.

Reiman, Jeffrey H. 1979. *The Rich Get Richer and the Poor Get Prison: Ideology, Class, and Criminal Justice*. New York: Wiley.

Reiss, Albert J., Jr. 1964. "The social integration of queers and peers." Pp. 181–210 in Howard S. Becker (ed.), *The Other Side*. New York: Free Press.

Reiss, Albert J., Jr., and Michael Tonry (eds.). 1986. *Communities and Crime*. Chicago: University of Chicago Press.

Rennie, Ysabel. 1978. *The Search for Criminal Man: A Conceptual History of the Dangerous Offender*. Lexington, Mass.: Lexington-books/Heath.

Robin, Gerald D. 1977. "Forcible rape: Institutionalized sexism in the criminal justice system." *Crime & Delinquency* 23 (April): 136–53.

Rodman, Hyman, and Paul Grams. 1967. "Juvenile delinquency and the family: A review and discussion." Pp. 188–221 in U. S. President's Commission on Law Enforcement and the Administration of Justice, *Task Force Report: Juvenile Delinquency and Youth Crime*. Washington, D.C.: U. S. Government Printing Office.

Rokeach, Milton. 1960. *The Open and Closed Mind: Investigations into the Nature of Belief Systems and Personality Systems*. New York: Basic Books.

Rosenbaum, H. Jon, and Peter C. Sederberg. 1976. "Vigilantism: An analysis of establishment violence." Pp. 3–29 in H. Jon Rosenbaum and Peter C. Sederberg (eds.), *Vigilante Politics*. Philadelphia: University of Pennsylvania Press.

Rosenberg, Charles E. 1968. *The Trial of the Assassin Guiteau: Psychiatry and Law in the Gilded Age*. Chicago: University of Chicago Press.

Rosett, Arthur, and Donald R. Cressey. 1976. *Justice by Consent: Plea Bargains in the American Courthouse*. Philadelphia: Lippincott.

Roshier, Bob. 1973. "The selection of crime news by the press." Pp. 28–39 in Stanley Cohen and Jock Young (eds.), *The Manufacture of News*. Beverly Hills, Calif.: Sage.

Ross, H. Laurence. 1960. "Traffic law violation: A folk crime." *Social Problems* 8 (Winter): 231–41.

Rossi, Peter H., Richard A. Berk, and Kenneth J. Lenihan. 1980. *Money, Work, and Crime: Experimental Evidence*. New York: Academic Press.

Rothman, David J. 1971. *The Discovery of the Asylum*. Boston: Little, Brown.

———. 1980. *Conscience and Convenience: The Asylum and Its Alternatives in Progressive America*. Boston: Little, Brown.

Rousseau, Jean Jacques. 1950. *The Social Contract* and *Discourses*. New York: E. P. Dutton. (Originally published 1750–1762.)

Rubin, Lillian B. 1986. *A Quiet Rage: Bernie Goetz in a Time of Madness*. New York: Farrar, Straus, and Giroux.

Rucker, Lila. 1991. "Peacemaking in prisons." Pp. 172–80 in Harold Pepinsky and Richard Quinney (eds.), *Criminology As Peacemaking*. Bloomington: Indiana University Press.

Rusche, Georg, and Otto Kirchheimer. 1939. *Punishment and Social Structure*. New York: Columbia University Press.

Sagarin, Edward (ed.). 1980. *Taboos in Criminology*. Beverly Hills, Calif.: Sage.

Schafer, Stephen. 1960. *Restitution to Victims of Crime*. Chicago: Quadrangle.

———. 1968. *The Victim and His Criminal: A Study in Functional Responsibility*. New York: Random House.

———. 1969. *Theories in Criminology: Past and Present Philosophies of the Crime Problem*. New York: Random House.

———. 1974. *The Political Criminal: The Problem of Morality and Crime*. New York: Free Press.

———. 1976. "The victim and correctional theory: Integrating victim reparation with offender rehabilitation." Pp. 227–36 in William F. McDonald (ed.), *Criminal Justice and the Victim*. Beverly Hills, Calif.: Sage.

Scharf, Peter. and Joseph Hickey. 1976. "The prison and the inmate's conception of legal justice: An experiment in democratic education." *Criminal Justice and Behavior* 3 (June): 107–22.

Scheingold, Stuart A. 1984. *The Politics of Law and Order: Street Crime and Public Policy*. New York: Longman.

Schlossman, Steven, Gail Zellman, and Richard Shavelson. 1984. *Delinquency Prevention in South Chicago: A Fifty-Year Assessment of the Chicago Area Project*. Santa Monica, Calif.: RAND Corporation.

Schmideberg, Melitta. 1960. "The offender's attitude toward punishment." *Journal of Criminal Law, Criminology, and Police Science* 51 (September–October): 328–34.

Schmidt, William E. 1990. "Prosecutors drop criminal case against doctor involved in suicide." *New York Times*, 15 December: 10.

Schneider, Anne L. 1986. "Restitution and recidivism rates of juvenile offenders: Results from four experimental studies." *Criminology* 24 (August): 533–52.

Schneider, Anne L., and Peter R. Schneider. 1981. "Victim assistance programs: An overview." Pp. 364–73 in Burt Galaway and Joe Hudson (eds.), *Perspectives on Crime Victims*. St. Louis: Mosby.

Schrag, Clarence. 1961. "Some foundations for a theory of correction." Pp. 309–57 in Donald R. Cressey (ed.), *The Prison: Studies in Institutional Organization and Change*. New York: Holt, Rinehart and Winston.

———. 1970. "Leadership among prison inmates." Pp. 429–34 in Norman Johnston, Leonard Savitz, and Marvin Wolfgang (eds.), *The Sociology of Punishment and Correction*. 2nd ed. New York: Wiley.

Schur, Edwin M. 1969. *Our Criminal Society: The Social and Legal Sources of Crime in America*. Englewood Cliffs, N.J.: Prentice-Hall.

———. 1971. *Labeling Deviant Behavior: Its Sociological Implications*. New York: Harper & Row.

———. 1973. *Radical Nonintervention: Rethinking the Delinquency Problem*. Englewood Cliffs, N.J.: Prentice-Hall.

Schwendinger, Herman, and Julia Schwendinger. 1967. "Delinquent stereotypes of probable victims." Pp. 91–105 in Malcolm W. Klein (ed.), *Juvenile Gangs in Context*. Englewood Cliffs, N.J.: Prentice-Hall.

———. 1977. "Social class and the definition of crime." *Crime and Social Justice* 7 (Spring/Summer): 4–13.

Scully, Diana, and Joseph Marolla. 1984. "Convicted rapists' vocabulary of motive: Excuses and justifications." *Social Problems* 31 (June): 530–44.

Sellin, Thorsten. 1938. *Culture Conflict and Crime*. New York: Social Science Research Council.

———. 1973. "The origin of the Pennsylvania system of prison discipline." Pp. 12–22 in George C. Killinger and Paul F. Cromwell, Jr. (eds.), *Penology: The Evolution of Corrections in America*. St. Paul: West.

Shaw, Clifford R. 1966. *The Jack Roller: A Delinquent Boy's Own Story*. Chicago: University of Chicago Press. (Originally published 1930.)

Shaw, Clifford R., and Henry D. McKay. 1969. *Juvenile Delinquency and Urban Areas*. Rev. ed. Chicago: University of Chicago Press.

Sheldon, William H., et al. 1949. *The Varieties of Delinquent Youth.* New York: Harper.

Sherman, Michael, and Gordon Hawkins. 1981. *Imprisonment in America.* Chicago: University of Chicago Press.

Shoham, S. Giora, and Giora Rahav. 1982. *The Mark of Cain: The Stigma Theory of Crime and Social Deviation.* Rev. and enl. ed. New York: St. Martin's.

Short, James F., Jr., and Fred L. Strodtbeck. 1965. *Group Process and Gang Delinquency.* Chicago: University of Chicago Press.

Shotland, R. Lance, and Lynne Goodstein. 1983. "Just because she doesn't want to doesn't mean it's rape: An experimentally based causal model of the perception of rape in a dating situation." *Social Psychology Quarterly* 46 (September): 220–32.

Shover, Neal. 1979. *A Sociology of American Corrections.* Homewood, Ill.: Dorsey.

Siegel, Larry J. 1989. *Criminology.* 3rd ed. St. Paul: West.

Simpson, Sidney P. 1949. "The problem of trial." Pp. 141–63 in Alison Reppy (ed.), *David Dudley Field: Centenary Essays.* New York: New York University School of Law.

Smigel, Erwin O. 1970. "Public attitudes toward stealing as related to the size of the victim organization." Pp. 15–28 in Erwin O. Smigel and H. Laurence Ross (eds.), *Crimes Against Bureaucracy.* New York: Van Nostrand Reinhold.

Smigel, Erwin O., and H. Laurence Ross. 1970. "Introduction." Pp. 1–14 in Erwin O. Smigel and H. Laurence Ross (eds.), *Crimes Against Bureaucracy.* New York: Van Nostrand Reinhold.

Smith, Adam. 1985. "The city as the OK Corral." *Esquire,* July: 62–64.

Sniderman, Paul M. 1975. *Personality and Democratic Politics.* Berkeley, Calif.: University of California Press.

Sondern, Frederic, Jr. 1959. *Brotherhood of Evil.* New York: Farrar, Straus, and Cudahy.

Sperber, Manes. 1974. *Masks of Loneliness: Alfred Adler in Perspective.* New York: Macmillan.

Staats, Gregory W. 1978. *Images of Deviants: Stereotypes and Their Importance for Labeling Deviant Behavior.* Washington, D. C.: University Press of America.

Stanciu, V. V. 1976. "Victim-producing civilizations and situations." Pp. 28–39 in Emilio C. Viano (ed.), *Victims & Society.* Washington, D.C.: Visage.

Steffensmeier, Darrell J., and Miles D. Harer. 1987. "Is the crime rate really falling? An 'aging' U. S. population and its impact on the national crime rate, 1980–84." *Journal of Research in Crime and Delinquency* 24 (February): 23–48.

Stephan, Walter. 1985. "Intergroup relations." Pp. 599–658 in Gardner Lindzey and Elliot Aronson (eds.), *The Handbook of Social Psychology*. 3rd ed. Vol. 2. New York: Random House.

Stinchcombe, Arthur. 1980. *Crime and Punishment: Changing Attitudes in America*. San Francisco: Jossey Bass.

Street, David, Robert D. Vinter, and Charles Perrow. 1966. *Organizations for Treatment: A Comparative Study of Institutions for Delinquents*. New York: Free Press.

Strick, Anne. 1977. *Injustice for All*. New York: Putnam.

Strodtbeck, Fred, and James F. Short, Jr. 1968. "Aleatory risks versus short-run hedonism in explanation of gang action." Pp. 273–91 in James F. Short, Jr., (ed.), *Gang Delinquency and Delinquent Subcultures*. New York: Harper & Row.

"Student group linked to 10 violent crimes." 1985. *New York Times*, 3 April: A16.

Suro, Roberto. 1990. "Louisiana lawmakers adopt toughest anti-abortion law in U. S." *New York Times*, 27 June: A14.

Sussman, Alan. 1978. "Practitioner's guide to changes in juvenile law and procedure." *Criminal Law Bulletin* 14 (July–August): 311–42.

Sutherland, Edwin H. 1937. *The Professional Thief*. Chicago: University of Chicago Press.

Sykes, Gresham M. 1958. *The Society of Captives: A Study of a Maximum Security Prison*. Princeton: Princeton University Press.

———. 1967. *Crime and Society*. 2nd ed. New York: Random House.

———. 1978. *Criminology*. New York: Harcourt Brace Jovanovich.

Sykes, Gresham M., and Sheldon L. Messinger. 1970. "The inmate social code." Pp. 401–8 in Norman Johnston, Leonard Savitz, and Marvin Wolfgang (eds.), *The Sociology of Punishment and Correction*. 2nd ed. New York: Wiley.

Szabo, Denis. 1979. *Criminology and Crime Policy*. Lexington, Mass.: Lexingtonbooks/Heath.

Taft, Donald R., and Ralph W. England, Jr. 1964. *Criminology*. 4th ed. New York: Macmillan.

Tageson, C. William. 1982. *Humanistic Psychology: A Synthesis.* Homewood, Ill.: Dorsey.

Tannenbaum, Frank. 1938. *Crime and the Community.* Boston: Ginn.

Tappan, Paul. 1949. *Juvenile Delinquency.* New York: McGraw-Hill.

Taylor, Ian, Paul Walton, and Jock Young. 1974. *The New Criminology: For a Social Theory of Deviance.* New York: Harper and Row.

Taylor, Lawrence. 1984. *Born to Crime: The Genetic Causes of Criminal Behavior.* Westport, Conn.: Greenwood.

Teeters, Negley. 1937. *They Were in Prison.* Chicago: Winston.

———. 1959. "Institutional treatment of juvenile delinquents." Pp. 671–87 in Sheldon Glueck (ed.), *The Problem of Delinquency.* Boston: Houghton Mifflin.

"Text of President's message on law enforcement and administration of justice." 1965. *New York Times,* 9 March: 20.

Thorvaldson, Sveinn A. 1980. "Does community service affect offenders' attitudes?" Pp. 71–88 in Joe Hudson and Burt Galaway (eds.), *Victims, Offenders, and Alternative Sanctions.* Lexington, Mass.: Lexingtonbooks/Heath.

Tillich, Paul. 1967. *Systematic Theology.* Vol. 7. Chicago: University of Chicago Press.

Tittle, Charles R. 1980. "Labelling and crime: An empirical evaluation." Pp. 241–63 in Walter R. Gove (ed.), *The Labelling of Deviance: Evaluating a Perspective.* 2nd ed. Beverly Hills, Calif.: Sage.

Tomasic, Roman (ed.). 1982. *Neighborhood Justice.* New York: Longman.

"Transcript of acceptance speeches by Nixon and Agnew to the G.O.P. convention." 1968. *New York Times,* 9 August: 20.

Trotter, Sharland. 1976. "Experimental prison opened in Butner, N. C." *APA* [American Psychological Association] *Monitor* 7, 7 (July): 5.

Twentieth Century Fund. 1976. *Fair and Certain Punishment.* New York: McGraw Hill.

Tyler, Gus (ed.). 1962. *Organized Crime in America: A Book of Readings.* Ann Arbor: University of Michigan Press.

U. S. Bureau of Justice Statistics. Published annually. *Criminal Victimization in the United States.* Washington, D. C.: U. S. Government Printing Office.

U. S. President's Commission on Law Enforcement and the Administration of Justice. 1967a. *The Challenge of Crime in a Free Society.* Washington, D. C.: U. S. Government Printing Office.

———. 1967b. *Task Force Report: Juvenile Delinquency and Youth Crime.* Washington, D. C.: U. S. Government Printing Office.

———. 1967c. *Task Force Report: Organized Crime.* Washington, D. C.: U. S. Government Printing Office.

———. 1967d. *Task Force Report: Police.* Washington, D. C.: U. S. Government Printing Office.

———. 1967e. *Task Force Report: Science and Technology.* Washington, D. C.: U. S. Government Printing Office.

van den Haag, Ernest. 1975. *Punishing Criminals. Concerning a Very Old and Painful Question.* New York: Basic Books.

———. 1982. "No excuse for crime." Pp. 69–75 in Leonard Savitz and Norman D. Johnston (eds.), *Contemporary Criminology.* New York: Wiley.

van den Haag, Ernest, and John P. Conrad. 1983. *The Death Penalty.* New York: Plenum.

Vaux, Kenneth. 1988. "Debbie's dying: Euthanasia reconsidered." *Christian Century,* 16 March: 269–71.

Verhouek, Sam H. 1990. "Inquiries held blocking aid in crime cases: Eligible victims denied funds, panel concludes." *New York Times,* 26 March: B1, B3.

"Victims' rights are supported at a memorial: Relatives hear appeals for a legal balance." 1990. *New York Times,* 23 April: B2.

"Visionquest." 1988. Segment of television program. Produced by Gail Eisen. *60 Minutes.* CBS. WCBS, New York. 10 July.

Vold, George B. 1958. *Theoretical Criminology.* New York: Oxford University Press.

Vold, George B., and Thomas J. Bernard. 1986. *Theoretical Criminology.* 3rd ed. New York: Oxford University Press.

von Hentig, Hans. 1948. *The Criminal & His Victim: Studies in the Sociobiology of Crime.* New Haven: Yale University Press.

von Hirsch, Andrew. 1976. *Doing Justice: The Choice of Punishments.* New York: Hill and Wang.

———. 1982. "Constructing guidelines for sentencing: The critical choices for the Minnesota Sentencing Commission." *Hamline Law Review* 5 (June): 164–215.

————. 1985. *Past or Future Crimes: Dangerousness and Deservedness in the Sentencing of Criminals.* New Brunswick, N. J.: Rutgers University Press.

Vorrath, Harry H., and Larry K. Brendtro. 1974. *Positive Peer Culture.* Chicago: Aldine.

Voss, Harwin L., and David M. Petersen (eds.). 1971. *Ecology, Crime, and Delinquency.* New York: Appleton-Century-Crofts.

Wagner-Pacifici, Robin E. 1986. *The Moro Morality Play: Terrorism as Social Drama.* Chicago: University of Chicago Press.

Walker, Nigel. 1981. *Punishment, Danger, and Stigma.* Totowa, N.J.: Rowman and Allenheld.

Warren, Marguerite Q. 1976. "Intervention with juvenile delinquents." Pp. 176–204 in Margaret K. Rosenheim (ed.), *Pursuing Justice for the Child.* Chicago: University of Chicago Press.

Weatherford, M. Stephen. 1980. "Politics of school busing: Contextual effects and community polarization." *Journal of Politics* 42 (August): 747–65.

Weihofen, Henry. 1956. *The Urge To Punish.* New York: Farrar, Straus and Cudahy.

West, Jessamyn (ed.). 1962. *The Quaker Reader.* New York: Viking.

Wheeler, Stanton (ed.). 1968. *Controlling Delinquents.* New York: Wiley.

Whyte, William F. 1981. *Street Corner Society: The Social Structure of an Italian Slum.* 3rd ed. Chicago: University of Chicago Press.

Wiehl, Liz. 1989. "Victim and sentence: Resetting justice's scales." *New York Times,* 29 September: B5.

Wilkinson, Rupert. 1972. *The Broken Rebel: A Study in Culture, Politics, and Authoritarian Character.* New York: Harper and Row.

Williams, Bernard. 1985. *Ethics and the Limits of Philosophy.* Cambridge: Harvard University Press.

Williams, Kristen M. 1976. "The effects of victim characteristics on the disposition of violent crimes." Pp. 177–213 in William F. McDonald (ed.), *Criminal Justice and the Victim.* Beverly Hills, Calif.: Sage.

Wilmer, Harry A. 1966. "Good guys and bad guys: A litmus paper concept of man." *Federal Probation* 30 (September): 8–15.

Wilson, James Q. 1977. "Crime in society and schools." Pp. 43–49 in James McPartland and Edward McDill (eds.), *Violence in Schools.* Lexington, Mass.: Lexingtonbooks/Heath.

———. 1983a. *Thinking About Crime*. Rev. ed. New York: Basic Books.

———. 1983b. *Crime and Public Policy*. San Francisco: ICS Press.

Wilson, James Q., and Richard J. Hermnstein. 1985. *Crime & Human Nature*. New York: Simon & Schuster.

Winer, David. 1984. "Trinity's way to keep students honest." Letter to the editor. *New York Times*, 24 October: A26.

Wolfgang, Marvin E. 1958. *Patterns in Criminal Homicide*. Philadelphia: University of Pennsylvania Press.

———. 1972. "Cesare Lombroso 1835–1909." Pp. 232–91 in Hermann Mannheim (ed.), *Pioneers in Criminology*. 2nd ed. Montclair, N.J.: Patterson Smith.

———. 1977. " Introduction." Pp. v–vi in Sarnoff A. Mednick and Karl O. Christiansen (eds.), *Biosocial Bases of Criminal Behavior*. New York: Gardner.

Wolfgang, Marvin E., and Franco Ferracuti. 1967. *The Subculture of Violence: Towards an Integrated Theory in Criminology*. London: Tavistock.

Wolfgang, Marvin E., Robert M. Figlio, and Thorsten Sellin. 1972. *Delinquency in a Birth Cohort*. Chicago: University of Chicago Press.

Wolfgang, Marvin E., Terence P. Thornberry, and Robert M. Figlio. 1987. *From Boy to Man, from Delinquency to Crime*. Chicago: University of Chicago Press.

Xenarios, Susan, Elaine Freedman, Jane Seskin, and Doris Ullendorf. 1987. "For battered women, a milestone case." Letter to the editor. *New York Times*, 27 October: A34.

Yablonsky, Louis. 1967. *Synanon: The Tunnel Back*. Baltimore: Penguin.

Yochelson, Samuel, and Stanton E. Samenow. 1976. *The Criminal Personality*. New York: Jason Aronson.

Zilboorg, Gregory. 1954. *The Psychology of the Criminal Act and Punishment*. New York: Harcourt, Brace.

Zimbardo, Philip G. 1972. "Pathology of imprisonment." *Society* 9 (April): 4–8.

Index

About the Author

DANIEL S. CLASTER is Professor of Sociology, Brooklyn College of the City University of New York. He has served as co-author of *The Dynamics of Residential Treatment* (1968).